The United Kingdom financial system in transition

Theory and practice

M. Buckle *and* J. L. Thompson

Manchester University Press
Manchester and New York
Distributed exclusively in the USA and Canada by St. Martin's Press

Copyright © M. Buckle and J. L. Thompson 1992

Published by Manchester University Press
Oxford Road, Manchester M13 9PL, UK
and Room 400, 175 Fifth Avenue, New York, NY 10010, USA

Distributed exclusively in the USA and Canada
by St. Martin's Press, Inc., 175 Fifth Avenue, New York,
NY 10010, USA

British Library Cataloguing-in-Publication Data
A catalogue record for this book is available from the British Library

Library of Congress Cataloging-in-Publication Data
Buckle, M.
    The United Kingdom financial system in transition: theory and
practice/M. Buckle and J. L. Thompson.
        p.   cm.
    Includes bibliographical references and index.
    ISBN 0-7190-3028-5. – ISBN 0-7190-3029-3 (paper)
        1. Finance – Great Britain.   I. Thompson, John L.   II. Title.
HG186.G7B83   1992
336.41 – dc20   91-31666

ISBN 0 7190 3028-5 *hardback*
       0 7190 3029-3 *paperback*

Typeset in Times 10/12 pt
by Best-set Typesetter Ltd., Hong Kong

Printed in Great Britain
by Billings Ltd, Worcester

Contents

Preface

In recent years there have been extensive developments in the UK
financial system. This book presents a review of of these developments
for second/third-year students of Accountancy, Business Studies, Economics and Finance. Chapters 1 to 6 are concerned with the various
financial institutions comprising the British financial system. Chapters 7 to
13 discuss the different financial markets located in the UK. The remaining chapters deal with a number of issues including the management of
risk, the development of a single European market in financial services,
the efficiency and regulation of the UK financial system.

We are grateful to Peter Franklin, Nottingham Polytechnic, Bryn
Gravenor, European Business Management School, Richard Harrington,
University of Manchester, Ken Holden, University of Liverpool, and
Kent Matthews, Cardiff Business School, for their help in the preparation
of the book. Any errors and omissions are the responsibility of the
authors.

To Margaret and Liza

Chapter 1

Introduction to the financial system

1.1 Introduction

We begin our study of the UK financial system with an introduction to
the role of a financial system in an economy. We start this introduction
with a very simple model of an economy and then extend the analysis
throughout the rest of this and the next chapter. A second objective is to
establish some of the basic financial concepts which will be drawn upon
throughout this book. Finally, we hope to introduce readers to the many
sources of data available relating to the UK financial system. In particular
we explain the relationships between the various sets of financial
statistics.

1.2 The role of the financial system

To help us to understand the role played by a financial system in a mature
economy such as that of the UK we start by constructing a simplified
model of an economy. In this model the economy is divided into two
distinct groups or sectors. The first is the *household sector*, which is
assumed to be the ultimate owner of all the resources of the economy. In
the early stages of development of an economy the household unit would
have undertaken production of any goods consumed. As economies
developed, a form of specialisation has generally taken place so that the
proximate ownership and control of much of the productive resources of
the economy, such as land, buildings and machinery, have been vested in
units making up the second sector, which we call the *firms sector*. We will
examine the financial relationships between these two sectors later. In our
simple model it is the firms sector which organises the production of
goods and services in the economy. In exchange for these goods and

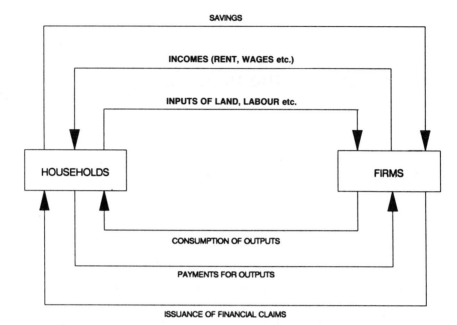

Figure 1.1

services, households hire out their resources of land, labour, etc. At this stage we ignore the role of the government and we assume that the economy is closed, so that there is no exchange of goods and services with other economies. The real flows in this simple economy are set out in the inner loop of figure 1.1.

In this simple economy it would not be an easy task for households to attempt to satisfy their wants. The greater the number of commodities available in the economy, the greater would be the task. This can be seen by considering the choices open to households. Households can consume the commodities they own, they can exchange these commodities for commodities owned by other households or they can use these commodities as inputs to create new commodities. In the last situation the household would have to hire out the commodities to an existing firm in exchange for the firm's output or alternatively create a new firm. In the case of exchanging commodities with other households there would clearly be many difficulties. For a successful transaction to take place between two parties in such a barter economy, it is necessary for each of the two parties to want simultaneously that which the other party is offering to exchange. This requirement is termed 'double coincidence of wants'. There would be considerable costs involved both in searching for a suitable party with which to trade and also in reaching an agreement over the terms of the trade. Such costs would limit the amount of trade taking place and would eventually lead to pressure for general agreement to use a single commodity as a standard unit of exchange into which all other commodities can be converted. The commodity used as the unit of exchange is known as money and various commodities have been used as money over time including cowrie shells, cattle, gold, silver, and cigarettes. The main criterion for development of a commodity as money is that it is generally acceptable in exchange for other commodities. With the development of money, the act of sale can be separated from the act of purchase.

We can now introduce money into our simple economy so that households are paid in money for the resources they hire out to firms and in turn households use that money to purchase the outputs of firms. These monetary flows are denoted by the middle circuit in figure 1.1 and are the flows corresponding to the real flows of goods and services occurring in the opposite direction. We should note that by aggregating all firms into one sector we are considering only flows taking place between firms and households and are therefore ignoring the considerable flows which take place between firms. That is to say, we are considering only inter-sector flows and ignoring intra-sector flows.

In this simple economy any expenditure in excess of current income by a household or a firm could occur only if the household or firm had accumulated money balances by not spending all of its income received in past periods. This is clearly a constraint on economic development since firms need to invest, that is, replace, maintain or add to existing real assets such as buildings and machinery. As the economy becomes more sophisticated, investment requires larger amounts of accumulated funds. Various expedients were developed to enable firms to overcome such constraints. For example, partnerships were formed so that accumulated savings could be pooled. The next major stage in the development of financing arrangements came with borrowing. Those households which did not spend all of their current income on consumption, that is, saved some of their income, could lend these funds to firms which in turn could use these funds to finance investment. In exchange for these funds, firms would issue claims, which are effectively sophisticated IOUs which promise some benefits to the lender of funds at some date or dates in the future. The nature of financial claims and the various types of claims in existence are discussed in the next section. The ability to finance invest-ment through borrowing undoubtedly encourages economic development, and the existence of financial claims would also stimulate household saving. The investment and saving flows in our simple economy are represented by the outer loop of figure 1.1. The non-spending of income (or saving) by households can be regarded as a leakage of funds from the circular flow of income and expenditure captured in the middle loop of figure 1.1. This household saving, though, finds its way into firms' investment and firms' investment involves the purchase of capital equipment from other firms, so the leaked funds are injected back into the circuit.

We can now see one of the main roles of a financial system, which is to provide the mechanisms by which funds can be transferred from those with surplus funds to those that wish to borrow. In other words, the financial system acts as an intermediary between surplus and deficit units. In terms of figure 1.1 this function is represented by the outer loop. It is clear therefore that the financial system plays an important role in the allocation of funds to their most efficient use amongst competing demands. In a market system such as the UK financial system this allocation is achieved through the price mechanism, with the various prices being set within the relevant financial markets, which are themselves part of the financial system. The existence of financial markets also enables wealth holders to alter the composition of their portfolios. A secondary role for a financial system is to provide the mechanisms for the inner money flows, i.e. the payments mechanism. A further function of a financial system is the provision of special financial services such as insurance and pension services.

Before we consider in more detail the lending and borrowing flows represented by the outer loop of figure 1.1, we examine in the next section the nature of the financial claims which underlie these flows.

1.3   Financial claims

A financial claim can be defined as a claim to the payment of a sum of money at some future date or dates. A borrower of funds issues a financial claim in return for the funds. The lender of funds holds the borrower's financial claim and is said to hold a financial asset. The issuer of the claim is said to have a financial liability. By definition therefore the sum of financial assets in existence will exactly equal the sum of liability. To take an example, a bank deposit is a sum of money lent by an individual or company to a bank. The deposit is therefore a liability of the borrower of funds, which is the bank. The depositor holds a financial asset, that is, a financial claim on the bank. Another term commonly used to denote a financial claim is a financial instrument.

The existence of a wide variety of financial instruments in a mature financial system, such as the UK system, can be explained by reference to consumer theory. Traditional consumer theory explains the demand for a commodity in terms of utility and a budget constraint, with the implication that a particular good can be identified as separate from other goods. In contrast Lancaster [1966] argues that:

(i)   all goods possess objective characteristics, properties or attributes, and

(ii) these characteristics form the object of consumer choice.

In the same way a financial instrument can be considered to be a 'bundle' of different characteristics. Because individual agents place different emphasis on the various characteristics, a wide range of financial instruments are supplied. It is now necessary to examine the different characteristics possessed by financial instruments. The most important of these are risk, liquidity, real value certainty, expected return, term to maturity, currency denomination and divisibility.

Risk

Risk is a fundamental concept in finance and it is one which we will return to many times throughout the book. What follows is a brief introduction to the nature of financial risk. When we talk about risk in relation to a financial instrument we are referring to the fact that some future outcome affecting that instrument is not known with certainty. The uncertain outcome may, for example, be changes in the price of the security or default with respect to repayment of capital or income stream. Although such outcomes are uncertain, an individual may have some view about the likelihood of particular outcomes occurring. Another way of stating this is that the individual will view some outcomes as more likely than others. Such views are likely to be formed on the basis of past experience of such outcomes occurring, although other relevant information may also be used. The next step in assessing the particular risk of the financial instrument is to assign subjective probabilities to the different outcomes that may occur. The resulting probability distribution provides us with the individual's view as to the most likely outcome, that is, the expected value of the distribution. The spread of the distribution indicates the degree to which the outcome will be much greater or much less than expected. The greater the spread, the greater the risk that an outcome far removed from that expected will occur. The most common measure of risk is in fact the standard deviation of the probability distribution, a measure which increases as the spread widens.

To take an example, a person invests £1,000 in the ordinary shares of a company. The value of the shares in one year's time, that is, the price of those shares plus any income received from them in the form of dividends, is uncertain. The value may have risen or fallen; however, this person will believe some range of values are more likely than others. For example he or she may believe that there is a 50 per cent chance that the value of the shares in one year's time will be in the range £1,000 to £1,200. Figure 1.2 illustrates one possible distribution of likely values.

The expected value of this distribution is £1,090 and the standard

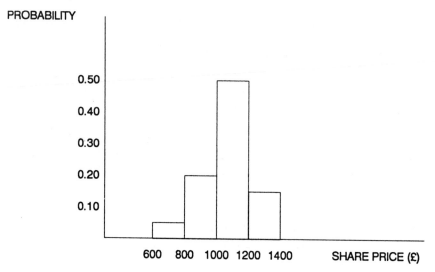

Figure 1.2

deviation, or measure of risk, is 161. A larger spread, that is, a larger standard deviation, would indicate the potential for a larger reward and, conversely, the potential for a larger loss around a particular expected value. In these introductory remarks on the nature of risk, two types of risk were mentioned, namely price risk and the risk of not being repaid the sum lent or any interest promised in the claim, known as default risk. During the course of this book we will consider many other types of financial risk.

Liquidity

Liquidity refers to the ease and speed with which a financial instrument can be turned into cash without loss. This will depend upon on the asset being redeemable or marketable on an organised market. Thus for example a bank sight deposit can be withdrawn or redeemed on demand and is therefore very liquid. In contrast listed shares can be sold on the stock exchange but the precise amount of cash obtained will depend on the market valuation at the time of sale. Hence listed shares are less liquid than sight deposits. As a final example a bank loan is an agreement between two parties, the bank and the borrower, and so there is unlikely to be a third party willing to purchase the loan from the bank before it matures. That is to say, the bank loan is not marketable. (Note that over the 1980s there has been a growing trend towards packaging loan-type assets, such as mortgages, to make them marketable so they can be sold on. This process is part of a larger phenomenon termed securitisation –

for further discussion see chapter 12.) The existence of an organised market for an instrument and the ability to deal at short notice therefore enhance the instrument's liquidity. It is possible to devise a spectrum of liquidity along which different financial instruments can be positioned. Such an analysis is crude and subject to a number of exceptions but is still illustrative. At the very liquid end we would find short-term deposits, moving through longer-term deposits where funds are tied up for longer periods, through bonds and shares where their marketability provides some degree of liquidity, to long-term loans, life policies and pension rights. Life policies and pension rights are considered to be very illiquid when they are held to maturity, although it has become increasingly easier to turn them into cash at short notice, albeit at considerable financial penalty, the further the date of encashment is from the maturity date.

Real value certainty
A third distinguishing characteristic of financial instruments is real value certainty, which refers to their susceptibility to loss due to a rise in the general level of prices. The maintenance of real value of an asset is likely to be an important consideration for those who are lending funds over a long time period. An individual acquiring assets to draw upon in retirement will want to ensure that the purchasing power of those assets is at least as great in retirement as when the assets were acquired. Financial instruments whose values are fixed in money terms, for example a bank deposit, will find their real value eroded when the rate of inflation exceeds the rate of interest earned. Over most of the 1970s, inflation exceeded the interest rate earned on bank and building society deposits in the UK and as a consequence the real value of such deposits was eroded. Ordinary shares are an instrument which, if held over a few years, have tended to increase in value in line with or above the rise in the general price level. The asset which has tended to provide the best protection against erosion in value by inflation is not a financial asset but the physical asset of property. This is not to say that there are not times when the real value of property does decrease, and a recent example of this is the decline in the real value of residential property in 1989/90. Rather it is to say that, if held over a number of years, the increase in value of property has tended to exceed inflation. This, as we shall see in chapter 6, explains why the long-term investment institutions are significant holders of property in their portfolios.

Expected return
Most financial instruments offer an explicit cash return to their holders. This return takes the form of a rate of interest or dividend and, for those

instruments subject to changes in their market price, there is an additional element of return in the form of an appreciation in their value. Instruments subject to changes in price are termed capital uncertain and include bonds and equities. For such capital-uncertain instruments it will be the expected return (see above section on risk) that is used to determine whether to purchase or hold on to the instrument. *Ceteris paribus*, the higher the expected return the greater the demand for the instrument. In practice, however, a high return on an asset may also indicate that there is a premium component to the return to compensate the holder for some disadvantage such as illiquidity or high risk.

Term to maturity
Financial instruments vary widely according to the characteristic of term to maturity. Sight deposits at banks have zero term to maturity as they can be withdrawn on demand. At the other end of the spectrum, 'consols' (a type of government bond) and equity have no redemption date and therefore possess an infinite term to maturity. Between these two extremes, financial instruments are issued with a wide range of maturities. In general, returns on instruments identical except for their term to maturity will reflect (i) expectations of future interest rate changes and (ii) the loss of liquidity in holding long-term as opposed to short-term instruments. This is examined in more detail in chapter 9.

Currency denomination
With the general reduction in restrictions on the movement of capital across national boundaries, the currency denomination of a financial instrument has assumed greater importance. This adds a further component to the return on non-domestic instruments in the form of the appreciation or depreciation of the relevant exchange rate.

Divisibility
This characteristic reflects the degree to which the instrument can be subdivided into small units for transaction purposes. For example, a sight deposit is fully divisible whereas treasury bills are sold in minimum denominations and hence are not divisible. The degree of divisibility is therefore an additional determinant of an instrument's liquidity.

The characteristics approach to analysing financial instruments can also provide some indication of why an economic agent, such as an individual or company, will desire to hold more than one type of financial asset. It is likely that an economic agent will hold their wealth in different forms so as to meet a number of different financial objectives. For example, an individual may be uncertain about their level of income or consumption in the near future and so can meet this uncertainty by holding wealth in a form which can be drawn on at short notice. That is, some wealth will be held as liquid assets such as bank deposits. The individual may also have the objective of holding wealth over a long period of time, for the purpose of providing income in retirement, and will want these funds to keep their purchasing power. This may lead to the holding of some funds in the form of ordinary shares. From this analysis we can see that an economic agent is likely to hold a collection or *portfolio* of assets where the mix of characteristics underlying the assets in the portfolio will satisfy the various objectives of the agent.

We have referred to some specific types of financial instruments in this section, such as a bank deposit and an ordinary share. These are examples of the two general types of claim, namely debt and equity, which dominate the types of financial instruments in existence. We shall finish this section with a look at the characteristics of these two general types of claim.

Debt

Debt is a financial claim which is normally due to be repaid on a specified future date, with interest being paid at regular intervals until the claim is repaid. Examples of debt instruments are deposits, loans, bills and bonds.

A deposit is a claim which records the liability of a financial institution to repay a sum of money in the future to the depositor (the lender of funds to the institution). A variety of deposit types exist, differing mainly in the arrangements for repayment; so, for example, a sight deposit with a bank would be repayable on demand whilst a time deposit is repayable after a given period of notice. Deposits are generally considered to be at the liquid end of the spectrum of liquidity, although there are some exceptions to this where a deposit may have a repayment date of up to five years from the date of issue. Deposits are susceptible to default risk, though such risk is considered to be low as financial institutions rarely default. Deposits can also be classified according to their size, so that retail deposits are small and wholesale deposits are large. Financial institutions have also issued Certificates of Deposit (CDs), which are instruments acknowledging the existence of a deposit for a fixed period but which can be sold in the money markets (i.e. possess the characteristic of marketability – see chapter 10 for further discussion).

The majority of loans are made by financial institutions and generally specify a fixed date for repayment. The term to maturity of the loan generally varies according to the purpose for which the finance is required, which may be up to thirty years hence in the case of a mortgage. Most bank loans, though, have a repayment date of under ten years from the date they are issued. Loans are susceptible to default risk, although, as we shall see in the next chapter, financial institutions attempt to minimise such risks through a variety of methods. Loans which are secured, such as a mortgage on property, have a lower default risk than unsecured loans, as in the event of non-repayment the holder of the claim can sell the security to recover the debt. Loans are generally considered to be illiquid as they are agreements between two parties and therefore not marketable.

Bills of exchange can be considered to be promises to pay a certain sum of money at a fixed date and are analogous to post-dated cheques. Commercial bills are used to finance trade and help to reconcile the competing interests of (i) the buyer of the goods who wishes to delay payment and (ii) the seller who desires prompt payments. The buyer issues a bill which promises to pay in the future but the seller receives a financial instrument which he can resell in the money markets (i.e. it is negotiable). The price received from the sale is less than the face value of the bill on maturity and so the bill is said to be discounted. For example, if a £1,000 bill due for redemption in three months' time is sold for £950, the rate of discount over three months is 5.3 per cent ((£50/950) × 100) or approximately 21 per cent per annum. Bills are also issued by central government (treasury bills) and local authorities.

Deposits and loans are claims which generally pay variable rates of interest. In contrast, a bond is a claim which pays a fixed rate of interest, known as a 'coupon payment', at regular intervals. The bond may have a known repayment date at which time the bond's par value, which is generally £100, is repaid. Some bonds, though, have no definite repayment date and are known as undated bonds, for example 2½ per cent consolidated stock (consols) issued by the UK government in 1888. In the UK, bonds are issued by central government, local government, public boards and companies. UK government issued bonds are commonly known as 'gilt edged', as the risk of default on such stocks is as close to zero as is possible on a financial instrument. Bonds issued by companies, known as debentures or loan stocks, do carry some risk of default, as do bonds issued by some foreign government. Another type of bond traded in London is the eurobond. These are issued by international companies, governments and government agencies and are distinguished by not being subject to the tax and other regulations of the country in whose currency they are issued. This freedom from restrictions has led to many innovations in the characteristics of eurobonds and so there exists a wide variety of interest, currency denomination and repayment terms for these bonds (see chapter 12 for further detail on this). All bonds have the characteristic of marketability, which enhances their liquidity. The yield to maturity on a bond can be defined as the rate of discount which equates the current market price of the bond with the future coupon payments and the repayment of the principle. Thus, for example, the yield to maturity on a five-year £100 bond with a coupon of 10 per cent paid once a year can be calculated by solving for i (the yield to maturity) in the following formula:

$$\text{Market price of bond} = \frac{10}{(1 + i)} + \frac{10}{(1 + i)^2} + \frac{10}{(1 + i)^3} + \frac{10}{(1 + i)^4} + \frac{10}{(1 + i)^5} + \frac{100}{(1 + i)^5}$$

The price at which bonds trade in a market will change as yields on other financial instruments change. It can be seen from the above formula that there is an inverse relationship between the price of a bond and its yield to maturity. If yields on competing financial instruments change then, given that the coupon is fixed, changes in the market price of bonds keep its yield in line with that of similar financial instruments. Consequently, if a bond is not held to maturity, there is a risk that the price at which the bond is sold is not the same as the price at which the bond was bought; that is, bonds are subject to price risk.

A final point about the characteristics of debt instruments is that they are normally susceptible to a reduction in real value due to general price inflation (when the nominal rate of interest is less than the rate of general price inflation). There are some exceptions to this where debt instruments have been issued with yields that are linked to the retail price index. In the UK, two examples of such instruments are index-linked government bonds and index-linked national savings certificates.

Equity
Equities differ from the types of financial instruments so far described in that they represent a claim to a share in the ownership of a company, rather than evidence of debts. The principal type of equity instrument is the ordinary share issued by limited companies. The main characteristic of ordinary shares is that the income to be received from them is not fixed in any way. This income payment, known as dividends, constitutes a share in the profits earned by the company. The amount of the total profits earned by the company which are distributed to shareholders is determined by the company's management. The factors determining the dividend payment will include the financial performance of the company and the extent to which the company wishes to retain profits to finance investment. In addition to uncertainty about the income payments on ordinary shares, known as income risk, ordinary shares are also subject to price risk. Ordinary shares are marketable, although it is easier to trade listed shares in the larger, well-known companies than it is in small companies. The liquidity of the particular ordinary share will therefore depend on its degree of marketability. In times of panic in share markets, for example October 1987, it may not be possible to sell a share without

incurring a significant loss. One characteristic of ordinary shares which is highly valued is their real value certainty, that when held over a sufficiently long period of time the value of shares have generally increased at a rate in excess of the rate of inflation.

1.4 Sectoral analysis of the financial system

In the simple circular flow model of the economy introduced in section one the economy was assumed to be made up of two separate groups of decision makers, or sectors, namely households and firms. To take our analysis of the financial system further we need to consider both a further disaggregation of these two sectors and an extension of the economy to introduce a government and trade with overseas economies. The further disaggregation involves splitting the firms sector into industrial firms and firms whose primary activity is financial. The other changes introduce a public sector and an overseas sector. We have now achieved a sectoral breakdown of the economy which roughly corresponds to that used by the Central Statistical Office (CSO) for the UK economy. The CSO in fact identifies six main sectors of the UK economy:

> Personal
> Industrial and Commercial Companies (ICC)
> Monetary
> Other Financial Institutions (OFI)
> Public
> Overseas

The personal sector is mainly made up of households, along with some other groups such as unincorporated businesses, charities, universities, etc. which the statisticians find difficult to separate out. Ideally we would like data relating solely to households; however, it is not thought that these other groups distort the overall picture of household behaviour to any significant degree. As described above, the firms sector is split into industrial and commercial companies (ICC) and financial companies. The CSO then further separates the latter group into monetary institutions, which are essentially banks, and other financial institutions (OFI). This is useful as the behaviour of banks, as creators of credit, sets them apart in some respects from the rest of the financial institutions that make up the financial system. The grouping of the remaining financial institutions in the OFI sector is not altogether desirable in terms of analysing the role and behaviour of the financial system. Attempts are being made by the CSO to separate out the different types of institution in the OFI sector and recent developments have seen the emergence of a separate building society sector. The public sector represents government institutions and in some analysis by the CSO this is further split into central government, local government and public sector corporations. For most of the analysis which follows it is this CSO sector breakdown of the economy which is adopted.

1.5 National wealth

We begin our examination of the financial relationships of the UK economy with a look at the extent of national wealth. We will then move on to examine a breakdown of this wealth by sector. The first ever assessment of wealth relating to the UK was the Domesday Book which, just over nine hundred years ago and using a census approach, set out the value of the land, animals and mills of England. Over the last thirty years government statisticians and academics have adopted statistical techniques to provide an assessment of the nation's wealth today.

The tangible wealth of a nation consists of its national resources and its stocks of goods, which include buildings, durable equipment which provides services to consumers and producers, stocks of finished goods, raw materials and work in progress. In addition a nation also possesses intangible wealth, which includes the skill, knowledge and character of its people, otherwise described by economists as human capital. The final component of a nation's wealth is its claims on wealth in other countries net of other countries' claims on its own wealth. The statisticians have encountered many problems in estimating the value of these various components of national wealth and these are discussed in detail in an article in *Economic Trends* written by Bryant [1987]. The main problems identified by Bryant are those of putting a value on natural resources such as oil, coal and gas and of valuing human capital. As a consequence these items are left out of the final national accounts published by the CSO. The UK national balance sheet for the end of 1987 is summarised in table 1.1.

From table 1.1 we can note that the net national wealth of the UK at the end of 1987 was just over £2,000 billion. This is just over four times gross domestic product for the UK for that year. This figure for net national wealth is of course only an estimate because of the exclusion of certain items, mentioned above, and because many of the included items are measured with error.

In a capitalist economy such as the UK most of the appropriable wealth is owned privately. The breakdown by sector of the ownership of national wealth for 1985 is given in table 1.2. Thus private sector ownership of net national wealth was estimated to be just over 86 per cent at the end of 1985. Persons are in fact the ultimate owners of most private sector wealth (i.e. more than the 71.5 per cent owned directly) through the

Table 1.1   *UK national balance sheet, 1987 (£bn)*

Tangible assets		1,797.0
Intangible assets[a]		131.0
External assets of the UK	706.3	
External liabilities of the UK	617.7	
Net external assets		88.6
Net national wealth		2,016.6

Note:
[a] Non-marketable tenancy rights (includes housing and
   agricultural tenancy rights).
Source: CSO,   *UK   National   Accounts*,   1989,
Table 12.1.

Table 1.2   *Ownership of the national wealth by sector, 1985*

Sector	*% share of wealth*
Personal	71.5
Industrial and commercial companies	11.3
Monetary sector	1.5
Other financial institutions	2.1
Total private sector	86.4
Total public sector	13.6
	100.0

Source: Bryant [1987], Table 6.

equity claims they hold, either directly or indirectly, on the other parts of
the private sector.

1.6   Sector balance sheets

The national balance sheet shown in table 1.1 hides most of the financial
wealth held by the various groups of decision makers which make up the
UK economy. A person may be wealthy without possessing any of the
wealth counted in national wealth. This is because, to take an example,
wealth held in the form of a bank deposit by a person (i.e. an asset to that
person) will have a corresponding liability held by the bank. So, assuming
that the bank deposit is not held outside the UK, then aggregation of the
net wealth of the personal sector (which contains the person's bank
deposit as an asset) with the net wealth of the monetary sector (which
contains the bank deposit as a liability) to form national wealth causes the

asset and liability to cancel each other out. The financial relationship between the person and the bank is said to be netted out. It therefore follows that the only financial wealth appearing in the national balance sheet is those assets held by UK residents which are claims on the overseas sector (i.e. the corresponding liability is held overseas). These are included in the item 'external assets' in table 1.1. As we move down to the sectoral level of the economy, the more financial wealth is revealed. In this connection balance sheets have recently been constructed for the five domestic sectors of the UK economy identified in the earlier section and it is to these which we now turn our attention.

(i) *Personal sector*
The personal sector balance sheet showing how its wealth is made up for 1987 is shown in table 1.3. Tangible assets of the personal sector are principally houses, with consumer durables such as cars and washing machines also forming a significant share of such assets but not included for reasons noted in the table. Intangible assets are as defined in table 1.1 above. The financial assets and liabilities of the personal sector are many and varied and will be examined more closely later in this chapter when financial transactions acounts are considered, as well as in chapter 2.

There are a number of important points to note about the personal sector's balance sheet. Firstly its financial assets greatly exceed its financial liabilities; therefore the sector has been a net lender of funds to other sectors of the economy. This is to say not that all members of the

Table 1.3   *Personal sector balance sheet, 1987 (£bn)*

Tangible assets	846.7
Intangible non-financial assets	131.0
Financial assets	831.1
Financial liabilities	283.2
Net financial wealth	547.9
Net total wealth	1,525.6
Memo. item: Consumer durables[a]	137.1

Note:
[a] There are many difficulties with defining and measuring consumer durables so the figure given here is tentative and hence not included in the total for personal sector tangible assets (see Calder [1978] for more discussion).
Source: CSO, *UK National Accounts*, 1989, Table 12.2.

Table 1.4   *Personal sector balance sheet, 1987: conventional format (£bn)*

Financial liabilities		Financial assets	
Net wealth	1,525.6	Tangible assets	846.7
Financial liabilities	283.2	Intangible assets	131.0
		Financial assets	831.1
	1,808.8		1,808.8

Source: CSO, *UK National Accounts*, 1989, Table 12.2.

personal sector have been net savers but that in aggregate the personal sector has been a net saver. This highlights again the point about aggregation hiding information and that a disaggregation of the households of the personal sector by, for example, age would reveal more information about the ultimate lenders and ultimate borrowers in the economy. A second point not revealed by the figures in table 1.3 is that over the period 1975 to 1987, when personal sector net wealth rose by over £1,200 billion, over four-fifths of this increase was due to price changes of its tangible assets (mainly houses) and financial assets (mainly equities, held directly and indirectly). Therefore most of the increase in personal sector wealth in recent years has been due to positive changes in the value of assets already held rather than to increases in the quantity of assets held.

The balance sheet described in table 1.3 can be rewritten in the more conventional format for balance sheets as in table 1.4, which shows us that net wealth, sometimes known as net worth, is the item that brings assets and liabilities of the sector into balance. This format of balance sheets is the one we adopt for the rest of this chapter.

(ii)   *Industrial and commercial companies (ICC)*
The balance sheet for the ICC sector for 1987 is shown in table 1.5.

Tangible assets for the ICC sector are mainly the buildings, plant and machinery which provide the means of production, along with any stocks of raw materials, finished goods and work in progress. Financial assets held by this sector are mainly funds held to meet short-term needs, loans to subsidiaries and trade credit provided. On the liabilities side the main item is issued share capital or equities, with the rest made up of loans from banks and trade credit received (this is approximately balanced by trade credit provided). The ICC sector, in contrast to the personal sector, has generally been a net borrower, as evidenced by the excess of financial liabilities over financial assets outstanding at the end of 1987. It should be

Table 1.5 *Industrial and commercial companies balance sheet, 1987 (£bn)*

Financial liabilities		Financial assets	
Net wealth	182.1	Tangible assets	482.8
Financial liabilities	610.2	Financial assets	309.5
	792.3		792.3

Source: CSO, *UK National Accounts*, 1989, Table 12.3.

Table 1.6 *Monetary sector balance sheet, 1987 (£bn)*

Financial liabilities		Financial assets	
Net wealth	27.4	Tangible assets	10.5
Financial liabilities	905.7	Financial assets	922.6
	933.1		933.1

Source: CSO, *UK National Accounts*, 1989, Table 12.4.

noted that as equities are a liability of companies then the value of these liabilities can change as the prices of shares change. This can lead to the rather curious result, seen over the 1980s, of an increase in equity prices, as the equity markets enjoyed a long period of boom, leading to an increase in the liabilities of companies greater than an increase in their assets, resulting in a reduction in the net wealth of the ICC sector.

(iii)   *Monetary sector and other financial institutions sector*
For the purpose of this analysis of sectoral wealth we will take the two financial sectors together as they are sufficiently similar in this respect. The balance sheets for these two sectors are summarised in tables 1.6 and 1.7.

The striking points about the balance sheets of these two financial institution sectors are the substantial financial assets and liabilities alongside a comparatively low net wealth. This follows from the nature of their activities as financial intermediaries. Their business is to lend and borrow funds, hence their substantial holdings of financial assets and liabilities. The near equality of the financial asset and liability positions again reflects the nature of their business as intermediaries. Unlike companies in the ICC sector they do not need substantial investment in plant, equipment and stocks to undertake this business, hence the relatively low

Table 1.7 *Other financial institutions sector balance sheet, 1987, (£bn)*

Financial liabilities		*Financial assets*	
Net wealth	33.6	Tangible assets	76.1
Financial liabilities	693.7	Financial assets	651.2
	727.3		727.3

Source: CSO, UK National Accounts, 1989, Table 12.5.

Table 1.8 *Public sector balance sheet, 1987 (£bn)*

Financial liabilities		*Financial assets*	
Net wealth	242.1	Tangible assets	381.2
Financial liabilities	282.7	Financial assets	143.6
	524.8		524.8

Source: CSO, UK National Accounts, 1989, Tables 12.6, 12.7, 12.8 (own calculations).

level of tangible assets. These tangible assets are mainly buildings, for example the branch networks of the banks and building societies, and equipment such as computers.

(iv) *The public sector*

The balance sheet data that are published by the CSO for the public sector are separated into its three component parts of public corporations, local government and central government. For this overview type of analysis, these components are approximately aggregated to provide a public sector balance sheet, shown in table 1.8.

The public sector's tangible assets have risen slowly in value over the 1980s and hence its share of national wealth has declined from 18 per cent in 1980 to under 14 per cent in 1985 (see table 1.2 above). This is due in the main to the policies of privatisation (sales of public corporation assets) and sales of council houses (sales of local authority tangible assets) initiated by the Conservative administration over this period.

1.7 Sectoral flow of funds

The analysis of sectoral financial relationships has so far examined balance sheets. These show the breakdown of wealth by sector and the financial relationships between sectors at one moment in time – the day the balance sheet is constructed, which for the above was 31 December 1987. This is useful information but it is only a 'snapshot' of the financial relationships at a particular point in time and does not show us how the relationships have been arrived at or how they are changing. Therefore, in addition to information on stocks of assets and liabilities it is also useful to have information on flows of funds into and out of these stocks, recorded over periods of time. By comparing the balance sheets of a sector at two different points in time and noting the changes that have taken place over the intervening time period, balance sheet data can be converted from stock to flow form. Abstracting from price changes, if we compare a sector's balance sheet as of 31 December 1986 with that for 31 December 1987, for example, we would see the net changes that have taken place between the beginning and end of 1987 and these net changes provide the basis for flow of funds accounts. To introduce the construction of sector flow of funds accounts from balance sheets we will revert to our simple economy made up of only two sectors; households and firms. After this introduction we will move on to examine a complete flow of funds account for the UK economy.

The real and financial flows of a sector of an economy are related in the following manner. Over some period, say one year, the sector will receive income (Y) and will spend some proportion of this on consumption (C), with the remainder being termed saving (S).

$$Y - C = S$$

A sector's saving can be used in three ways:

(i)   to finance investment (I) in tangible assets
(ii) to acquire financial assets
(iii) to reduce financial liabilities.

Thus, after accounting for funds used for investment, the remainder of a sector's savings determine the net financial transactions it can undertake. That is,

$$S - I = \text{financial balance}$$

If a sector's financial balance is positive, then it is said to have financial surplus, which implies it has funds available to add to its financial assets or to reduce its financial liabilities. If a sector's financial balance is negative, then it is said to be in financial deficit, which implies it needs to raise funds by selling its holdings of financial assets or increasing its financial liabilities by borrowing.

We can now consider a simple two-sector – households and firms – economy which has two financial instruments available for transactions –

trade credit and equity. Trade credit is an asset of firms, that is, it
represents funds lent from firms to households. Equity on the other hand
is an asset of households. At 31 December 1986 our imaginary household
sector is described by the following balance sheet.

Households
Balance sheet at 31 December 1986

Liabilities		Assets	
Net wealth	1,400	Tangible	800
Financial	200	Financial	800
	1,600		1,600

Over 1987 the following flows are undertaken by the household sector.

Household flows over 1987

Income	=	500
Consumption	=	300
Saving	=	200
Investment	=	100
Financial balance	=	100

So over 1987 the household sector had a financial surplus of £100
million, which implies that it has funds available to enable it to acquire
more financial assets or reduce existing liabilities or both. For this
example we take the situation where households acquire £200 million of
company-issued equities as well as increasing their liabilities by £100 by
borrowing from companies through the medium of trade credit. Any
other collection of financial flows is possible though, as long as the net
effect is consistent with the financial surplus. At the end of 1987 the
household sector will have the following balance sheet arising out of these
flows.

Households
Balance sheet at 31 December 1987

Liabilities		Assets	
Net wealth	1,600	Tangible	900
Financial	300	Financial	1,000
	1,900		1,900

The increase in tangible assets is the result of investment over the
period. The values of financial assets and liabilities have increased by the

value of the flows over the period. The change in the value of net wealth comes about to bring the balance sheet of households back into balance. Another way to see the increase in net wealth is that it is equal to the value of saving over the period. Saving, which is the value of funds coming into the sector which are not consumed, is one way in which the size of the balance sheet of the sector can increase. The other way is for the value of assets already held to increase. In the case of households, the value of housing may increase as a result of an increase in house prices. So it is possible for the net wealth of a sector to increase without it saving any funds out of its income. However, changes in the value of assets are not captured within flow of funds accounts as they are not actual flows passing between sectors.

If we now consider the firms sector in our imaginary economy, its balance sheet for the end of 1986 is given below.

Firms
Balance sheet at 31 December 1986

Liabilities		Assets	
Net wealth	300	Tangible	500
Financial	400	Financial	200
	700		700

The firms sector flows over 1987 are given below.

Firms flows over 1987

Income	=	200
Consumption	=	___
Saving	=	200
Investment	=	300
Financial balance	=	−100

The firms sector has retained earnings of £200 over 1987 but invests £300 million, leaving it with a financial deficit of £100 million. This implies that firms must sell existing assets or borrow new funds to finance the deficit. The financial decisions of the firms sector are implied by the household sector flows described earlier. This is because, in a two-sector economy, as one sector increases its asset holdings the other sector must be increasing its liabilities by the same amount, for reasons explained in section 1.3. The financial decisions of firms are therefore to borrow funds through the issue of £200 million of equities and at the same time to increase holdings of financial assets by £100 million. The resulting balance sheet for the firms sector for the end of 1987 is given below.

Firms
Balance sheet at 31 December 1987

Liabilities		Assets	
Net wealth	500	Tangible	800
Financial	600	Financial	300
	1,100		1,100

These flows, in particular the financial flows, can be brought together in a flow of funds matrix as shown in table 1.9.

Income and consumption flows are not shown in flow of funds accounts, but the residual of these flows, namely saving, provides the starting point for the account. The top section of the account showing the saving and investment flows of each sector is known as the capital account. The bottom part of the account showing the net flows in each financial instrument by each sector is known as the financial transactions account. The financial balance is the item that links these two accounts. There are some conventions which need to be stated before we can begin to interpret this or any other flow of funds account. The main convention refers to signs on the figures given in the financial transactions account and is:

A positive sign implies an increase in financial assets or a decrease in financial liabilities.

A negative sign implies an increase in financial liabilities or a decrease in financial assets.

So, in the flow of funds account below, a negative sign on trade credit transactions for the household sector implies that this sector is increasing its liabilities, that is, it is borrowing more from companies through the medium of trade credit. It should be clear from this example that in order

Table 1.9 *Flow of funds matrix for a two-sector economy*

	Households	Firms
Saving	200	200
Investment	100	300
Financial balance	100	−100
Trade credit	−100	100
Equities	200	−200
Net financial transactions	100	100

to interpret a particular figure in the financial transactions account we need to know, not only the conventions stated above, but whether the instrument transacted is an asset or a liability of that sector.

From this simple flow of funds matrix we can discern the accounting rules which underlie its construction and in fact the construction of all flow of funds accounts. First, the sum of the financial surpluses and deficits equals zero, which reflects the fact that the financial assets of one sector are by definition the financial liabilities of another. Second, the net financial transactions of a sector will equal its financial balance. Third, the sum of transactions in a particular financial instrument will equal zero. This again follows from the fact that increased holdings of an asset of one sector will be balanced by increased liabilities of another. Finally, the sum of saving across sectors, that is, for the economy, will equal the sum of investment across sectors. In other words, all saving will find its way into investment.

Some caution needs to be exercised when interpreting flow of funds accounts. First of all there are practical problems in constructing actual flow of funds accounts, as opposed to our imaginary account above, and these relate to the nature of the available data. These problems are discussed below. However, there is also a conceptual problem in that the construction of a flow of funds account suggests a hierarchy of decision taking, with the consumption decision presented as being made before the investment decision, which in turn is made before any financial decisions. This hierarchy is established only for accounting purposes as these real and financial decisions are quite likely to be made simultaneously. A presentation of real and financial sectoral flows that avoids this hierarchy problem is a sector sources and uses statement where all of a sector's sources of funds – savings, borrowing and proceeds of asset sales – are grouped separately from the sector's uses of funds – investment, purchases of financial assets and repayments of past borrowing. Sector sources and uses accounts constructed along these lines are published by the CSO.

With these cautions in mind we now turn to examine the construction of flow of funds accounts for the complete UK economy.

1.8 Flow of funds accounts for the UK economy

Both the Bank of England and the CSO publish flow of funds accounts for the UK. Attention here is focused on the Bank of England flow of funds matrix which is published annually in the 'Sector Financing' article in the *Bank of England Quarterly Bulletin*.

The flow of funds matrix for 1988 is presented in table 1.10. This matrix is essentially made up of seven sectors, although the public sector is

Table 1.10 *Flow of funds: annual matrix, 1988 (£m)*

	Line	Central government	Local authorities	Public corporations	Public sector	Banks	Building societies	Other financial institutions	Industrial and commercial companies	Personal sector	Overseas sector	Residual error
Capital account												
Saving	1	+7,425	+1,653	+5,769	+14,847		+14,753		+43,445	+13,393	+14,672	
Taxes on capital and capital transfers	2	+779	−2,243	+787	+1,949		−403		−210	−1,336	−	
less:												
Gross fixed capital formation at home	3	−3,714	−2,243	−4,882	−10,839		−12,167		−40,062	−25,451		
Increase in value of stocks and work in progress	4	+322		−276	+46		−		−9,409	−1,101		
Financial surplus+/deficit−	5	+4,812	−207	+1,398	+6,003		+2,183		−6,236	−14,495	+14,672	−2,127
Changes in financial assets and liabilities												
Assets: Increase+/decrease−												
Liabilities: increase−/decrease+												
Notes and coin	6	−1,476		−3	−1,479	+270	+120	+4	+94	+945	+46	
Sterling Treasury bills	7	−1,277	+2	+120	−1,155	+1,185	+10	+4	−70		+26	
British government securities	8	+5,032	+25	−4	+5,053	−2,365	+560	−1,674	−420	−1,996	+842	
National savings	9	−1,536		−48	−1,488		+5	+1	+73	+1,409		
Certificates of tax deposit	10	+1,034	−	+63	+1,097	−313	−379		−434	+29		
Net government indebtedness to Banking Department	11	−138		+138	+138	+138						

	Code	1	2	3	4	5	6	7	8	9
Northern Ireland central government debt	12	+8	+8						−5	−3
Government liabilities under exchange cover scheme	13	−188	−6	+179	−15			+15		
Other public sector financing:										
Non-marketable debt	14.1	−450	+450							
Short-term assets	14.2	+1,081	+450				−247		−70	
Issue Department's transactions in bills	15	+435	+435			+657	−677		−596	+181
Government foreign currency debt	16	+449	+449			+172				−621
Other government overseas financing	17	+73	+73							−73
Official reserves	18	+2,761	+2,761							−2,761
Local authority debt	19	+4,860	−3,404	+1,422	−445	+214	−96		−681	−12
Public corporation debt	20	+716	+47	+877	−523	−30			−13	−311
Deposits with banks:										
Sterling sight	21.1	+83	−106	+107	+82	−12,095	+1,959		+1,895	+8,159
Sterling time	21.2	+94	+1,734	+879	+2,707	−27,508	+4,543	+7,426	+4,293	+8,539
Foreign currency	21.3	−99	+8	+3	−88	−2,768	+2,380		+254	+222
Banks' net external transactions	21.4					−14,342				+14,342
Deposits with building societies	22				+403	−21,153	+200	−92	+20,165	+477
Bank lending (excluding public sector):										
Foreign currency	24.1					+9,650		−1,028	−8,333	−289
Sterling	24.2					+44,134	−391	−8,927	−22,163	−12,653
Credit extended by retailers	25								+260	−260
Identified trade credit:										
Domestic	26.1	+7	−1,106			−1,099	+300		+823	−24
Import and export	26.2		−32			−32			+320	−288
Loans for house purchase:										
Building societies	27.1	+153							−415	−23,178
Other	27.2	−313	−9		−169	+10,893	+23,593	+5,804		−16,528

Table 1.10 *Continued*

		Central govern-ment	Local authori-ties	Public corpora-tions	Public sector	Banks	Building societies	Other financial institu-tions	Industrial and commer-cial companies	Personal sector	Over-seas sector	Resi-dual error
Other public sector lending	28	+254	+40	-2	+292	-	-	-	-124	+21	-189	
Other lending by financial institutions	29			-	-	-	+280	+1,122	-759	-643		
Unit trust units	30							+540		-540		
UK company securities	31	-6,192	+118	-74	-6,148	-2,379	-2,889	+6,370	-2,254	-2,046	+9,346	
Overseas securities	32	-		-	-	+1,734	-	+5,952	+5,553	+2,904	-16,143	
Life assurance and pension funds	33	-869			-869			-20,927		+21,796		
Miscellaneous domestic instruments	34	-	-88	+88		-123	+257	+1,968	-3,385	-276	+1,559	
Direct and other investment abroad	35					-552		+428	+9,549	-30	-9,395	
Overseas direct and other investment in the United Kingdom	36					-339		+24	-3,541	-445	+4,301	
Miscellaneous overseas instruments	37	-174		+49	-125	-39	-	+781	-3,445		+2,828	
Accruals adjustment	38	+1,306	-276	-225	+805	-47	-499	-2,101	+162	+1,680		
Financial transactions	39	+4,866	-1,140	+611	+4,337	+5,398	+2,896	-133	-22,911	+6,258	+4,155	
Balancing item	40	-54	+933	+787	+1,666	-5,978			+16,675	-20,753	+10,517	-2,127

Source: Bank of England Quarterly Bulletin, February 1990.

further disaggregated into its three components. The total number of financial instruments is thirty-nine. Whilst the matrix in table 1.10 is larger and more disaggregated than the matrix for our imaginary economy in table 1.9, its structure is essentially the same. Taking the capital account, made up of lines 1 to 4, the starting point is again saving. Line 2, which was not included in our simple flow of funds matrix, simply captures any fund transfers between sectors which do not involve a corresponding transfer of goods and services. Lines three and four together make up investment. The financial transactions account consists of lines 6 to 38, with the financial balance, line 5, providing the link between the two accounts.

It was mentioned above that there are problems with the data used to construct both national income and flow of funds accounts. The figures making up these accounts are recorded with varying degrees of error. A sector's overall financial position, after calculating all income, expenditure and capital flows, is shown in its financial balance. If these flows were accurately recorded and if the sector's financial transactions were likewise identified in full, then the sum of financial transactions, shown in line 39, should equal the financial balance. The effects of the errors and omissions in the flows recorded above and below line 5 lead to a difference between the financial balance and the sum of financial transactions. This difference is recorded in line 40 as the balancing item, although its appearance adjacent to the financial transactions account should not be interpreted as meaning that all or even most of the errors occur in this account. The sum of the balancing items across each sector is equal, necessarily, to the residual error, which accounts for the discrepancy between the recorded national income and expenditure flows. For the public sector and financial institutions, where most transactions have to be accurately recorded for policy or supervisory purposes, then the balancing items have generally been small. For the other sectors, where there is less direct collection of statistics, the balancing items are large and have been particularly large in the latter part of the 1980s. Whilst there is a practice of revising recently published data as new information comes to light, which tends to reduce the balancing item, the large size of recent balancing items has tended to undermine the value of the accounts. This can be seen in table 1.11, showing the balancing items for the three sectors most prone to this problem.

The CSO has recently (1990) taken steps to reduce the deficiencies in its published statistics by, among other things, increasing its number of statisticians by 25 per cent.

There are other deficiencies with the Bank of England flow of funds matrix, although none as serious as that just described. One problem, which can be seen from the matrix in table 1.10, is that the available data

Table 1.11   *Balancing items, 1990, (£bn)*

Sector	1986	1987	1988
Personal	−8.1	−24.9	−20.8
ICCs	−0.2	+7.0	+16.5
Overseas	+9.9	+10.0	+10.5

Source: *Bank   of   England   Quarterly   Bulletin*, February 1990.

do not allow a separation of the capital account transactions of the three sub-groups of financial institutions. A further problem is that the data are published on a net basis, that is, a figure presented in the financial transactions account represents the net result of purchases and sales (new borrowing and repayments) of an asset (liability). We cannot therefore infer whether a larger than normal figure for, say, acquisition of company securities by other financial institutions is due to greater purchases or lower sales during the period. However, despite all these drawbacks, there are still many interesting points that can be drawn from a study of a flow of funds account. One fundamental thing that the accounts show is that those people who save in an economy are not the same as those people who invest in physical assets. The flow of funds account thus demonstrates one of the reasons for the existence of financial institutions, which is to channel funds from savers to investors, and it shows the various routes by which the funds flow. This will be considered in more detail in the next chapter. The flow of funds account, by setting the flows for each sector together in a consistent framework, also allows us to obtain a more complete picture of financial relationships compared with looking at each sector's flows individually. For example, if we examine row 21.2 in the accounts for 1988 in table 1.10, we can see each sector's transactions in bank time deposits. Here we see that of the approximately £27.5 billion net flows into bank time deposits over 1988, roughly 30 per cent came from the personal sector, 15 per cent from companies, 27 per cent from other financial institutions and 16 per cent from building societies. The banks in fact attracted a lot of new funds into time deposits in 1988 (the figure for 1987 was £19 billion) for various reasons, but in particular because the stock market crash of October 1987 had made private (in the personal sector) and institutional (in other financial institutions) investors wary of equities. They therefore placed a larger proportion of their surplus funds in liquid assets, thereby enabling them to obtain a reasonable return whilst being in a position to switch funds back into equities or other investments once those markets looked more attractive.

Another interesting feature of the financial picture in 1988 revealed by this flow of funds account is that the personal sector, whilst acquiring more liquid assets, such as bank and building society deposits, than usual, still showed a financial deficit. Historically it is unusual for the personal sector to show a financial deficit, with a long period of financial surplus being obtained for the years 1972 to 1985. The main explanation for this change from net lender to net borrower for the personal sector can be seen by looking at lines 24.2, 27.1 and 27.2 in table 1.10. These lines show that the borrowing undertaken by the personal sector is large and in fact increased at a rapid rate over the 1980s following the removal of controls on lending in 1980 and the general liberalisation of the financial system that followed. These borrowed funds have financed a boom in both consumption and housing expenditure by the personal sector. These trends will be examined in greater detail in the next chapter. One of the implications of the consumption boom is also revealed in the flow of funds account. This is the financial surplus of the overseas sector, which implies a current account deficit (i.e. imports exceed exports) on the balance of trade with overseas economies.

This discussion of some of the features of the 1988 flow of funds accounts was intended to show that, bearing in mind the caveat on data deficiencies, some interesting insights into changing financial relationships can be obtained from a study of such accounts.

1.9 Conclusion

In this chapter we have started our examination of the role of a financial system in an economy, we have established some fundamental concepts of finance and we have introduced data on wealth and financial transactions in the UK and shown the relationship between these. In the next chapter we build on this and examine further the role of a financial system in intermediating between savers and investors, before looking at how financial systems evolve.

Chapter 2

Financial intermediation

2.1 Introduction

In this chapter we aim, first of all, to describe the process of financial intermediation, a process which provides the *raison d'être* for financial institutions. Our second aim is to examine the general evolution of financial systems and in particular distinguish between the more bank-oriented financial systems of Germany and Japan and the more market-oriented systems of the United States and the UK. Our final aim is to provide an overview of the many significant changes that have taken place in the UK financial system over the last twenty years and the 1980s in particular. This will provide a framework for the more specific discussion of changes to financial institutions and financial markets which make up the remainder of this book.

2.2 Financial intermediation

In developed economies, decisions to invest are often taken separately from decisions to save. There are some exceptions to this; for example, firms which do not distribute all profits as dividends but retain some to finance investment are both saving and investing. However, even when saving and investment are carried out by the same economic agent, the timing of the decisions will often be different. Saving may precede the investment as sufficient funds are accumulated, or the saving may follow the investment as debts used to finance it are paid off. However, it is a general feature of developed economies that a high proportion of saving that takes place is not used immediately by the saver but is made available to investors elsewhere. In the last chapter, one of the roles of a financial system was described as the channelling of funds from those who save to those who invest. To be more precise, we are concerned with the channelling of funds from those economic agents with a financial financial surplus (lenders) to those economic agents with a deficit (borrowers). Whilst most borrowing is used to finance investment, this more precise statement acknowledges that there will be some economic agents who borrow to finance a deficit which has arisen not from investment but from an excess of consumption over income.

A financial system essentially consists of financial markets and financial institutions. In this section we will examine in some detail the role of financial markets and institutions in the process of channelling funds from lenders to borrowers. To begin the analysis we will return to our simple economy, introduced in section 1.2, which consists of households and firms only. This highlights more clearly the benefits which a financial system brings to this process. Assuming that households in aggregate are lenders and firms in aggregate are borrowers, then the only way in which funds can flow from lenders to borrowers is directly, as shown in figure 2.1.

In this simple economy, firms will finance some part of their investment by borrowing funds from households and in return households will hold the financial claims issued by firms. Investment, which takes the form of the acquisition of durable real assets such as buildings or machinery, will generally be long term in nature so that the returns to the firm generated by the investment will take some time to meet the promised repayment to the claim holder. Further to this, investment by firms is an inherently risky activity. The returns produced by the investment are uncertain. The firm making the investment may have misjudged the market for the

Figure 2.1

product, or the costs of producing the product may be higher than anticipated. Both these factors would cause returns to be less than the anticipated level. Furthermore, the acquired real assets are generally highly specialised, making them difficult to sell, if problems occur, except at a loss.

The characteristics which borrowers seek in the claims they issue are likely to reflect these features of investment. That is, they will seek to issue long-term claims, such as a long-term loan, which will provide a reasonable prospect of the investment generating sufficient returns to repay the claim. Given the uncertainty of the returns from investment, firms are also likely to seek to finance some part of the investment in the form of equity, where the claim can be remunerated according to the profitability of the firm.

Whilst some (wealthy) lenders will be happy to hold long-term, risky claims, it is likely that the majority of lenders will seek different characteristics in the claims they hold. As we saw in chapter 1, there are many motives for saving. Some economic agents save in order to even out income and consumption flows or to provide a cushion against unforeseen circumstances and, in such cases will have a short time horizon. Other saving may be directed towards long-term needs such as retirement. Such motives for saving will have a bearing on the characteristics of the financial claims that savers will seek to hold. For most savers, an important characteristic will be safety, that is, the risk of loss of the sum lent should be low. For savings directed towards short-term purposes, the characteristic of liquidity will be important.

It is clear from the preceding discussion that the requirements of borrowers and lenders are in general different. Borrowers are looking to issue long-term, risky claims. Lenders will be seeking to hold low-risk and, in many cases, short-term claims. In addition, borrowers are likely to be seeking a sum of money which in general will be greater than the sum provided by one lender. In the absence of organised financial markets or financial institutions, as presented in figure 2.1, lending/ borrowing will occur as a result of direct negotiation between two parties. The claims that occur as a result of such transactions will be highly illiquid since it would be difficult to sell them to a third party in the absence of an organised market. There will also be significant search costs as borrowers seek out willing lenders and vice versa. For the borrower seeking a large loan such costs will be greater as a number of lenders will have to be found. There will also be costs relating to the drawing up of any agreement confirming the terms of the transaction. There are also additional costs involved in carrying out a financial transaction which are generally not encountered in trade in physical goods and services. This is because the potential lender will have to assess whether the borrower can meet the promises of future payments over the relatively long time period which are inherent in financial claims. Thus the lender will have to assess the financial standing of the borrower and also whether the use to which the loaned funds are put is likely to generate sufficient returns to repay the claim. A particular problem here is that borrowers have more information about the likely return and riskiness of the investment project than a direct lender. This problem is one of a class of general problems of trade in financial markets, referred to since Akerlof [1970] as that of asymmetric information. A related problem is that of moral hazard, which here refers to the incentive for borrowers to exaggerate the returns or play down the risks involved in the use of the borrowed funds; that is, they may behave differently when using borrowed rather their own funds. Therefore a lender will incur costs in acquiring information and the information obtained may not be complete or honest. In addition, after the loan is made, the lender will incur further costs relating to monitoring the performance of the borrower until the loan is repaid.

If we now consider the situation where an organised financial market emerges where standard equity-type instruments are issued and acquired. Such a market is called a capital market as it deals in claims which are used to finance the acquisition of capital or physical assets. A capital market where claims are first issued is called a primary market, as distinct from a secondary market which deals in the purchase and sales of existing claims. We shall consider this distinction in more detail in chapter 8. The existence of organised primary and secondary capital markets overcomes some of the obstacles to the flow of funds from lenders to borrowers. The ability to sell on claims in a market will enhance the liquidity of such claims and so encourage more lending of funds. In addition, a central feature of organised markets is the existence of specialist brokers who bring together buyers and sellers and so reduce the search costs outlined above. However, many of the problems which reduce the incentive to lend and borrow remain; in particular, the risk of the claims on offer to lenders is still high. It is the existence of financial institutions which provides the means to overcome such problems and so stimulate and smooth the flow of funds from lenders to borrowers. Financial institutions achieve such an intermediation by holding the long-term, risky claims of borrowers whilst financing the lending that accompanies this by issuing claims which are attractive to lenders. For example, a financial institution such as a bank lends funds in the form of loans, which are generally risky and long term, whilst at the same time it borrows funds in the form of low-risk, short-term deposits – see figure 2.2.

So, instead of households only being able to deal directly with firms, they can now also deal indirectly through an intermediary such as a bank.

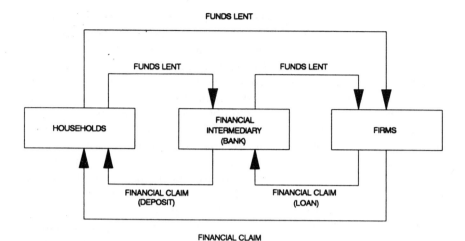

Figure 2.2

To acknowledge the indirect nature of the flow of funds from households to firms in this example, households can be labelled the ultimate lenders and firms the ultimate borrowers. We can seem from this example that the process of financial intermediation, that is, the process by which financial institutions intermediate to reconcile the conflicting require-ments of lenders and borrowers, involves not only a channelling of funds from ultimate lenders to ultimate borrowers but also a transformation of the characteristics of those funds as they pass through the intermediary. We now turn to examine in greater detail the ways in which financial institutions can achieve this transformation of the characteristics of funds, how they reduce transaction costs involved in channelling funds from lenders to borrowers and finally the implications of financial inter-mediation for the economy.

2.3   Features of financial intermediation

Maturity transformation
On average, financial intermediaries have liabilities with a shorter term to maturity than that possessed by their assets. A good illustration of this phenomenon is provided by the practice of building societies, which accept deposits largely repayable on demand and make loans repayable over twenty-five or thirty years (note that this overstates the degree of maturity transformation since many mortgages are in fact repaid before maturity). This is known as mis-matching their balance sheets or

borrowing 'short' and lending 'long'. Mis-matching exposes the institution to liquidity risk, which is the risk that they have insufficient liquidity to meet their commitments. Financial institutions can accomplish such mis-matching by relying on the 'law of large numbers' and holding a structured asset portfolio. The law of large numbers applied here means that a bank, for example, by attracting a large number of depositors, knows that in any period, whilst some depositors will be withdrawing funds, others will be making new deposits, thus keeping the net withdrawal of funds small in relation to total liabilities. Banks can then cover against the potential net withdrawal by holding some assets in liquid form which it can turn into cash at short notice if required. This is not the only method by which banks can manage liquidity risk and further discussion of this problem is left until chapter 3.

Risk transformation
Financial institutions such as banks hold mainly loans in their asset portfolio, but issue mainly deposits to finance these assets. Loans inevitably carry some risk of default, yet bank deposits are generally considered to be of low risk. Financial institutions can transform risky assets into virtually riskless deposits by minimising the risk of the individual loans it takes on, by spreading the risks over a large number of loans and by holding sufficient capital to meet any unexpected losses.

There are many ways in which a bank can control the risk of any individual loan it takes on going into default. First of all the bank can consider the purpose of the loan and allow funds to be lent only for what the bank considers to be legitimate. Secondly, it can consider the financial circumstances of the borrower. An important consideration here would be the borrower's income, although other factors are also taken into account for consumer lending where credit scoring is increasingly used. Such factors include other financial commitments, age and whether the borrower is a home owner. Under credit scoring, on the basis of their answers to a standard set of questions, borrowers are given a score which determines the risk involved and therefore whether to make the loan. The use of credit scoring has largely replaced judgement in determining loan entitlement, and can indeed be automated, so reducing costs of acquiring information to judge borrower suitability. A third method of reducing individual loan risk is for the bank to ask for security over the borrower's assets. In the event of the borrower getting into difficulties and being unable to meet the loan repayments, the bank can sell the secured assets and recover the loan. A well, known type of secured lending is mortgage lending, where the house is used as security.

Even when such methods of risk control are used there is still some residual risk of loan default. Further techniques of risk management can be used by banks to manage such risks. One particular technique is to pool risks by making a large number of small loans rather than a small number of large loans. In addition, financial intermediaries can spread their loans across different types of borrowers and geographical region. If, for example, a bank lent funds only to firms involved in the construction industry, then it is open to the risk of a large number of defaults if there is a recession in the construction industry. By spreading its loans across different types of firms, firms in different regions and consumers as well as firms, it achieves a greater independence of default risks. Of course, if the whole economy goes into recession then it will incur a relatively large number of defaults. International diversification of its loans may help to reduce this problem.

Use of these techniques of risk management increases the accuracy of the bank's predictions of its loan losses in any one period. Knowledge of its probability distribution of loan losses allows the bank to incorporate a charge in its lending rate to cover the expected value of such losses. Any loan losses in excess of its expected losses, that is, any unexpected losses, are then covered by the institution's own capital and it is only in the event of losses in excess of the institution's capital that the depositors' funds are threatened. It is quite rare for a bank or similar financial institution to default on its deposits and hence deposits are considered to be safe financial instruments. There are occasions when a loss of confidence may lead to large net withdrawals from an institution or a particular group of institutions. For example, Kindleberger [1978] reports that in the US over the depression years of 1930–33, such a loss of confidence occurred leading to 9096 bank suspensions. This is known as systemic risk and is one of the reasons for the detailed prudential controls over financial institutions seen in most countries. This is discussed in chapter 17.

Another type of risk transformation is carried out by financial institutions which hold mainly ordinary shares in their asset portfolios. In the UK, such institutions are unit trusts and investment trusts. These institutions hold portfolios of ordinary shares, which as we saw in section 1.3 are particularly risky assets. By holding a large number of different shares in the portfolio, particularly if these shares are spread over different types of company and even different countries, as with bank loans described above, the overall riskiness of the portfolio can be reduced without any corresponding loss in the overall return of the portfolio. An additional advantage in portfolio construction held by institutions such as unit trusts and investment trusts over all but the most wealthy individuals is that the proportionate transaction costs in buying and selling shares are smaller for larger blocks of shares. The claims issued by such institutions therefore offer the advantage of lower risk that comes from a diversified portfolio with lower costs of achieving and maintaining the portfolio.

Collection and parcelling

When describing the requirements of lenders and borrowers above it was noted that lenders tend to lend smaller amounts of funds relative to the amounts that borrowers generally wish to borrow. A third feature of financial intermediation then is the way in which many financial institutions collect the small amounts of funds made available by lenders and parcel these into the larger amounts required by borrowers. Institutions such as banks and building societies achieve this collection by convenient location of their branches in high streets, but more generally the various institutions achieve this collection by offering claims which are tailored to meet the lenders' requirements. The convenient location of institutions and the standard products offered by such institutions can reduce the search and information costs to both lenders and borrowers. Related to this feature of collecting small amounts to onlend as larger amounts is the feature of size intermediation. This refers to the process by which financial intermediaries can offer the small lender the benefits which would come from lending large amounts. An example of size intermediation was referred to in the last section on risk transformation whereby institutions such as unit trusts provide the advantages which arise from a diversified portfolio to the small lender. Another example is the money market deposits provided by most banks in the UK and many other countries. Such accounts offer the high rates of interest available on large wholesale money market deposits to lenders without the requirement of providing the large outlay.

2.4 Rationale for the existence of financial intermediaries

We will now attempt to bring together the various strands of the analysis introduced above and so provide the main reasons suggested to explain the existence of financial intermediaries. One of the main obstacles to direct financing of ultimate borrowers by ultimate lenders was presented as the conflicting requirements of lenders and borrowers in terms of the characteristics of the financial claims sought by lenders and the characteristics of the financial claims that borrowers would prefer to issue. Financial institutions are therefore able to find a role in bridging this gap by holding the primary claims issued by borrowers but financing these by issuing secondary claims which have characteristics which are more attractive to lenders. Financial intermediaries therefore in effect transform the characteristics of the funds as they pass from ultimate lender to ultimate borrower.

The costs involved in ultimate lenders transacting with ultimate borrowers are likely to be high. There are various types of costs involved in such direct transactions including (i) searching out suitable agents to transact with, (ii) drawing up contracts, (iii) obtaining information on borrowers to enable the assessment of the likelihood of repayment of the loan, and (iv) monitoring and enforcing the terms of the contract. Where a lender and borrower have agreed to transact at a particular rate of interest, the existence of transaction costs implicitly reduces the return earned by the lender below that of the agreed interest rate and increases the charge paid by the borrower to above the agreed rate. The existence of a differential between the net return to lending and the total cost of borrowing provides additional scope for the emergence of financial intermediaries.

Many reasons have been presented in the discussion above to suggest that the involvement of financial intermediaries reduces these transaction costs, including convenient location and provision of standard products. In general, though, there are two main advantages that financial inter-mediaries bring to the process that are likely to lead to lower transaction costs. First, their size brings economies that generally accompany a large scale of operations. Second, by specialising they obtain expertise and experience of obtaining and interpreting information which enables them to assess and manage the various risks involved. By significantly reducing transaction costs, the intermediary is able to enter the market and earn a profit on its operations by charging an interest rate on lending (loan rate) which is higher than that paid on borrowing (deposit rate). As long as the differential between the financial intermediaries' lending and borrowing rates is lower than the differential created by transaction costs in the process of direct transacting then all parties gain from the existence of intermediaries. More formally, defining the rate of interest as R and the search transaction costs as T_L and T_B for the lender and borrower respectively (note these costs are calculated as a percentage on the loan):

$$\text{The net return for the lender } (R_L) = R - T_L$$
$$\text{The cost for the borrower } \quad (R_B) = R + T_B$$

then

$$R_B - R_L = T_B + T_L$$

Introduction of a financial intermediary introduces a new element of cost C, which we, for convenience, assume is paid by the borrower and is again expressed in percentage terms. Thus now:

$$R_L = R - T'_L$$
$$R_B = R + T'_B + C$$

where the prime indicates search/transaction costs after the introduction of the intermediary. Hence

$$R_B - R_L = T'_B + T'_L + C$$

The gap between lending and borrowing rates will be lower and benefit both parties provided:

$$(T_B + T_L) - (T'_B + T'_L) > C,$$

that is, providing the introduction of the intermediary has lowered search/transaction costs by more than its charge.

Competition between intermediaries serves to keep down operating costs and therefore the margin charged by the intermediaries. The competitive pressures have increased over the 1980s following widescale deregulation within the financial system and we will return to this topic later in this chapter.

It is likely that the reduction in costs involved in lending and borrowing through financial intermediaries has increased the level of lending and hence saving and borrowing and hence investment compared to a situation of no intermediation. The stimulation of investment has also been achieved through the improvement in the characteristics of financial instruments available, which is likely to have made saving more attractive, again increasing the level of aggregate saving. A more rigorous economic analysis of the implications of financial intermediation is provided in Bain [1981, chapter 4].

In addition to conflicting requirements of borrowers and lenders and transaction costs, a further reason to explain the existence of financial intermediaries which is increasingly stressed in the literature is the existence of informational asymmetries. Direct lenders do not have the experience or skills necessary to gather information on borrowers and monitor their performance and so lenders delegate these functions to an intermediary which can specialise in this role. Leland and Pyle [1977] and Diamond [1984] analyse such market imperfections as a basis for the existence of intermediaries.

In the traditional view of finance, the emergence of financial intermediaries is seen as the final stage in the evolution of a financial system. A new view has been presented though (see, for example, McCulloch [1981] and Tobin [1984]) which argues that financial intermediaries can in some circumstances distort the workings of the system and, further, that they should be seen as a transitory phase in this evolutionary process. The final phase under the new view is a complete set of spot, futures and options markets embracing all commodities and all contingencies. Such markets are referred to as Arrow–Debreu markets following the Arrow–Debreu general equilibrium model (for an exposition of this see Arrow and Hahn [1971]) and are markets characterised by negligible transaction costs. The nature of futures and options markets is covered later in this book (see chapter 13). Essentially, though, futures markets allow trade in commodities for delivery in the future. The existence of a complete set of such markets allows borrowing to take place by selling goods now for delivery at a future date. Similarly, lending takes place by buying goods now for future delivery. Options markets are essentially markets in contingent claims, that is, they provide the holder of an option with insurance against the risk of a particular contingency occurring. The existence of a complete set of such contingent markets removes the uncertainty from transactions. With negligible transaction costs and little risk involved in lending and borrowing, there is no role for financial intermediaries and transactions would return again to direct barter. The existence of a complete set of options and futures markets with negligible transaction costs is, of course, a theoretical construct. Such markets, however, are expanding in both volume of transactions and number of products traded. Advances in computer and telecommunications technology are reducing costs of financial transactions. This new view of finance may therefore provide some indication of the likely future direction of financial systems. Indeed, there is some evidence of a move away from financial intermediation by large companies to raising funds directly through international capital markets. This phenomenon is referred to as securitisation and is discussed in more detail in chapter 12.

2.5 Evolution of financial systems

The financial systems that have emerged in the major developed countries of the world have some important differences in structure. The differences that exist, in particular the different relationships between the financial system and the corporate sector, have been suggested as one explanation of the different economic performances of these countries since the second world war. We will examine this debate in some detail in chapter 16 of this book. However, to provide some background to this debate we will consider here the relationship between the evolution of a financial system and the different phases of economic growth (see Rybczynski [1988] for further discussion).

In the early stages of the growth of an economy, that is when an economy transforms itself from agrarian to industrial, it is banks which act as the main intermediary providing the external finance for the investment required for this restructuring. During this **bank-oriented** phase of the financial system, ownership of the productive resources of the economy is concentrated in few hands and there is little separation of ownership and control of these resources.

As industrialisation continues it is usual for firms to obtain a larger proportion of their externally raised funds through the capital markets. This inevitably leads to a separation of ownership from control of firms, with ownership (i.e. holders of the equity claims issued by firms through the capital market) held by households both directly and increasingly indirectly, through non-bank financial companies. The control of firms is delegated to professional managers subject to satisfactory performance of the company. In this **market-oriented** phase of the financial system, the role of the banks in providing finance for firms is less important and generally passive. As industrialisation reaches a peak, there is greater restructuring of economic activity, that is, redirection of resources in the economy through a change in the ownership and control of firms. This active restructuring takes place through the capital markets.

As the economy moves into what has been termed the de-industrialisation phase, where the relative importance of the traditional manufacturing industries declines and the relative importance of service industries increases, there is a much greater level of economic restructuring. This places greater demands on the financial system which, it is argued, moves into the **securitised phase**. The functions of the financial system expand under this phase so that enhanced capital and credit markets emerge along with markets for corporate control and venture capital. The financial system is more complete under the securitised phase and, more importantly, plays an active role in the re-structuring of the economy. This restructuring takes place through the new markets in corporate control and venture capital. The market for corporate control is concerned with changing the ownership and control of existing firms and is increasingly carried out through the use of takeovers. Such takeovers are often hostile (that is, the bid from the company proposing the takeover is opposed by the target company's management) but the takeover process may be seen as providing a discipline on companies, allowing control to be transferred from inefficient to efficient management – see chapter 16 for further discussion of this. The market for venture capital is concerned with the provision of finance to the new firms which emerge in this restructuring process.

The preceding description of the evolution of financial systems was very general and does not apply to all countries. The description is probably most applicable to the United States (US) and the UK, with the transformation to a securitised financial system taking place earlier in the US. In contrast, countries such as Germany, Japan and to a lesser extent France have continued to operate with a financial system which more closely represents the bank-oriented system. In such countries, banks can and do act in an active way in industrial restructuring, providing risk capital (equity) to companies and then working closely with those companies. This close relationship also involves performance monitoring of the management of the company and where necessary banks may initiate a change in the management or ownership of companies. Such changes though, in contrast to the market or securitised systems, are generally carried out without hostile confrontation.

The foregoing discussion of the evolution of financial systems presents a clearcut distinction between bank-oriented and market-oriented or securitised systems. In recent years certain developments have blurred this distinction. As countries loosely associated with bank-oriented systems have moved into the de-industrialisation phase, the accompanying increased level of restructuring has tended to encourage a transition to more market-oriented or securitised financial systems. Countries experiencing such a transition are France and Italy. Also, companies in both Germany and Japan are now increasingly making greater use of capital markets, with a greater proportion of risk capital provided by non-bank institutions. Finally, countries more strongly associated with bank-oriented systems have recently experienced hostile takeover activity, although the regulatory and institutional impediments to hostile takeovers in such countries suggest that such activity is unlikely to grow at a significant rate.

2.6 Recent developments in the UK financial system

In the last section we identified that the UK system has recently moved into a securitised type of financial system. There has in fact been a vast amount of change in the UK financial system in recent years, and in particular over the 1980s. The changes that have taken place are not random and can be analysed in a systematic way. In this section we will provide an overall perspective of the main forces leading to change and the major changes that have taken place. This analysis (adapted from Llewellyn [1985]) will provide a framework for the more specific assessment and interpretation of events in the various financial markets and institutions throughout the rest of this book.

Some of the main forces leading to change in any financial system are:

(i)   Changes in the market environment.
(ii)   Changes in the portfolio preferences of the users of financial intermediation services.
(iii) Changes in the portfolio preferences of and constraints on the providers of financial intermediation services.

The interaction of these forces produces (a) financial innovation, which is essentially the development of new financial instruments, markets and techniques of intermediation, and (b) changes in the structure of the financial system, with new markets appearing, and changes in the organisation and behaviour of institutions. With this general framework in mind we can now examine the main changes in the financial system.

Over the postwar period up to the end of the 1960s the UK financial system was characterised by strict demarcation between the various types of financial institution. So, for example, it was rare for the banks to operate in the housing finance market, which was seen as the sole province of the building societies. There are therefore very little competition between the different types of financial institution. There was also little internal competition within a particular financial market as, for example, banks and building societies operated cartels which controlled the setting of interest rates. Similarly within the stock market, restrictive practices, in particular the existence of minimum non-negotiable commissions, had the effect of reducing competition. Towards the end of the 1960s however, the first competitive pressures were felt by banks as the relaxed requirements of entry to the City of London saw penetration by foreign banks into the UK banking system. In 1971 the first substantial official reforms of the financial system, known as Competition and Credit Control, were introduced. These reforms were aimed at the banking system and were designed to remove the banking cartel and encourage competition between banks. These reforms heralded the beginning of a long period of deregulation of the financial system, mostly officially sanctioned, which has increased competition throughout the financial system. Most of the deregulation of the financial system has, though, taken place over the 1980s and has been a feature of financial systems in most other countries. Before we analyse the changes that have taken place, we will first of all examine the broad forces inducing change referred to above.

Changes in the market environment
The main environmental factors over the 1970s and 1980s which brought about changes in the financial system can be summarised as follows:

(i) These was a strong trend over this period, particularly the 1980s, towards deregulation of the financial system. The aim here was to introduce greater competition into the financial system with a view to increasing efficiency. Alongside this deregulation was a parallel trend to tighten up the prudential regulation of the financial system, with the aim here of protecting the user of financial intermediation services. So this period saw deregulation as far as pricing of services was concerned accompanied by increased regulation for purposes of prudential control and investor protection. The key events in this process are presented in table 2.1.

The deregulation of banking in 1971 was the starting point for the wave of deregulation that was to come later in the 1980s. The delay before the deregulation of building societies is partly explained by the controls that

Table 2.1   *Key events in the market environment since 1970*

1971	Introduction of competition and credit control – banking cartel removed
1973/4	Secondary bank crisis – led to rethink of bank regulation
1975	'Mayday' at the New York Stock Exchange – deregulation
1979	Exchange controls abandoned
1979	Banking Act – introduced a system of controls by which the Bank of England could monitor and control banks' activities
1980	Medium Term Financial Strategy – new system of monetary control – also controls on bank lending ('the Corset') abandoned
1983	Building Societies Association cartel abandoned
1984	Collapse of Johnson Mathey bank – further rethink of bank regulation
1986	'Big Bang' at the London Stock Exchange – deregulation
1986	Building Societies Act – deregulation of building societies
1986	Financial Services Act – investor protection
1988	Convergence Accord – international agreement on measuring banks' capital

were intermittently placed on banks (for example 'the Corset') over the 1970s. With the removal of these controls in 1981, banks were free to compete with building societies in the market for housing finance. The competitive pressures on building societies led in 1983 to the breakdown in the cartel arrangement whereby interest rates were set, and later in 1986 to the Building Societies Act, which allowed societies to pursue a much wider range of financial services. The pressure for deregulation in the stock market arose partly from competitive pressures following the deregulation of the New York Stock Exchange in 1975, which led to lower costs of transacting in New York, and also from the general philosophy of the Conservative administration from 1979 in favour of unrestricted markets. The abolition of exchange controls in 1979, allowing the big institutional investors to invest funds abroad, particularly using the lower-cost New York exchange, led to some loss of business for London. Preparations for deregulation of the London Stock Exchange began in 1979, following the decision of the Director General of Fair

Trading to take the rule book of the Exchange before the Restrictive Practices Court, but it was not until 1986 that full deregulation occurred.

(ii) The economic environment, particularly in the 1970s and 1980s, was very volatile. High and volatile inflation and interest rates led to great uncertainty in financial decision taking. This led to changes in the portfolio preferences of users and the development of new financial instruments to manage the greater risks. These are discussed below.

(iii) A substantial rise in domestic and international imbalances led to a greater demand for financial intermediation services. International imbalances on a large scale occurred following the oil price increases of 1973/4, which led to OPEC country surpluses and balance of payments deficits for many developing countries. In the 1980s, Germany and Japan, continuing a long-run trend, have accrued large surpluses and the US and to a lesser extent the UK have had balance of payments deficits.

(iv) The taxation system played a major role in determining the portfolio preferences of the users of the financial system. One obvious example of this is the tax incentives provided to saving through life assurance (up until 1984) and pension funds. This has led to a greater proportion of personal sector investment being directed through investment institutions.

Changing portfolio preferences of users
Here we examine the main changes in the portfolio preferences of the three domestic sectors which use the financial intermediation services provided by financial institutions.

Personal sector The personal sector has been in financial deficit since 1987, reversing a long run of financial surpluses since the early 1970s (shown in table 2.2). However, some caution is needed here because, as explained in chapter 1, the figures for saving and financial transactions for the personal sector are subject to a wide degree of error.

It is likely, though, that significant changes took place in personal sector behaviour over the 1980s and a number of reasons have been

Table 2.2 *Financial surplus/deficit of the personal sector, 1972–89 (£m)*

1972	1974	1976	1978	1980	1982	1984	1986	1987	1988	1989
636	2,584	4,096	5,585	11,643	10,314	8,816	3,017	−6,424	−15,357	−9,519

Source: CSO, *Financial Statistics*, various issues.

Table 2.3 *Savings ratio of the personal sector, 1980–89 (%)*

1908	1981	1982	1983	1984	1985	1986	1987	1988	1989
13.2	12.6	11.6	9.8	10.2	9.5	8.2	5.7	4.1	5.0

Source: *Economic Trends*, various issues.

Table 2.4 *Components of personal sector net wealth, 1981 and 1988 (£bn)*

	1981	1988	% growth 1981–8
Dwellings	401	1,129	181
Financial assets	340	921	171
Financial liabilities	108	340	215

Source: CSO, *Financial Statistics*, various issues.

suggested to explain these developments. Firstly, personal sector saving reduced (see table 2.3), so that a savings ratio of 13.2 per cent in 1980 had reduced to 5 per cent by 1989. One suggested explanation for this development is the decline in inflation over the 1980s, which means that households do not need to save as much to maintain the real value of their nominal assets such as bank deposits. A second possible explanation is the growth in the wealth of the personal sector resulting from large rises in the prices of housing and equities (up to the stock market crash of 1987). It can be argued that the greater feeling of wealth created by these capital gains may lead households to decide to save less. Another factor is that households are borrowing more following the liberalisation of financial markets, particularly the mortgage market, early in the 1980s. The growth in liabilities over the 1980s is shown in table 2.4. As households have found it easier to borrow they have used this to finance an increase in consumption. Some of the finance for consumption expenditure may have 'leaked' out of the equity built up in housing through the phenomenon of equity withdrawal (explained further in chapter 5).

Companies sector   The sources of finance for companies over the 1970s and the 1980s are compared in table 2.5 (refer to table 8.1 in chapter 8 for more detail). It is clear from these figures that, whilst internally generated funds are the dominant form of company finance, externally raised finance became more important over the 1980s. Issues of ordinary shares increased over the 1980s, taking advantage of a bull market in shares until

Table 2.5   *Company sources of finance in the 1970s and 1980s (% of total)*

	Internal funds	*Bank loans*	*Ordinary shares*	*Debentures % preference shares*	*Other*
1970s	69.0	15.0	2.8	0.7	12.5
1980s	55.0	24.0	7.2	1.6	11.4

Note: See table 8.1 for more details.
Source: COS, *Financial Statistics*, various issues.

the stock market crash in October 1987. In fact, in the year of the stock market crash, issues of ordinary shares were the main source of externally raised finance. Since the stock market crash, companies have turned increasingly to bank-raised funds to finance the large numbers of take-overs that occurred in 1988 and 1989. As a consequence, companies' gearing ratios have increased, although gearing of UK companies has typically been lower than other industrialised countries, in particular Germany and Japan. Debentures and preference shares, essentially fixed-interest marketable debt, declined in importance over the 1970s as historically high interest rates discouraged issues. Issues of this type of debt showed some signs of recovery in the 1980s and issues in 1989 exceeded issues of ordinary shares. The growth in issues of company fixed-interest debt at the end of the 1980s is partly explained by investors seeking alternative types of fixed-interest debt following the reduction in the amount of government debt – see below.

Public sector   In 1980 the government introduced the Medium Term Financial Strategy, which stressed the need to reduce public expenditure. The original aim was to reduce the public sector borrowing requirement (PSBR) to 1–2 per cent of GDP. This aim has been exceeded as the policy of reducing public sector spending, combined with greater revenues from a growing economy over the mid 1980s, combined with proceeds from privatisation sales, brought about a government budget surplus in 1988 resulting in the PSBR giving way to a public sector debt repayment (PSDR). The PSDR permits the government to redeem maturing debt without making new issues and to buy in outstanding debt. This has reduced the amount of debt available for investing institutions to hold. A downturn in the UK economy in 1990/91 is expected to lead to an end to the run of budget surpluses. The Treasury on Budget day 1991 predicted a PSBR of £8 billion in 1991/92 rising to £12 billion in 1992/93. The latter figure is equal to 2 per cent of GDP, which is at the top end of the original target for the PSBR set in 1980.

Changing portfolio preferences of the suppliers of financial intermediation services

The banks were the first institutions to be affected by the waves of deregulation described above, and as a consequence banks have gone through more change and produced more innovation than other financial institutions. The removal of controls on bank activity in 1971 led to greater competition between banks, which became more growth oriented, more profit conscious and more innovative. An early development involved the switch from a strategy of asset management whereby the asset portfolio is managed on the basis of a given level of deposits, to a strategy of liability management whereby liabilities are managed to fund a desired level of assets. In response to a more volatile economic environment and the changing nature of portfolio preferences of companies, banks developed term loans, which came to replace fixed-interest debt issued by companies. The growing international financial imbalances, largely arising from the oil price rises in the 1970s, saw banks substantially increasing their role as international financial intermediaries. This, however, turned out to be an unsuccessful episode in the history of international banking as the high interest rates and slowdown in world trade in the early 1980s produced the sovereign debt crisis (examined in chapter 4).

In response to capital controls imposed on banks and the greater competitiveness of the traditional banking business of taking in deposits and making loans, banks have increasingly undertaken fee-generating business such as underwriting security issues. A large proportion of this business does not appear on the balance sheet and in response to the growth of off-balance sheet business the regulatory authorities have had to rethink the capital controls on banks. Greater international competition between banks led to pressure for these new capital controls to be harmonised across borders to create a 'level playing field', resulting in the Convergence Accord in 1988. These issues are considered in more detail in chapter 17.

Another development, mentioned above, was the move by banks into the mortgage market, previously dominated by building societies, following the removal of lending constraints on banks. This in turn contributed to pressures for the deregulation of building societies to allow them to compete in the more competitive climate created by banks. A development affecting the portfolio preferences of the investing institutions, namely life assurance companies and pension funds, was the abandonment of exchange controls in 1979, which led to a greater proportion of foreign securities in the asset portfolios of these institutions.

The interaction of the forces described above led to changes in market structure and financial innovation. The main developments are summarised below.

2.7 Market structure and financial innovation

Financial conglomeration

Deregulation and the greater competition it produced have resulted in a steady erosion of the traditional demarcation between different types of financial institutions. Over the 1980s we have seen banks enter the housing finance market, traditionally dominated by building societies, and building societies lending on an unsecured basis and offering cheque book accounts, activities traditionally associated with banks. This diversification of the activities of the different financial institutions, largely encouraged by the authorities, is leading to the development of financial conglomerates or financial supermarkets. Banks again are furthest along this road, with interests in broker–dealer firms operating on the stock market, insurance companies, foreign currency dealing, unit trusts, etc.

Whilst the development of financial conglomerates brings greater competition to the financial markets and can reduce search costs for users of financial intermediation services, it also poses difficulties. One problem that has been identified is the greater potential for conflict of interest; for example, the new market-making entities on the stock exchange which combine the old (separate) functions of broking and market making. The broking section of these bodies may provide the advice to a client of buying the shares held by its market making section even though these shares may not be the most ideal available for that client. A further problem posed by conglomeration is that of the appropriate regulatory authority for the different activities of the conglomerate. A related problem is that of cross-infection, where the failure of a bank's subsidiary operating in a nonbanking field and regulated by a different authority from the regulator of banks may lead to difficulties for the parent company.

Growth of non-bank financial institutions

Over the 1970s and 1980s the non-bank institutions grew at a rapid rate. This is illustrated by the figures in table 2.6, which show all the main non-bank financial institutions achieving a higher rate of growth of assets than the banks.

The growth of all the financial institutions reflects the greater need for intermediation services as a result of the growing domestic financial imbalances. The growth of building societies and investment institutions also reflects certain tax advantages which are obtained by the use of the services of these institutions. Tax relief on mortgage interest payments is one of the factors which contributed to the steady growth in home ownership over the 1970s and 1980s and hence to the assets of building societies. Contributions to pension schemes and life assurance policies (up to 1984) also benefited from tax advantages. The consequent growth

Table 2.6 *Growth of assets of UK financial institutions, 1976–88 (£bn)*

	1976	1980	1984	1988	% growth 1976–88
Banks[a]	70.8	117.4	271.4	401.8	468
Building societies	28.1	54.3	103.3	189.8	575
Unit and investment trusts	8.7	12.5	31.1	60.9	600
Insurance companies:					
General		11.5	19.9	39.6	
Life	29.9[b]	53.7	114.2	198.3	696[c]
Pension funds	16.9	52.6	130.3	214.5	1,169

Notes:
[a] Combined retail, merchant and other British banks.
[b] Figure for combined life and general insurance assets.
[c] Growth of combined life and general insurance.
Source: CSO, *Financial Statistics*, various issues.

in funds flowing to these institutions from the personal sector has resulted in greater indirect investment in company shares and other marketable securities by the personal sector at the expense of direct investment.

Growth in use of new technology
Developments in computing and telecommunications technology applied to financial intermediation services have been both a consequence of the greater competition fostered by deregulation, as institutions have sought to cut costs and introduce new products, and at the same time an enabling factor allowing the development of new products and services. One of the main areas where new technology has so far had the most impact is in the area of payments and cash dispensing systems. Banks and building societies have introduced large numbers of automated teller machines (ATMs) into their branches. It is argued that the development of ATMs makes the branch networks of banks and building societies largely re-dundant. However, the diversification of the product base of these in-stitutions, described above, provides one reason for these institutions to hold on to these high street financial supermarkets where the range of products they provide can be marketed. The numbers of staff involved in the payments services side of banks and building societies are likely to decrease, though, as more of the service is automated. The greater automation of payments services should reduce entry costs into this traditional area of banking activity. Further developments in automation of banking services, for example EFTPOS (electronic funds at point of transfer) and home banking through a computer/modem link, have

not been introduced as quickly as forecast. Another area where new technology has found an application is in the automation of dealing in stock markets. In the London Stock Exchange, the SEAQ (Stock Exchange Automatic Quotation) system is at present only a price information system but has the capability of being upgraded to an automated dealing system.

Internationalisation

Another trend in the provision of intermediation services is internationalisation. London has always had relaxed entry requirements in relation to foreign banks. This helped London to develop as one of the main centres for international banking, in particular euro-banking. Some of the foreign banks which established themselves in London, however, have increasingly competed for domestic UK business in the area of wholesale banking, mortgage lending and securities trading. At the same time, UK-based banks have increasingly sought business in other countries. The development of a European single market in a wide range of financial services (see chapter 15) should encourage greater cross-border activity and therefore greater international competition in financial services. The removal of exchange controls in the UK in 1979 has increased cross-border investment by UK investment institutions. This development, the reforms of the London Stock Exchange and London's time zone position in the 'golden triangle' of New York, London and Tokyo have enabled London to become one of the major centres in international equities trading. The developments in new technology, enabling prices to be transmitted around the world in seconds, have also contributed to the globalisation of equities trading.

Financial innovation

In addition to the structural changes in the financial system described above, the last twenty years have also seen considerable innovation in financial instruments, techniques and markets. Many of the innovations have been mentioned in the above discussion. For example, the volatility and high level of interest rates in the 1970s saw companies withdraw from issuing fixed-interest debt and banks develop term loans to fill the gap. Gap filling is one of the many determinants of financial innovation and at the risk of over-simplification can be seen as institutions and markets combining the various characteristics that make up financial instruments to create a new instrument for which there is a demand.

Growth of the UK financial services industry

The 1980s saw a rapid growth in the UK financial services industry, which mirrored the decline in the manufacturing sector. This is reflected in table

Table 2.7
(a) *Gross domestic product (at constant factor cost) by industry as a % of total,*
     1980–88

	1980	1981	1982	1983	1984	1985	1986	1987	1988
Manufacturing	26.5	24.8	24.7	23.5	23.7	23.7	23.6	23.3	23.7
Financial services[a]	12.5	12.5	13.0	14.0	14.6	15.9	17.6	18.4	19.5

(b) *Employment by industry as a % of total employees, 1980–88*

	1980	1981	1982	1983	1984	1985	1986	1987	1988
Manufacturing	30.2	28.4	27.4	26.2	25.5	25.0	24.3	23.6	23.2
Financial services[a]	7.4	7.9	8.4	8.9	9.3	9.7	10.2	10.7	11.2

Note:

[a] Financial services is defined as banking, finance, insurance, business services and
  leasing. This definition includes accounting and computing services and is
  therefore wider than the traditional perception of financial services. However, it
  is narrowest category to which GDP data refer.

   Financial services' contribution to GDP includes net interest receipts. In the
  aggregate measure of GDP (where net interest flows within the economy must
  sum to zero) these interest receipts are excluded.

Source: CSO, *UK National Accounts*, 1989.

2.7, which shows the relative contributions to gross domestic product and
employment by manufacturing and a widely defined (see notes to table)
financial services sector over the 1980s.

   This provides support for the hypothesis that the UK has been going
through a process of de-industrialisation, as described in section 2.5, with
a relative decline in the manufacturing sector and a relative growth in the
services sector.

2.8 Conclusion

In this chapter we have described the role of a financial system in intermediating between lenders and borrowers and set out in broad terms the
tremendous changes that have taken place in the UK financial system in
recent years. In chapters 3 to 14 of this book we will describe in greater
detail the changes to the various institutions and markets that make up
the UK financial system.

Chapter 3

Retail banking

3.1 Introduction

In this chapter we examine the nature of retail banking as distinct from wholesale banking. Whilst such a distinction has in recent years become less relevant in practice, as most retail banks also undertake wholesale business, we feel there is still some advantage to be gained from some aspects of retail banking being considered separately from wholesale banking. In particular we examine why retail banks combine payments services with intermediation services, the risks inherent in retail banking and the strategies adopted by banks to manage these risks. We then finish this chapter by outlining the main functions of the Bank of England. Wholesale banking will be discussed in chapter 4.

3.2 Nature of retail banking in the UK

The traditional business of banking involves taking in deposits which are then packaged and on-lent as loans. Retail banking refers to the large-volume, low-value end of this business where deposits are typically attracted from individuals and small businesses and loans are made to the same groups. This is in contrast to wholesale banking where transactions are typically small volume but large value. In practice it is difficult to distinguish between retail and wholesale banks in the UK, as most of the banks operating in the retail markets also operate in the wholesale markets. In fact one of the issues we focus upon in section 3.4 is why retail activities are typically combined with wholesale activities.

To operate in the retail markets, banks require an extensive branch network. The Bank of England in fact defines retail banks, with a few exceptions, as those banks 'which either have extensive branch networks

Table 3.1 *The combined balance sheet of UK retail banks as at 30 June 1990 (£bn)*

Liabilities		Assets	
Notes outstanding	1.4	Notes and coin	2.9
		Balances with Bank of England	1.1
Total sterling deposits	284.8	Market loans	50.8
(*of which sight deposits*	*136.7*)	Total bills	11.6
Foreign currency deposits	61.4	Investments	12.3
Items in suspense and transmission plus capital and other funds	61.5	Advances	229.2
		Other currency and miscellaneous assets	99.7
		Banking Dept lending to central govt (net)	1.4
Total liabilities	409.2	Total assets	409.2
(*Eligible liabilities*	*234.4*)		

Source: Bank of England Quarterly Bulletin, August 1990, Table 3.2.

in the United Kingdom or participate directly in a UK clearing system'. At 30 June 1990 the Bank of England classified twenty-one banks as retail. The largest of these are the four London clearing banks, namely, Barclays, Lloyds, Midland and National Westminster, along with the recently transformed Trustee Savings Bank and the Abbey National, which in 1989 transferred from the mutual status of a building society to plc status, and hence a bank. The rest include banks whose operations are largely confined to Scotland (Bank of Scotland, Clydesdale and the Royal Bank of Scotland) and Northern Ireland (Bank of Ireland, Ulster and Northern).

By examining the combined balance sheet for retail banks in the UK we can discern their main activities (see table 3.1). Examining the liabilities side of the balance sheet first, we find the small item of 'notes outstanding', which refers to private bank notes issued by Scottish and Northern Ireland banks. The bulk of a bank's liabilities are deposits, accounting for 85 per cent of total retail bank liabilities, with 18 per cent of these deposits being in foreign currency. There are no figures available for the retail banks as a whole showing a breakdown of sterling deposits into retail and wholesale deposits (which are deposits mainly raised through the inter-bank market – see section 3.4), although some indication is provided by table 3.2, which shows that 64 per cent of London clearing bank group sterling deposits at the end of 1985 were wholesale. It should be noted, however, that the figures in table 3.2 are

Table 3.2 *The balance between wholesale and retail funding for London clearing banks, 1976–85*

Year	Retail funds as a % of total sterling deposits	Wholesale funds as a % of total sterling deposits
1976	59	41
1978	56	44
1980	56	44
1982	43	57
1984	38	62
1985	36	64

Source: Committee of London Clearing Banks, *Abstract of Banking Statistics*, 1985.

likely to misrepresent to some extent the position of the retail banking sector as a whole as, firstly, they relate to both parent and the wholesale subsidiaries of clearing bank groups and, secondly, in the latter half of the 1980s the clearing banks competed more actively for retail deposits, seeing these as a base for selling other financial products (see chapter 5). The other main liabilities are 'items in suspense and transmission', which refer for example to cheques drawn and in the course of collection, and 'capital and other funds', which refer mainly to banks-issued share capital, long-term debt and reserves. These latter capital funds are important items when it comes to assessing a bank's capital adequacy in relation to the risks it faces. Finally, eligible liabilities are essentially defined as non-bank sterling deposit liabilities with an original maturity up to two years, plus net sterling inter-bank transactions plus any sterling resources obtained by switching foreign currencies into sterling.

Turning now to the assets side of the balance sheet, we find a small item referring to 'balances with the Bank of England'. This relates to a compulsory 'cash ratio' requirement whereby all banks with eligible liabilities greater than £10 billion are required to hold 0.40 per cent of their eligible liabilities in a non-interest-bearing account at the Bank of England. This has little relevance to any prudential assessment of a bank but is simply a tax on banks which is used to finance the various activities of the Bank of England. The cash balances held outside of the Bank of England (notes and coins) account for roughly 0.7 per cent of total assets, which is a very low cash base. Additional liquidity is provided by 'market loans', which refer to short-term loans made through the money markets. Traditionally, banks' market loans were call or overnight loans to the discount houses. These loans are used to even out cash positions within the banking system. However, the retail banks' involvement in the inter-bank markets since 1971 has reduced the importance of this function and inter-bank loans now account for approximately 72 per cent of total market loans. Dealings between banks and the discount houses, however, continue to take place in order to smooth out shortages or surpluses of cash arising out of dealings between the banking system as a whole and non-banks, as clearly the inter-bank market cannot perform this function. This is dealt with in more detail in chapter 10. Further liquidity is provided by the next item on the assets side, which is 'bills'. These are mainly treasury bills and bank bills eligible for re-discounting at the Bank of England via discount houses. The item of 'investments' refers to retail banks' holdings of marketable securities. These are mainly government bonds or government-guaranteed stocks and therefore have the characteristics of low default risk and marketability. The main assets of retail banks are sterling advances, which accounted for approximately 56 per cent of total assets or 74 per cent of sterling assets. The majority of advances are the traditional 'overdraft facility' made to business borrowers. However, since the mid-1970s banks have increasingly made term loans to businesses, with an average original term to maturity of around seven years. In addition, over the 1980s following the removal of controls on bank lending, the banks increasingly targeted personal sector customers with both long-term mortgage lending and unsecured term loans. The remaining items on the assets side of the retail banks' balance sheet are 'other currency' and 'miscellaneous assets'. Of the other currency assets, around 21 per cent is accounted for by advances, with the remainder being made up of mainly market loans and investments. Miscellaneous assets includes the banks' physical assets, mainly premises and equipment, which provide the infrastructure of the business. The final item is 'Banking Department lending to central government', which refers to the Banking Department of the Bank of England, which is included in the retail banks classification due to its involvement in the clearing system. We consider the function of the Banking Department and the other functions of the Bank of England in section 3.5.

It follows from the Bank of England's definition of a retail bank, quoted above, that, in addition to providing intermediation services, most retail banks provide transaction or payments and cash distribution services. In the next section we examine the nature of the payments system in the UK and consider why it is that banks combine payments with intermediation services.

3.3 Payments services

Banks until very recently have been the sole provider of payments services. A payments service is merely an accounting procedure whereby transfers of ownership of certain assets are carried out in settlement of debts incurred. Payments facilities generate a desire for instruments that (i) serve as a medium of exchange enabling consumers to acquire goods, (ii) serve as a medium of payment to effect payment for the goods acquired, and (iii) act as a temporary store of purchasing power since income receipts and payments are generally not synchronised. As we saw in chapter 1, a commodity that takes on these three characteristics is termed money, and any commodity can act in this role as long as it is generally accepted. In most developed economies, the payments system that has evolved is based on government-issued paper money and cheques drawn on a bank deposit. The reasons for this are covered adequately in most texts on money and banking. What we propose to examine here are some recent developments in the UK payments system.

Recent financial innovation has made it possible to 'unbundle' the three functions of money so they can be separately carried out using different instruments. So, for example, a credit card may serve as the medium of exchange enabling goods to be purchased. A direct debit from a bank deposit account may then be used to effect payment at a later date and in between the purchase and payment the funds used for payment may be held in a high-yielding account. Developments in technology are also bringing about changes in the payments system. In particular, the ongoing developments in electronic funds transfer, whereby electronic signals replace paper cheques in undertaking the accounting transfers, are lowering the entry barriers to the provision of payments systems.

As we have noted above, payments services are generally provided together with portfolio services by an institution. This is because there are certain advantages in combining the two services. The funds which are held in bank accounts, before being used to finance purchases – although customers will attempt to keep these at a minimum as they can most likely obtain a higher return by lending them elsewhere – can in aggregate be used to on-lend profitably. Thus intermediation emerges as a by-product of payments services. The profits from the intermediation services have generally been used to cross-subsidise the costs of providing the payments service. Various schemes have been adopted by banks in the past to enable the profits earned by the bank from the use of the idle balances of a customer to reduce or eliminate charges for the use of the payments service. For example, customers who kept a positive minimum and average account balance were then exempt from charges for payments services. Another method used was the calculation of implicit interest on a customer's idle balances which was used to offset charges.

The policy of deregulation of the financial system over the 1980s has affected these arrangements. In particular, deregulation of the building societies – covered in chapter 5 – allowed them to offer payments services. A number of building societies have to date set up deposit accounts with a cheque book facility with the feature of paying interest on the idle funds in the account whilst at the same time not charging for the payments service. This additional competition for banks has induced them to introduce cheque accounts which either pay interest or involve no bank charges. Deregulation and the increased competition it brings has so far not led to the removal of cross-subsidisation whereby explicit rates of interest are paid on account balances but payments services are fully charged for (as suggested by e.g. Fama [1980]), but instead appears to have reduced the overall profitability of retail banking type services. The provider of payments services, though, obtains certain advantages which enable them to be more efficient in their intermediation operations. In particular, they will obtain valuable information about the financial circumstances of the customer. This enables them to judge whether it is suitable to extend that customer credit and once the loan is extended the transactions account can be used as a source of information in the monitoring process. Such specialised information, as we saw in chapter 2, provides part of the explanation for the existence of financial intermediaries. Also the access to transactions details enables an institution to target other financial services at customers. These advantages therefore partly explain why institutions such as building societies have sought to introduce payments services.

3.4 Risks in retail banking

Banks, like all financial intermediaries, as we saw in chapter 2, are involved in managing risk. The principal risks that are managed by retail banks are:

(i)   liquidity risk – this is a consequence of issuing liabilities that are largely payable on demand or at short notice whilst holding assets which have a longer term to maturity.

(ii) asset risk – the risk that assets held by the bank may not be redeemable at thier book value owing to default, price risk or forced sale risk.

An additional source of instability in the banking system arises from banks' increasing undertaking of business which involves contingent commitments. This business is known as off-balance sheet as it does not appear on the balance sheet until the contingency arises. This is a feature of banking which relates more to the wholesale side, although it is relevant to retail banking to the extent that most retail banks also undertake wholesale business. However, we leave discussion of the nature of off-balance sheet business and its implications for regulation until the next chapter.

In this section we will examine the nature of the two risks identified above and briefly examine the methods used by banks in their management. In chapter 17 we will discuss the methods adopted by the Bank of England to ensure that these sources of instability in the banking system are controlled.

Liquidity risk
Bank deposits can be withdrawn at call or very short notice, whereas a large proportion of a bank's assets are illiquid (advances make up 74 per cent of sterling assets – see above). This practice of mis-matching or maturity transformation, discussed further in chapter 2, exposes the bank to liquidity risk and as a consequence it is important that banks manage the inflow and outflow of their funds. The inflows and outflows of much of the funds passing through a bank are uncertain. Deposit inflows and outflows are largely uncertain and, on the assets side of the balance sheet, overdraft commitments introduce another element of uncertainty. The inflow and outflow of funds through a bank will be predictable to some extent on the basis of what has happened in the past. However, there will be a stochastic element to these flows and banks will have to structure their balance sheet in such a way that they can manage this uncertainty. A fundamental element in a bank's management of this uncertainty comes from the large scale of its operation and more importantly from a diversified base of deposit accounts. When a large number of uncertain net flows (deposit accounts) are combined, then a greater degree of predictability is achieved. The basic principle here is that it is better to have a large number of small accounts than a small number of large accounts. This reduces the uncertainty of the bank's cash flows, but the remaining uncertainty still needs to be managed.

We will examine the requirements set out by the Bank of England to ensure that banks adequately cover this liquidity risk in chapter 17. What we concentrate on here are the two main strategies that banks can adopt to manage this liquidity problem.

Reserve asset management The diagram in figure 3.1 simply illustrates the reserve asset management approach to liquidity risk. Inflows in the form of new deposits and loan repayments are added to the holdings of cash and liquid assets. Loan repayments will clearly be a more predictable element of cash inflows, determined by the loans made in the past, although the bank will have to allow for potential default on repayment of the loan. The outflows, in the form of deposit withdrawals and new loans made, will deplete the holdings of cash and liquid assets. The illiquid loan portfolio is protected from an unexpectedly large net outflow of funds by the holding of a buffer stock of cash and liquid assets. That is,

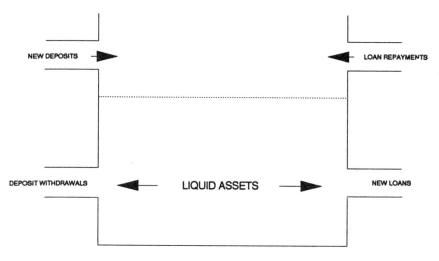

Figure 3.1

the bank will hold cash and liquid assets at a level above that which is required to meet the expected volatility of cash flows.

The assets held in liquid form do not have to be composed only of cash with a zero rate of interest, and a tiering or maturity ladder approach is generally adopted whereby some of the reserve assets held are short-term and therefore easily realisable assets such as callable or overnight deposits and others are longer term and therefore less easy to realise but still liquid because of their marketability, such as bills, Certificates of Deposit, government securities, etc. By holding these liquid assets rather than just cash the bank is at least obtaining some return on its funds. However, the return is still less than that it would obtain on its main earning asset which is advances.

Liability management   Liability management involves relying on instruments bearing market rates of interest to fund activity. At its most general it involves determining a desired quantity of assets and then adjusting interest rates to attract the desired level of deposits to fund this. This is in contrast to reserve asset management where interest rates are held constant, at least in the short term, and the scale of the asset portfolio is adjusted in line with the quantity of deposits attracted at that rate.

The form that liability management takes depends on the market for funds where existing deposits are drawn. If a bank is reliant on retail deposits then, leaving aside its ability to vary other characteristics of the deposits such as term, in order to attract new deposits it has to increase the interest rate on all deposits. This makes the marginal cost of the additional funds raised high. The existence of a market for deposits where the bank is effectively a price taker, so that its borrowing does not lead to a rise in the interest rate, means the marginal cost of the funds raised is reduced. As we describe in chapter 10, the inter-bank market is such a market in the UK. Banks can therefore use the inter-bank market as a marginal source and use of funds so that at the end of a working day if the bank has a shortage of funds it can borrow short term from the inter-bank market, or if the bank has a surplus of funds it can lend short term. The existence of an inter-bank market means that banks can raise additional funds at a lower marginal cost than raising interest rates across the board and also more quickly than from retail sources. As a consequence, retail banks in the UK have largely moved away from reserve asset management to liability management as a technique of managing liquidity risk. It has to be noted though that inter-bank markets are not perfect and that banks are not pure price takers in these markets. There is therefore some uncertainty about the quantity and price of funds raised through these markets and hence banks still require some level of reserve assets as a back-up. Note also that if there is a net shortage of funds in the banking system then banks have to look outside the inter-bank market to relieve this shortage.

Asset risk

The Bank of England (*Bank of England Quarterly Bulletin*, September 1980) identifies three ways in which a bank's assets are subject to the risk of a fall in value below that recorded in the balance sheet (their 'book value'). First, and most important in terms of the structure of the bank's assets, is the risk of default on the part of borrowers on the advances made by the bank. In chapter 2 we examined the ways in which a bank can manage the risk of default on its advances and we summarise these again here. As a first step a bank can minimise the risk of default on an individual advance by, for example, considering the use of the loaned funds and the financial circumstances of the borrower. Second, a bank can increase the predictability of default by spreading its loan portfolio over many borrowers, therefore enabling it to incorporate a premium in its lending interest rate to cover the effects of default. Finally a bank can minimise the overall risk of default on its loan portfolio by diversifying over different types and regions of borrower.

A second asset risk considered by the Bank of England is investment risk, which relates to capital-uncertain assets and refers to the risk of a price fall thus reducing the value of the asset. The main capital-uncertain asset held by banks is government securities and if the general level of interest rates increases then the value of the banks' government securities will decline.

The final risk considered by the Bank of England is forced sale risk, which refers to the risk that the realisable value of the asset may fall below its book value if the asset has to be sold at short notice.

A bank's exposure to these risks is an important consideration in determining its solvency and we consider this in detail in chapter 17 which examines regulation and prudential control of banks by the Bank of England.

3.5   The role of the Bank of England

The Bank of England (hereafter just termed the Bank) performs a wide range of activities in the UK financial system. In the remainder of this chapter we will outline these activities, some of which we will discuss in greater detail in later chapters of this book.

The Bank of England was formally recognised as a central bank by the 1946 Bank of England Act, which effectively nationalised the Bank. Prior to this Act, from its establishment in 1694, the Bank had carried out the functions of a central bank but operated as a private concern. Under the Act the subordinate status of the Bank to the Treasury was statutorily established. In practice, whilst the Bank and the Treasury may arrive at policies, for example on when to cut interest rates, by discussion, it is ultimately the politically controlled Treasury which holds sway. This had led to some discussion as to whether the Bank should be made independent of the government, as some other central banks operate, and we will briefly examine the arguments later in this section. First of all,

Table 3.3   *Bank of England balance sheet as at 27 June 1990 (£m)*

Liabilities		Assets	
Issue Department:			
Notes in circulation	15,676	Government securities	13,304
Notes in Banking Department	4	Other securities	3,376
Banking Department:			
Public deposits	38	Government securities	1,458
Special deposits	0	Advances and other accounts	731
Bankers' deposits	1,757	Premises, equipment and other securities	1,511
Reserves and other accounts	1,895	Notes and coin	4

Source: *Bank of England Quarterly Bulletin*, August 1990, Table 1.

though, we will describe the structure of the Bank and then outline its main functions.

The Bank is separated into two departments for accounting purposes; the Issue Department, which is treated as being part of the government, and the Banking Department, which is a public corporation (see table 3.3). The Issue Department has as liabilities notes in circulation or held by the Banking Department. Whilst it was possible to call upon the Bank to redeem these notes for gold up until 1931, since that date the note issue has been a fiduciary one backed by securities. These securities, held as assets by the Issue Department, include government securities as well as privately issued securities such as commercial bills.

The Banking Department obtains its deposits from two main sources. First, acting as banker to central government, it has the item referred to as 'public deposits' which represents the consolidated accounts of the various revenue-collecting and spending departments of the government. Second, it has 'bankers' deposits', which include the mandatory deposits of UK banks, set at 0.40 per cent of eligible deposits – discussed in section 3.2 above, as well as additional balances held by retail banks which form part of their cash reserves as they are redeemable for notes and coins on demand. The remainder of the Banking Department's liabilities are made up of accounts held by other bodies such as overseas governments and central banks, capital and reserves. The assets of the Banking Department include, first, government securities, which comprise government bonds, treasury bills and ways and means advances to the government; second, advances and other accounts, which includes short-term loans to discount houses and holdings of commercial bills; third, notes and coin, which represents the reserve held by the Bank to meet any deposit withdrawals.

Bankers' bank

By holding balances at the Bank of England, banks are able to settle any inter-bank indebtedness in a convenient way. This works through the operation of a Clearing House, so that at the end of a working day the net debts between any two banks are settled by means of an appropriate transfer of funds between the two banks' accounts at the Bank of England. A further role played by the Bank under this heading is that of note issuing. If the general public increase their demand for notes then this will show up as a decrease in notes held by the banks. The banks can then replenish their stocks by exchanging their balances held at the Bank for notes. The Banking Department in turn can replenish its stock of notes, if required, by authorising a change in the fiduciary issue from the Issue Department. The resulting transfer of notes from the Issue

Department to the Banking Department will generate a corresponding balancing transfer of securities in the opposite direction.

Lender of last resort

The Bank's role here works on two levels. On a day-to-day basis when the banking system as a whole runs short of cash then it is ultimately the Bank which restores the cash position of the banks. However, unlike many other countries, the banks do not borrow cash directly from the Bank but receive assistance via the discount houses. Thus a cash shortage for the banks would be reflected by the banks recalling loans made to the discount houses. The discount houses obtain the cash to pay the banks from the Bank, which stands ready to offset any cash shortages by open market purchases of bills from or by lending to the discount market. As the Bank is acting as lender of last resort in this situation, the terms at which the Bank is prepared to lend have implications for the level of short-term interest rates and ultimately for the level of interest rates generally. We examine the operation of the discount market in greater detail in chapter 10.

The Bank also adopted the role of lender of last resort to any bank or group of banks experiencing liquidity problems. The Bank's aim here is to maintain the stability of the banking system. As the banking system is based on confidence, the failure of one or more banks can rapidly lead to a collapse in confidence in the banking system generally. A classic example of the Bank acting in this role was the operation of the 'lifeboat' to help a number of secondary banks in 1974/75. We examine the 'lifeboat' operation in more detail in chapter 17.

Regulation of banks

As the Bank ultimately guarantees the stability of the banking system through its role as lender of last resort, then in order to minimise any moral hazard problems which may result from this, (that is, banks acting imprudently as they know they will be bailed out if they get into difficulties) the Bank also undertakes prudential regulation of banks. Prudential regulation in the UK is based on flexible supervision of individual banks. Supervision by the Bank has tended to concentrate on two areas of banking: (i) the entry and establishment of banks, and (ii) the risks of the activities undertaken by banks. With regard to the first aspect of supervision, the Bank has required authorisation of banks subject to specified criteria, with the ability to revoke such authorisation in the event of wrongdoing. Supervision of the risks of banks' activity has focussed on monitoring the liquidity and capital adequacy of banks. We consider such prudential regulation in chapter 17.

Managing monetary policy

The Bank is the agent of government policy. In this role it manages the marketable securities, mainly government bonds, which form the bulk of the outstanding government debt. It regulates the redemption of maturing issues and the issue of new securities so as to preserve an orderly market. The main techniques of the Bank's operations in this regard are considered in chapter 9. The other channel through which the Bank pursues government monetary policy is through its operations in the discount market. As we have indicated above, the Bank can alter the level of short-term interest rates through its dealings with the discount houses. Government international monetary policy is administered by the Bank's management of the Exchange Equalisation Account (EEA). This account comprises the nation's gold and foreign currency reserves and, by intervention in the foreign exchange markets, that is, by buying or selling sterling through this account, the official policy on the exchange rate can be pursued. The role of the EEA has assumed greater importance following the entry of sterling into the Exchange Rate Mechanism (ERM) of the European Monetary System (EMS) in October 1990. Further consideration of the ERM and the EMS is relegated to chapter 15.

Independence of the Bank of England

As we have noted above, the politically controlled Treasury has the ultimate say on the monetary policy objectives which are pursued by the Bank. In such a situation there is a temptation for a government to finance its current borrowing requirement and to reduce its real burden of accumulated debt through increasing the money supply, thereby leading to inflation. There is also some suggestion that over the 1980s the government relaxed monetary policy at politically convenient times, for example in the period leading up to a general election, rather than pursuing the monetary policy most appropriate for reducing or controlling inflationary pressures. This has prompted serious consideration of the question of central bank independence. Examples of independent central banks are the German Bundesbank established in 1957 and the US Federal Reserve System ('the Fed') established in 1913. The legislation governing both these central banks includes the pursuit of price stability. However, this is just one of many economic and monetary objectives in the governing legislation and neither central bank is legally required to make price stability always its prime concern. The legislation does assign a great deal of power over economic and monetary policy to these unelected bodies, which inevitably brings them into conflict with the elected government of the country. Indeed, the lack of accountability of an independent central bank is often cited as a counter-argument to independence. However – this argument fails to take into account the fact that the independence of a central bank is not permanently guaranteed, as the government could introduce new legislation to remove their independence. Central banks such as the Bundesbank and the Fed maintain their autonomy by being accepted as legitimate. The Bundesbank obtains its legitimacy through the widespread popular support it enjoys in Germany, which has come from its achievement of low and stable inflation, which, in turn, has assisted the economic success of the country. The legitimacy of the Fed has been achieved largely as a result of successive Fed chairmen exploiting the conflict between President and Congress built into the US constitution.

The debate has taken on a new dimension following the entry of the UK into stage one (i.e. entry into the EMS) of European economic and monetary union (EMU), as stage three of the Delors plan for EMU envisages an independent European central bank coordinating a system of the domestic central banks, which logically would also need to operate independently of national government influence. At the time of writing however, the UK has expressed reluctance about proceeding to stages two and three of EMU as represented by the Delors plan, and an Inter-Governmental conference on the details of EMU has only recently commenced. Nevertheless it is clear that there is now greater pressure on the UK government to cede control of monetary policy to an independent central banking institution (see chapter 15 for further discussion).

3.6 Conclusion

In this chapter we have considered the nature of retail banks, the risks involved in retail banking and the strategies available to banks to manage these risks. We have also outlined the main roles of the Bank of England. We pointed out at the beginning of this chapter that it has become increasingly difficult to separate retail banks from wholesale banks in practice, as most retail banks also undertake wholesale banking operations. To complete our picture of banking we therefore turn in the next chapter to consider the nature of wholesale and international banking and some of the issues that have affected such banking over the 1980s.

Chapter 4

Wholesale and international banking

4.1 Introduction

In the last chapter we examined the nature of retail banking in the UK and noted that the distinction between this type of banking and wholesale banking has become increasingly blurred over recent years. To complete our discussion of banking we therefore turn in this chapter to examine the nature of wholesale banking. This type of banking can be further separated into domestic and international. We begin by examining the general nature of wholesale banking in section 4.2. This examination relates to activities which are captured on the balance sheet. An increasing amount of business of wholesale banks does not appear on the balance sheet and is termed 'off-balance sheet' business. We discuss the nature, causes and consequences of this type of business in section 4.3. In section 4.4 we discuss the nature of eurocurrency banking, which is now the most dominant form of international banking. Finally, in section 4.5 we consider the issue of sovereign lending, that is, lending by banks to sovereign countries. A boom in this type of lending over the 1970s led to consequences which blighted the international banking system over the 1980s and the problems are still far from being resolved.

4.2 Nature of wholesale banking

A large number of banks which operate in the UK do not come under the category of retail banks as defined in the last chapter. These banks are a heterogeneous group, and the Bank of England, in its statistical analysis, separates them on the basis of the country where the headquarters are located and then, for the non-retail UK banks, further subdivides these to identify those operating as merchant banks. At 30 June 1990 the breakdown of non-retail banks operating in the UK was as follows:

British merchant banks (30) – members of the British Merchant Bankers and Securities Houses Association (formerly the Accepting Houses Committee). Merchant banks have traditionally financed commerce and trade by the 'accepting' of bills. Their activities are now much broader and include direct lending to industry, underwriting new issues and providing advice on mergers, acquisitions, portfolio management, etc.

Other British banks (166) – this group captures all financial institutions registered as banks which are not included in the retail and merchant bank categories. As a consequence the activities of these institutions are diverse, ranging from small regional banks to finance houses, leasing companies and other specialised institutions, some of which are the subsidiaries of retail banks.

American banks (43)

Japanese banks (28)

Other overseas banks (279)

Most banks today are to some degree multi-product banks. As we noted in chapter 3, most retail banks also operate in the wholesale markets, but the converse is not true since the non-retail banks tend to operate solely or mainly in wholesale markets. We now examine the balance sheets of these different categories of wholesale banks so as to identify some of the aspects of wholesale banking and in particular those features which distinguish it from retail banking. The sterling and foreign currency breakdown of the deposits of the different categories of banks is provided in table 4.1.

One salient feature of wholesale banking revealed in this table, which contrasts with retail banking, is the large size of deposits and loans and consequently the smaller number of depositors and borrowers. Minimum values for sterling deposits and loans are typically £250,000 and £500,000 respectively. The structure of the sterling deposits of these wholesale

Table 4.1 *Sterling and foreign currency breakdown of the deposits of non-retail banks as at end June 1990 (£m)*

	Sterling	*Foreign currency*	*Sterling sight as a % of total sterling*
British merchant banks	31,178	15,800	23
Other British banks	41,944	10,078	10
Japanese banks	36,067	212,423	4
American banks	20,131	88,743	22
Other overseas	90,982	237,757	12

Source: *Bank of England Quarterly Bulletin*, August 1990, Tables 3.3, 3.4, 3.5, 3.6, 3.7.

banks is also quite different from retail banks. For sterling deposits, the sight element is considerably lower for non-retail banks, with merchant banks and American banks showing the largest proportions at 23 per cent and 22 per cent respectively (see table 4.1), compared with 48 per cent for retail banks. This reflects the absence of these banks from retail banking. Approximately 30 per cent of sterling wholesale deposits are inter-bank (i.e. deposits of one bank placed with another bank – see chapter 10 for further discussion), the remainder being mainly time deposits from UK private companies and overseas companies and banks. For the foreign currency business, a much larger proportion (approximately 70 per cent) of wholesale deposits are inter-bank.

One other feature of wholesale banking indicated in the table is the greater extent of foreign currency business for both British and overseas banks when compared to retail banks (where foreign currency deposits accounted for approximately 18 per cent). The overseas banks though, whilst engaging in a considerable amount of sterling wholesale business, are more heavily involved in foreign currency business. The reasons why overseas banks locate in the UK but deal mainly in foreign currencies is explored in section 4.4.

Table 4.2   *Assets of non-retail banks operating in the UK at 30 June 1990 (£m)*

	British merchant banks	Other British banks	Japanese banks	American banks	Overseas banks
Sterling:					
Notes and coin & balances at the Bank of England	71	117	106	65	290
Market loans	16,383	14,465	16,634	7,650	37,048
Bills	453	279	36	995	789
Advances	12,678	32,397	16,881	12,591	54,424
Investments	2,011	2,524	2,083	1,063	4,250
Total sterling assets	31,596	49,782	35,740	22,364	96,801
Foreign currency:[a]					
Market loans	11,523	8,146	161,218	52,832	160,699
Advances	4,609	2,764	36,791	30,491	61,693
Bills, investments, etc.	3,632	983	15,184	4,414	16,574
Total foreign currency[a]	19,764	11,893	213,193	87,737	238,966

Note:
[a] Selected foreign currency assets – some miscellaneous assets excluded.
Source: *Bank of England Quarterly Bulletin*, August 1990, Tables 3.3, 3.4, 3.5, 3.6, 3.7.

The assets held by non-retail banks are summarised in table 4.2, again broken down by type of bank. Non-retail banks, because of the nature of their business which is low volume, large value and hence unlikely to be conducted through cash transactions, require little in the way of cash balances. Much of the first item in table 4.2 is made up of the compulsory cash balance with the Bank of England required of all banks. In terms of sterling assets, market loans are clearly important, with the main item here being inter-bank loans – the counterpart to inter-bank deposits. Compared to retail banks, a larger proportion of sterling assets of non-retail banks is accounted for by market loans. The extent to which overseas banks based in the UK have become involved in domestic UK activity is revealed in table 4.2. Taken together, overseas banks accounted for 23 per cent of total sterling lending to the UK private sector. A significant part of this lending was directed towards large construction projects begun in recent years, including the Canary Wharf development in the London Docklands and the Channel Tunnel. As is also the case for the liabilities side of the balance sheet, foreign currency assets form a significant proportion of total assets. This is particularly pronounced for non-British banks. Reference back to table 4.1 illustrates a fair degree of currency matching, since foreign currency assets for each category of bank are similar in total to foreign currency liabilities.

A common hypothesis about wholesale banks is that they aim to 'match' the term to maturity of their liabilities and assets. So, for example, a £100,000 three-month certificate of deposit in its liability portfolio may be used to finance the purchase of a three-month commercial bill of value £100,000. Under this hypothesis, wholesale banks are simply liquidity distributors or brokers of liquid assets and do not produce liquidity by undertaking maturity transformation. It is sometimes argued that wholesale banks cannot mis-match because, unlike retail banks, they typically have a small number of large-value deposits and therefore cannot rely on the law of large numbers effect which comes from having a large number of small-value deposits. This effect, as we saw in chapter 3, makes net withdrawals of deposits more predictable and so it is claimed that in the face of uncertainty wholesale banks will aim to match the maturity of their assets with those of their liabilities. If wholesale banks are simply distributing liquidity, then the justification for the existence of such banks is dependent solely on their ability to reduce the costs of liquidity distribution to a lower level than would exist if borrowers and lenders sought out each other directly. As we saw in chapter 2, banks can reduce costs in credit markets through specialisation, which enables them to achieve economies of scale in their lending and borrowing operations. However, unlike the normal type of financial intermediation described in chapter 2, there will be no reflection of the liquidity generated by the bank in its

Table 4.3 *Maturity analysis of sterling and foreign currency business with non-bank customers of retail and wholesale banks in the UK as at end January 1987 (%)*

Maturity	Sterling					
	Retail banks		British non-retail banks		Overseas banks	
	A	L	A	L	A	L
0–7 days	3.54	83.51	13.98	52.83	12.64	41.29
8 days–1 month	3.49	7.89	3.09	18.74	12.75	21.97
1–3 months	6.18	6.28	6.27	15.61	15.35	20.88
3–6 months	5.01	1.00	6.19	4.36	5.69	5.16
6 months–1 year	5.91	0.67	10.42	4.70	7.20	4.03
1–3 years	10.21	0.24	18.11	1.83	12.65	2.37
3 years +	65.68	0.41	41.94	1.93	33.72	4.30

Maturity	Foreign currency			
	All banks		British banks	
	A	L	A	L
0–7 days	11.96	38.15	11.11	47.95
8 days–1 month	11.00	23.97	8.20	20.70
1–3 months	13.71	18.15	10.21	17.19
3–6 months	9.33	6.87	7.86	6.71
6 months–1 year	6.09	2.68	6.61	2.29
1–3 years	13.11	2.02	15.20	1.74
3 years +	34.80	8.16	40.81	3.42

Notes: A = Assets
L = Liabilities
Source: Bank of England, 'Sterling Business Analysed by Maturity and Sector', March 1987; Bank of England, 'Maturity Analysis by Sector of Liabilities and Claims in Foreign Currencies', March 1987.

interest rate margin as no liquidity is being generated. Of course this does not preclude other types of transformation such as, for example, risk transformation.

We now turn to examine whether there is any evidence to support the hypothesis of matching by wholesale banks. The Bank of England has published the results of a survey of retail and non-retail banks operating in London which show the maturity profiles of the aggregate asset and liability portfolios at the end of January 1987. These results (also presented in Lewis and Davis [1987]) are shown in table 4.3.

It should be noted that the figures in table 4.3 refer to business with non-banks, that is, the inter-bank positions are netted out as these positions will be matched positions in aggregate. The figures for business with non-banks reveal considerable mis-matching by wholesale banks, with the overwhelming majority of deposits having a maturity of under three months whilst a majority of assets have a maturity of over one year. The main features of this mis-matching are: (i) similarity in the degree of maturity mis-matching between sterling and foreign currency business, (ii) wholesale banks, whilst significantly mis-matching, appear do this to a lesser extent than retail banks (for example, for retail banks roughly 84 per cent of deposits fall in the category 0–7 days and 66 per cent assets have a maturity of over three years, whereas for British merchant banks the figures are 53 per cent and 42 per cent respectively), and (iii) British wholesale banks appear to mis-match to a greater extent than overseas banks – in their operations in London.

This evidence therefore does not support the view that wholesale banks are only liquidity distributors but rather that they transform the maturity characteristic of the funds flowing through the institution, albeit to a lesser extent than for retail banks. This result begs the question of how they are able to engage in maturity transformation and hence liquidity production for their non-bank customers when they do not have the advantage of the retail banks of the law of large numbers effect. That is, how do wholesale banks manage their liquidity risks? A related problem is that, given the small number of advances on the assets side of the balance sheet, there is less scope for pooling and diversifying default risks than with retail banking.

The solution to the problem of liquidity risk is provided firstly by the practice of liability management, which, as we discussed in chapter 3, involves banks having access to inter-bank borrowings and other market-based deposits as an immediate source of funds to replace any shortfall in the event of maturing or withdrawn deposits. A second strategy which became increasingly available to banks over the 1980s is the securitisation or marketisation of assets. This involves transforming previously illiquid assets such as mortgages into marketable instruments which can then be sold on to a third party. This is one aspect of the phenomenon of securitisation which also refers to the switch away from indirect bank financing to direct financing through the capital markets observed over the 1980s (discussed in chapter 12). The solution to the problem of default risk has been for wholesale banks to form 'syndicates' to spread the default risk of a large loan over a number of banks. This is examined further in section 4.4.

The discussion of wholesale banking so far has focussed on the activities which appear on the balance sheet. We now examine the growing phenomenon of off-balance sheet business.

4.3 Off-balance sheet business

Off-balance sheet business refers to business undertaken by a bank which generates a contingent commitment and generally an income to the bank without the business being captured on the balance sheet under conventional accounting procedures. This type of business has long been undertaken by banks but grew rapidly in both volume and scope over the 1980s. In this section we will examine the nature of off-balance sheet business and the reasons for its growth in recent years. In order to consider the latter we broaden the picture to examine more generally the causes of financial innovation. Finally we examine some of the implications of off-balance sheet business, in particular its implications for the regulation of banks.

Types of off-balance sheet business
If we consider first of all the narrow definition of off-balance business, that is, activities giving rise to contingent commitments, then four broad areas can be identified:

(i) *Loan commitments*. This covers any advance commitment by a bank to provide credit. Examples are revolving lines of credit, where a bank provides a line of credit to which it is committed often for several years ahead, overdrafts, where a bank has agreed a facility but can withdraw it in certain circumstances, and note issuance facilities (see chapter 12), where the bank provides credit only in the event of others being unable to. Provision of these commitments generates a fee income for banks.

(ii) *Guarantees*. This involves a bank in underwriting the obligations of a third party, thus relieving the counterparty from having to assess the ability of the customer to meet the terms of the contract. Examples of such guarantees are acceptances, whereby the bank guarantees payment of a customer's liability to a holder of its debt, and performance bonds, which support the good name of a customer and their ability to perform under a particular contract. The bank receives a fee for providing such guarantees.

(iii) *Swap and hedging transactions*. These involve the bank in a transaction using one of the recently developed 'derivative' instruments such as swaps, forward contracts, options, financial futures, interest caps, collars, etc. The nature of many of these instruments is discussed further in chapters 11, 13 and 14. The transaction can be hedged (to neutralise a position exposure) or unhedged (left open to exposure).

Table 4.4   *Fee or commission income*[a] *as a % of net interest income for Barclays Bank Group, 1980–89*

1980	1982	1984	1986	1988	1989
29	34	41	45	52	53

Note:
[a] Fees or commissions from banking and related services plus foreign exchange trading income plus securities trading income (since 1986 when, after Big Bang, banks have been allowed to own a securities trading firm).
Source: published accounts.

(iv) *Securities underwriting.*   Investment banks and merchant banks are involved in underwriting issues of securities whereby they agree to buy a set amount of the securities which are not taken up in an issue. This guarantees the issuer that the whole of the issue is taken up and a fee is paid to the banks providing the underwriting service.

All the above examples involve the bank in a commitment which may or may not lead to a balance sheet entry in the future. There are a wide range of other financial services provided by banks which generate fee income and where the business does not lead to a balance sheet entry. These include loan origination, trust and advice services, brokerage and agency services and payments services such as the provision of credit cards and cash management systems. The total income of a bank can be roughly split into net interest income, that is, the margin between their lending and borrowing rates, and fee or commission income. The relative growth in fee or commission income and other non-interest income (excluding capital gains from selling investments) over the 1980s for Barclays Bank Group, shown in table 4.4, illustrates a general trend for the UK clearing banks.

The relative growth in fee or commission income reflects both a growth in contingent commitment business and attempts by banks to diversify into related financial services such as selling insurance policies and securities trading. In the remainder of this section we concentrate on the nature of contingent commitment banking, which we will call off-balance sheet business whilst recognising that this term covers a wider range of activities.

Nature of contingent commitment banking
It is traditional to view a bank as a collection of assets and liabilities making up its balance sheet. We have already discussed in chapters 2 and

3 why banks engage in the traditional business of borrowing and lending, in terms of lenders delegating the collection and use of information to banks and sharing risks with banks, in return for a charge obtained from the interest rate spread. Banks are able to perform these services at a lower cost than ultimate lenders because they can specialise in collecting and skilfully using information about credit risks thereby leading to a better selection of risks and because their size of operations enables them to pool and diversify risks more effectively.

Lewis [1987] argues that banks perform similar information and risk-sharing roles when they undertake off-balance sheet activities. For example, the establishment of a loan commitment, such as an overdraft, reduces the liquidity risk faced by the customer but exposes the bank to greater liquidity risk, which it is better able to bear through its size of operations and access to the wholesale markets. When a bank provides a guarantee of a customer's ability to meet its debts, as with a bill acceptance, then this leads to a lower interest rate being required by the market. When looked at from the lender's or bill holder's viewpoint the effect is akin to a depositor accepting a lower rate of interest from a bank because of the safety provided by the bank compared with holding a primary security. Other transformations of asset characteristics performed on the balance sheet have their equivalent off-balance sheet. Note issuance facilities provide an example of maturity transformation where issues of short-term paper generate longer-term funding. When banks make available a syndicated loan, the borrower can negotiate the terms of the loan, including the interest rate basis, the currency and the date at which the loan is to be drawn down. All these choices can be made off-balance sheet as well by means of currency swaps, interest rate basis swaps and financial futures contracts to alter draw down dates.

Factors determining the growth in off-balance sheet business

The motives for banks' involvement in off-balance sheet business are many. One motive indicated in the above discussion is the desire for the fee income this type of business brings, thus diversifying the bank's income base. More generally banks have looked to diversify their operations, and the liberalisation of financial services in most countries in recent years has allowed banks to expand into new areas of business. Whilst some of the contingent commitments described above have long been a feature of commercial banking, for example loan commitments and guarantees, the banks have in recent years found more innovative uses for such activities. Other parts of contingent commitment banking, such as swaps and options trading, represent more recent innovations which banks, rather than creating, have encouraged their growth in use by being willing to run an unhedged position. Banks' involvement in financial innovation, and hence off-balance sheet business, is related to the changing policy and economic environment and the changing preferences of users of the financial system. In order to examine these motives in more detail we will now widen the discussion to consider the factors determining financial innovation.

As we saw in chapter 1, a financial instrument can be described by its underlying characteristics of liquidity, risk, etc. Financial innovation, as related to financial instruments, can be defined as the process of un-bundling the characteristics and repackaging them to create new instruments. Indeed, recent developments have made it easier to unbundle and repackage the characteristics of an instrument even after it has been issued. For example, a ten-year, fixed-rate, dollar-denominated eurobond represents a particular package of characteristics. Any of these characteristics can be unpackaged and traded separately. The holder of the bond can swap the currency to yen or swap the fixed-interest stream to a floating rate. This example illustrates the fungibility of financial instruments compared to physical products.

The **demand** for financial innovation can be explained by reference to a number of factors, which are discussed below (see Bank for International Settlements [1986] for further discussion).

Changes in the financial environment   Changes of policy regimes over the last twenty years have led to greater volatility of asset prices. In particular, the general move to floating exchange rates in the early 1970s after the breakdown of the Bretton Woods agreement and the adoption of monetary aggregates as intermediate policy targets have increased the scope for fluctuations in exchange rates and interest rates (see figures 14.1 and 14.2 for an illustration of this). The greater the volatility of asset prices and other prices, such as commodities, the greater the uncertainty about future prices and hence the greater demand for instruments for hedging exchange rate and interest rate risk. We examine hedging strategies in greater detail in chapter 14.

Greater perception of credit risks   There was a deterioration in the credit standing of banks which had large exposures to less developed countries' debt following the onset of the debt crisis in 1982 – discussed in section 4.5 of this chapter. One consequence of this was a desire by some banks to sell or swap some problem debts to diversify extreme exposures, and so a secondary market in LDC debt emerged (although not used to a significant extent to date). A further consequence of the decline in the credit standing of many banks was that investors were more wary of lending to banks and therefore were more willing to hold the direct securities of ultimate borrowers. In addition, large borrowers with good credit standing found they could obtain better terms by issuing their own securities through the capital markets rather than borrowing directly from banks. One result of this was some shift away from bank intermediation and towards capital market instruments as a source of financing – a process known as securitisation and discussed in chapter 12. Banks, however, sought to benefit from this trend by securitising packages of their own loans so they could be sold on and by expanding their role in guaranteeing and underwriting securities issues so as to increase their fee income.

Arbitrage opportunities in capital markets   The existence of barriers, such as exchange controls, interest rate controls and reserve ratios, separating banking markets in different countries led to the development of euro-currency banking. This in turn put pressure on domestic markets to lessen controls, thus eventually creating a global short-term money market. A similar process is occurring in the capital markets. Barriers separating capital markets have led to the emergence of eurobond and euronote markets – see chapter 12. However, the process of globalisation of capital markets is still incomplete, leaving banks to exploit arbitrage opportunities. The use of the swap transaction (see chapters 12 and 13) has enabled a borrower to raise funds in the capital market in which it has a comparative advantage and then swap the principal and interest on those funds to the currency in which it wishes to borrow. For example, a UK company which has a comparative advantage with its issues of sterling bonds but wanting to raise dollars can issue a sterling eurobond and then swap with a US company wishing to raise pounds but with a comparative advantage in the issue of dollar bonds.

Two factors which have had a major influence on the **supply** of innovations have been increased regulatory pressures and developments in technology.

Increased regulatory pressures   One consequence of the deterioration in bank credit ratings over the 1980s – see above – has been greater pressure from bank regulators for increased levels of capital in banking. The need to operate on higher capital ratios and the greater cost of raising additional capital due to their reduced credit standing led banks to pursue business that was not subject to capital adequacy controls, i.e. off-balance sheet business. Thus banks actively contributed to the development and growth in use of instruments such as swaps, options, note issuance facilities, etc. Another consequence of increased capital pressures was the development of securitisation whereby banks packaged up parts of their loan portfolio (for example mortgages) so that they could be sold on in markets.

Technology Advances in computing, information processing and tele-communications technology have enabled more complex instruments to be designed and priced on a continuous basis. In particular it has enabled the complex financial engineering of already issued financial products, as described above, to take place.

Implications of the growth in off-balance business

The growth in off-balance sheet business has been largely the result of the interaction of the demand and supply factors described above. An important implication of this growth stems from one factor in particular, which is the desire of banks to escape capital adequacy controls. This has concerned the regulatory authorities as banks have taken on risks which are not explicitly related to the banks' capital. These risks are similar to the risks faced by banks in their on-balance sheet activities but are heightened by the greater uncertainty arising from the novelty of many of the instruments traded. Such risks include, firstly, liquidity risk, which is the risk of banks having insufficient funding to meet their obligations as they fall due; second, credit risk, which covers both the risk of default by a loan counterparty and the risk of a customer whose performance is guaranteed by the bank failing to deliver; third, position risk, which is concerned with exposure to adverse movements in interest rates and exchange rates (in relation to swap and hedging transactions, banks are exposed to position risk when they take up an unhedged position); fourth, price risk. There was concern that banks may be underpricing new services in the sense that the income derived may not be sufficient to cover costs, including profit, over the long term. This fear was heightened by (i) keen competition which could force prices down to uneconomic levels and (ii) lack of past experience of sufficient duration on which an assessment of the risks could be made.

Regulators have addressed the credit risk of off-balance sheet trans-actions in their construction of a new risk assets ratio (a capital ratio where the capital of a bank is related to the risk-adjusted value of its assets – see chapter 17). In the construction of this ratio, off-balance instruments are converted to a credit equivalent and then risk weighted along with the on-balance sheet instruments. An illustration of banks' greater exposure to position risk as a consequence of the growth of off-balance sheet business is provided by the case of Midland Montague, the investment banking arm of the Midland Bank Group. Their treasury operations in 1989 were positioned towards declining interest rates which failed to materialise and as a consequence the net interest income of the group was considerably reduced. A further risk of off-balance sheet business is related to the novelty and complexity of the new instruments. This risk was highlighted in the swap market in 1989 when banks suffered sizeable losses following the ruling of the UK High Court that swap deals undertaken by local authorities, in excess of their underlying borrowing, were *ultra vires*. The banks which had entered into these swap arrangements had clearly not fully considered the risks arising from the special legal status of the local authorities.

4.4 International banking

As we have indicated in section 4.2 above, much of the business of wholesale banks based in the UK is concerned not with domestic sterling borrowing and lending, but with borrowing and lending in foreign currencies. The Bank of England defines international banking as all banking transactions in foreign currency – both cross-border and with local residents – plus cross-border transactions in domestic currency. From this definition we can identify two distinct types of international banking. The first is traditional foreign banking which, for UK-based banks, involves transactions in sterling with non-residents. The second type of international banking is termed eurocurrency banking, which, for UK-based banks, involves transactions in currencies other than sterling with both residents and non-residents. Traditionally the location of a bank determined the currency in which it would make loans. So to obtain dollar loans you would go to a US-based bank. Whilst such traditional foreign banking still exists, it has been largely replaced by eurocurrency banking where the location of the bank is unrelated to the currency of its transactions.

Eurocurrency banking
In this section we first of all define the term eurocurrency and then examine the nature and operation of eurocurrency markets. We then discuss eurocurrency lending before reaching a conclusion on the role of these markets in the international financial system.

A eurocurrency can be defined as a deposit or loan denominated in a currency other than that of the host country where the bank is physically located. Thus, for example, a deposit denominated in dollars placed with a bank located in London is a eurocurrency. In a similar manner, a deposit denominated in sterling placed with a bank located in Paris is a eurocurrency. Consequently the existence of eurocurrency markets permits the separation of location of the market and the currency and therefore political and currency risks. It is not surprising that the main currency employed in eurocurrency markets is the dollar (about 75 per cent of the total market) given the importance of the dollar in the international payments mechanism. Because of this dominant role, much of the following exposition will be in terms of the eurodollar market, though it can easily be extended to other currencies.

In order to demonstrate the operation of the eurodollar market we will trace the effect of a series of hypothetical transactions on the balance sheets of (i) the consolidated US banking system and (ii) two eurobanks designated A and B respectively. Assume initially that a UK customer of Eurobank A receives a payment of $1 million in respect of the sale of goods and he places this as a demand deposit with the bank. The impact of this on the two sets of balance sheets is as follows:

Consolidated US banking system

Liabilities	$m	Assets	$m
US resident demand deposit	−1		0
Eurobank A demand deposit	+1		0
Net change	0		0

Eurobank A

Liabilities	$m	Assets	$m
UK company time deposit	+1		+1
Net change	+1		+1

These changes represent the first round, with the customer lodging the receipt of dollars with his own bank as a time deposit. Suppose for the sake of exposition that Eurobank A has no immediate use for the funds so they are placed in the market via a broker with Eurobank B in the form of a time deposit earning a rate of interest higher than that paid to the bank's UK customer. The second-round impact of these changes on the various balance sheets is shown below:

Consolidated US banking system

Liabilities	$m	Assets	$m
Eurobank B demand deposit	+1		0
Eurobank A demand deposit	−1		0
Net change	0		0

Eurobank A

Liabilities	$m	Assets	$m
		Demand deposit with US bank	−1
		Time deposit with Eurobank B	+1
Net change			0

Eurobank B

Liabilities	$m	Assets	$m
Time deposit with Eurobank A	+1	Demand deposit with US bank	+1
Net change	+1		+1

If Eurobank B then lends the $1 million to a customer, the only changes recorded to the balance sheets would refer to the consolidated US banking system and Eurobank B recording the change of ownership of the demand deposit and the loan. These would be as follows:

Consolidated US banking system

Liabilities	$m	Assets	$m
Customer	+1		0
Eurobank B	−1		0
Net change	0		0

Eurobank B

Liabilities	$m	Assets	$m
		Demand deposit with US bank	−1
	—	Loan to customer	+1
Net change	0		0

This completes the chain of transactions in our hypothetical example. Note that these changes are simplified to the extent that we have assumed that the total sum, i.e. $1 million, has been moved around the system, whereas in practice the various banks will have retained some portion as a reserve for their own protection. Secondly, we have not included the situation after the customer has used the loan. If this is paid to a US exporter for goods, then the demand deposit at the US bank will have reverted back to a US resident and the chain completed. These caveats do not invalidate the general principle of the analysis. The points to note are that (i) no extra demand deposits have been created on the US banking system, (ii) total eurodollar deposits are now $2 million (original customer with Eurobank A, Eurobank A with Eurobank B) so that an extra $1 million deposit has been created by the operation of the eurobanks. This demonstrates the tiering in the eurocurrency markets, with the original demand deposit creating an additional deposit of $1 million. In practice, the quantity of extra deposits created would depend on the ratio of the reserves held by eurobanks in the form of deposits on banks within the US banking system against eurodollar deposits. Also illustrated by this example is the difference between gross and net measures of the size of the eurocurrency markets. The gross size is $2 million, but the net size is $1 million, i.e. the gross size less the quantity of inter-bank lending.

The interesting question posed is why the market developed outside the US, since, in our example, the original recipient of the deposit could have held it with a US bank rather than with Eurobank A. A number of reasons have been put forward. One suggestion is that the eastern bloc

countries wished to hold dollar deposits for international payment purposes but were reluctant to hold them in the US for fear that they could
be 'blocked' in time of dispute. A second reason put forward is the
existence of regulations in the US covering interest rates payable on
deposits and capital flows.

Since their development in the early 1960s the eurocurrency markets
have experienced a fast rate of growth. One of the main reasons for this is
an advantage in terms of cost. As noted above, US banks were restricted
in terms of interest rates that could be paid on bank deposits and this
restraint became more onerous as interest rates rose on a world-wide
basis. Furthermore, other regulations in the form of reserve requirements
and deposit insurance raised the cost of banking in the US as compared
with a centre such as London where prudential control was more relaxed.
Banks' costs were also lower in the eurocurrency markets since they
operated as wholesale banks with no branch network. The impact of
these cost advantages was that eurobanks could offer rates on deposit and
charges on loans that were marginally more attractive than those relevant
to similar transactions with banks located in the US. This raised the
attractiveness of the eurocurrency markets and stimulated a fast rate of
growth.

A second factor was the growth in international banking itself. This was
stimulated by two factors. First there was the growth in world trade
necessitating a corresponding growth in the international payments
system. Second there was a growth of financial imbalances on a world-
wide basis. In particular, the vast surpluses earned by OPEC members
following oil price increases in the early 1970s was an important factor.
OPEC members placed their surplus dollar revenue from the sale of oil
with eurobanks. It is often claimed that the large US balance of payments
deficits over recent years also aided the development of the market. The
importance of this factor may be over-estimated since, whilst it increased
the total quantity of dollars, it does not explain why these dollar balances
were held outside the US. The main reason for the continued growth
of the market appears to be the cost advantage and it remains to be
seen whether the market will continue to grow as quickly once the
relative advantage of off-shore centres is reduced following the proposed
harmonisation of prudential regulation noted in chapter 17.

We now briefly examine the general nature of the market. The first
point to note is that it is a wholesale market with transactions typically of
$1 million or more. As illustrated in our hypothetical example, the second
point to note is that there is a significant volume of inter-bank lending,
so that the gross size of the market is larger than the net size obtained
when the inter-bank transactions are netted out. Interest rates are clearly
related to those charged in domestic markets. Thus the rate charged on

dollar loans by banks situated in the US sets an upper limit to the rates charged for similar loans in the eurocurrency markets. Similarly there is a relationship between the rates ruling in a particular location. Interest rate parity requires the following relationship to hold between rates on sterling in the domestic market and those on dollars in the London eurodollar market for transactions of similar maturity and risk, etc.:

Nominal rate of interest on sterling	=	nominal rate of interest on eurodollars in London	±	expected appreciation/ depreciation of the dollar versus sterling

Arbitrage will ensure that this relationship holds provided the market is efficient – see chapter 7 for a fuller discussion of this point.

The market is essentially a market for short-term deposits, with the average maturity of a deposit being in the region of three months. The main depositors and borrowers are governments, multinational corporations and banks from a wide range of countries including the US. Lending appears on the other side of the banks' balance sheet. It is estimated by the Bank for International Settlements that at the end of 1989 approximately 80 per cent of outstanding gross international bank lending was of the eurocurrency type. The reasons for this dominance of eurocurrencies in international lending follow from those discussed above for the growth of the eurocurrency markets. It is difficult to obtain separate figures for net eurocurrency lending, so the figures reported below refer to total international lending.

The figures for the volume of new international lending over the 1980s are presented in table 4.5. The net international lending figures exclude lending between banks and so provide us with a view of new international lending to companies, governments and government agencics. The eurocurrency part of this net international lending figure can be further sep-

Table 4.5 *Gross and net international lending, 1981–89 ($bn)*[a]

	1981	1982	1983	1984	1985	1986	1987	1988	1989
Gross international lending	336	229	127	152	297	657	760	501	704
Net international lending[b]	165	95	85	90	105	200	300	225	330

Notes:
[a] Figures are adjusted to exclude estimated exchange rate effects.
[b] Net figure excludes inter-bank lending but allows for banks' own use of external funds for domestic lending.
Source: Bank for International Settlements annual report, various years.

Table 4.6   *International syndicated lending, 1981–89 ($bn)*

	1981	1982	1983	1984	1985	1986	1987	1988	1989
International syndicated credits	101	88	38	30	19	30	89	102	149

Source: 'Developments in the international syndicated loan market in the 1980s', *Bank of England Quarterly Bulletin*, February 1990.

arated into syndicated loans, which are large long-term loans, and the rest, which are mainly shorter-term credits for financing trade, etc. The figures for international syndicated credits, which are mainly euro-currency syndicated credits, are presented in table 4.6.

Eurocurrency loans and syndicated loans in particular were the method of financing the international imbalances of the 1970s following the oil price rises of 1973/74. Sovereign borrowers from the less developed countries (LDCs) and the newly industrialising countries (NICs) in Latin America became important borrowers in this market. When the debt crisis broke in 1982 (see section 4.5) this had two main effects on the syndicated loan market. First, banks became reluctant to lend new money to LDCs and NICs unless forced to as part of an IMF restructuring package ('involuntary lending'). Second, those banks with a high ratio of sovereign debt to capital found their credit rating reduced, which made raising funds in the capital markets more costly, leading to higher lending charges. One consequence of this was that highly rated borrowers found they could raise funds at lower cost through the international capital markets than through borrowing from banks. This led to the phenomenon known as securitisation, which is discussed in chapter 12. The overall effect of the debt crisis was to bring about a dramatic reduction in the volume of new syndicated lending which continued until 1985. From 1986 to 1989 the market has grown again, reversing the trend of the early 1980s which many commentators predicted would continue. Most of the growth of syndicated credits in the late 1980s has come from a greater use of this type of financing by industrial borrowers. By 1989 industrial borrowers accounted for over 80 per cent of total syndicated credits, compared with approximately 60 per cent in the early 1980s.

Syndicated loans are loans spread among many, sometimes over 100, banks. They are generally medium-term loans with maturities ranging from three to fifteen years, although the average maturity of new loans is around six to eight years. Interest rates on the loans are floating, with the interest rate related to a reference rate such as the London Interbank

Offer Rate (LIBOR), plus a margin representing risk, etc., and adjusted several times a year. Syndicated loans can be denominated in any currency, although the US dollar is the most popular currency. Given the large number of banks involved in syndicated lending, it is natural that one bank will act as a 'lead' bank organising the arrangements of the loan. The lead bank will receive a fee for this service in addition to the normal interest rate charge.

There are a number of advantages for borrowers using the syndicated credits market compared to international capital markets. First, the loan provides a steady source of funds, unlike some of the short-term underwritten instruments of the euronote markets (considered in chapter 12). Second, borrowers can generally raise larger sums of money than through the capital markets. For example, a $13.6 billion credit was raised for Kohlberg Kravis Roberts for the leveraged takeover of RJR Nabisco in 1989. Third, deals can be arranged quickly. For example, in 1987 BP sought to raise a syndicated loan to finance its offer to purchase the remainder of the stock of Standard Oil. A consortium of banks, led by Morgan Guaranty, took just five days to arrange $15 billion, which was $10 billion more than BP actually required. The syndication of a loan across many banks also brings advantages compared to a loan from one bank in that an individual bank in the syndicate will be less affected by a default. The lower risk implies that the cost of a syndicated loan should be lower.

The recent surge of corporate restructuring using the vehicle of mergers and acquisition, particularly in the US and UK, has been one of the driving forces behind the recent growth of syndicated lending. An increasing proportion of the financing of such activity has been debt, partly marketable debt in the US ('junk bonds') but largely loans raised through the method of syndicated lending. The advantage of syndicated loans in this activity is the speed with which funds can be raised and the ability to raise these funds more discreetly than through the capital markets.

Another development in the syndicated credit market over the 1980s has been the emergence of a secondary market, in particular of LDC debt. This involves banks securitising the debt so that it can be sold on to a third party. The recent Basle agreement on capital adequacy (see chapter 17) means that banks have either to raise more capital or to remove some assets from the balance sheet. A number of banks have chosen the latter course and this raises the prospect of the emergence of a general secondary market in syndicated credits. Allen [1990] states that this 'could be regarded as part of a more general process in the euromarkets, where in recent years innovation and securitisation have led to gradual dissolving of the boundaries between money, credit and capital markets'.

Finally in this section we consider the consequences of the development of the eurocurrency market. The market clearly carries out many of the facets of financial intermediation discussed earlier in chapter 2. Maturity transformation is obviously present, with loans being of a longer term than deposits. Similarly asset transformation is evidenced by the change of almost riskless deposits into more risky loans. This creates some dangers for the financial system given the interdependence of the operators within the market due to the presence of inter-bank lending built on a relatively small base of deposits held in US banks. Failure of one bank may have a large knock-on effect, creating problems for national supervisors of the domestic monetary system. In fact, as we have argued earlier for the parallel sterling markets, such operations may enjoy *de facto* support since national supervisory authorities are loathe to allow a major bank to default on its liabilities. There is also a concern arising from the overhang of sovereign lending financed by borrowing in the eurocurrency markets. Furthermore, it is sometimes argued that the creation of such a large pool of acceptable currencies creates the potential for movement of funds which could lead to the destabilisation of exchange rates and the frustration of monetary policy.

A final concern has been expressed over the role of the eurocurrency markets in the propagation of inflation on a world-wide basis. It is sometimes argued that the creation of these markets has led to an expansion of the world money supply, which in turn leads to higher world inflation rates. However, an examination of the hypothetical examples at the outset of this section suggests that there was no expansion in the quantity of US dollars held at US banks but that secondary deposits were created in the manner of non-bank financial intermediaries building up credit on the base of bank deposits. This analogy suggests that the existence of the eurocurrency markets has permitted a growth of credit rather than of the money supply per se, and as such may have increased the efficiency of the allocation of credit on a world-wide basis. This is also evidenced by the the existence of syndicated lending, which permits the sharing of the risks of international lending amongst different banks from different locations.

In the next section we examine one of the consequences of the growth of international lending over the 1970s.

4.5 Sovereign lending crisis

In the 1960s and early 1970s most lending to developing countries was carried out by official institutions such as the World Bank and the International Monetary Fund (IMF). This position changed largely as a result of oil price increases between October 1973 and January 1974 which saw oil prices rise by over 400 per cent. These price increases were initiated by the Organization of the Petroleum Exporting Countries (OPEC), a cartel whose member countries as a consequence experienced a dramatic increase in their foreign currency receipts. Oil-importing countries, however, experienced balance of payments deficits. Some of the developed countries were supported by direct capital flows from OPEC countries; for example, $6 billion was placed in investments in the UK in the years shortly after the oil price rises. The oil-importing developing countries suffered the most problems and those with access to the international financial markets generally chose to borrow to cover their balance of payments deficits in order to sustain growth. However, unlike the borrowing of the period prior to the oil price rises, developing countries turned increasingly to commercial banks. Developing countries were reluctant to borrow from the IMF because any funds provided were usually given as part of a reconstruction package which, because they were generally deflationary, were politically unpopular. The international agencies such as the IMF and the World Bank would in any event have been unable to support the scale of lending required as the basis of their funding was the developed countries' governments, in particular the US, which were themselves experiencing problems. Since oil is priced in dollars, the commercial banks received a massive flow of liquid funds from the OPEC countries in the form of eurodollar deposits and therefore had the ability to meet the developing countries' demands for funds.

Much of this lending was to governments or was government guaranteed and was therefore termed sovereign lending. There was a widespread belief amongst the banking community that this lending was relatively safe as countries could not go bankrupt. As a consequence, any credit assessment was superficial and there was little monitoring by the banks as to the purpose to which the funds were put. Part of the blame for the crisis which came later can therefore be placed with the banks which were imprudent in their lending. However, in mitigation, the banks were encouraged by western governments to recycle the OPEC surpluses to offset the effects of higher oil prices on the world economy. Much of this lending was to the newly industrialising countries of Latin America. The poorer developing countries, particularly in the Sub-Saharan region of Africa, generally did not have sufficient credit standing to gain access to loans from commercial banks. To sum up this section, the developing countries borrowed heavily in dollars at floating rates of interest to finance balance of payments deficits (i.e. consumption) rather than investment. Consequently, adjustment to the higher oil prices was delayed and servicing the debt necessitated current account balance of payment surpluses to earn the required dollars to meet the interest payments and repayment of principal.

There was little sign of problems resulting from this sovereign lending over the rest of the 1970s, partly because of negative real interest rates on the debt. Over the latter half of the 1970s though, the surpluses of the OPEC countries reduced as a result of dramatically increased imports. In 1979, OPEC decided on a further sharp rise in the price of oil, which more than doubled the spot price from $11 to $24 a barrel. Further increases also occurred in 1980.

The response of the developed countries to this second round of oil price rises, however, was different. Around this time the governments elected in the UK, US and Germany adopted monetarist policies and so attempted to control inflation arising from higher oil prices by monetary restraint. This time there was no attempt to borrow and spend a way out of the problem. The policy of monetary restraint, however, contributed to a world recession, making it much more difficult for developed countries to expand exports to earn foreign currency. As part of the policy of monetary restraint, interest rates were increased, which led to a further deterioration in the debt-servicing capacity of the debtor countries. Thus the combination of higher interest payments yet declining exports led to increased pressure on debtor countries. The first public sign of a crisis did not occur until 1982 though, when Mexico, one of the leading borrowers and a country with proven reserves of oil which had achieved rapid economic growth in the previous four years, announced a moratorium on principal payments until the end of 1983. Pressure from the IMF on commercial banks with exposure to Mexico to provide new money prevented an actual default. However, the incident brought home to the international banking system the nature of the risks of sovereign debt.

The years between 1982 and 1985 have been termed the years of debt crisis management, with the IMF orchestrating commercial bank loan reschedulings along with 'concerted' lending packages. At the same time the debtor countries receiving help from the IMF were forced to accept politically unpopular austerity programmes. Whilst this period of management achieved stability for the international banking system, it did little to help the problems faced by the debtor countries. Although there was some narrowing of the balance of payments positions for many debtor countries, this was at the expense of a sharp fall in investment and growth. Net resource transfers to Latin American countries over the period 1982 to 1985 were in fact away from these countries to the developed countries as debtors paid back more than they received in new loans – see table 4.7.

The next initiative came in 1985 when James Baker, the US Secretary to the Treasury, announced a new package which was aimed at improving economic growth in the debtor countries. With this package, additional funds were to be provided to finance supply-side reforms, such as en-

Table 4.7 *Net resource transfers to Latin America,*
1981–85 ($bn)

Year	Net capital inflow	− Interest repayments and foreign profits	= Net resource transfer
1981	49.1	27.8	21.3
1982	27.6	36.8	−9.2
1983	6.1	34.9	−28.8
1984	11.6	37.1	−25.5
1985	4.1	36.7	−32.6

Source: Inter American Development Bank.

couraging inward investment, tax reform and the encouragement of competition in their economies. The Baker plan was aimed at fifteen heavily indebted countries, mostly based in South America, with a total of $29 billion targeted over three years. Of this additional funding, $20 billion was to come from commercial banks and $9 billion from international agencies. However, as Sachs [1986] states, 'The Baker plan was significant not as a new policy, but rather an admission by the United States that the debt strategy up to 1985 had not generated adequate economic growth in the debtor countries'.

Whilst the commercial banks cautiously welcomed the Baker plan, a number of problems were identified. In particular the smaller banks which had already been withdrawing credit lines or writing off LDC loans since the crisis broke were not anxious to increase their exposure again. This meant that the burden of new lending had to be taken up by the larger banks, which were already heavily exposed. At the same time, these banks were being put under pressure by their central banks to increase capital ratios because of the greater risks. As the new lending under the Baker plan envisaged 'soft' terms, these new loans would likely be classified as high risk thereby requiring greater capital backing. As a consequence little new lending, from either official institutions or commercial banks, materialised. In addition, the supply-side reforms proved difficult to sustain and continuing high interest rates increased the pressure on debtor countries. To prevent defaults, banks were forced to agree to extensive rescheduling of the debt. Many debtor countries, faced with growing social problems and political unrest began to impose conditions on the servicing of the debt. In March 1987, Brazil, the largest debtor country, declared a moratorium on interest payments on $68 billion of its outstanding foreign private sector debt. Against this background the commercial banks began to acknowledge the serious consequences of

Table 4.8   *UK banks' exposure to outstanding debt of*
Mexico, Argentina, Brazil and Venezuela as a % of
capital as at end 1984

Barclays	62
Lloyds	165
Midland	205
National Westminster	73

Source: Estimate in Lever and Huhne [1985].

Table 4.9   *UK banks: exceptional provisions against*
LDC debt, 1987–89 (£m)

	1987	1988	1989
Barclays	740	10	983
Lloyds	1,148	53	1,763
Midland	1,016	–	877
National Westminster	562	49	1,040

Source: published accounts.

default. To illustrate the potential for insolvency of UK banks in the mid-
1980s, the exposure of the four main clearing banks to the four largest
Latin American debtors, as a percentage of their capital base, is shown in
table 4.8.

Citicorp became the first bank, in May 1987, to establish substantial
reserves against poor-performing LDC debt. Other US banks with large
exposures quickly followed the example of Citicorp. UK banks, led by
National Westminster and under pressure from the Bank of England and
the stock market, which had started to mark down the price of bank
shares, also announced substantial provisions – see table 4.9.

Further substantial provisions were set aside in 1989 in response to a
deterioration in debt servicing by many debtor countries, discussed
below. Whilst this provisioning acknowledged the dangers of default of
LDC debt, it did not in itself help the debtor countries as the provisions
represented funds set aside in case of default rather than any write-off of
the debt. A problem with increased provisioning against poor-performing
LDC debt is that it may provide an indication to the debtor nations
that banks expected non-payment. This may act as an incentive towards
further deterioration in the servicing of the debt and lower the value of
the debt on the secondary market (see below). Over the latter half of the
1980s a number of market-based solutions were used by the banks to

Table 4.10   *Secondary market prices for selected LDC debt, 1986–90*

Country	Price for $100 claim ($)				
	August 1986	April 1987	October 1987	March 1989	May 1990
Argentina	66	60	34	17	15
Brazil	76	63	38	34	25
Mexico	56	59	47	41	46

Source: Sachs and Huizinga [1987] and *Barclays Bank Review*, August 1990.

reduce their exposure to LDC debt. Three of the solutions which have been often used are discussed below.

Selling the debt in the secondary market in LDC debt   A secondary market in LDC debt began in late 1983 and although much of the activity in this market is inter-bank trading, with banks having the aim of adjusting their portfolio of risks, it has also been used as a basis for debt buy-backs by the debtor countries and as an intermediate stage for debt–equity swaps. The price of a country's debt in the market does provide some indication of the current and future performance of the debt and table 4.10 illustrates the generally deteriorating position for the three main Latin American debtors over the latter half of the 1980s.

The fact that a debtor's servicing record can influence the secondary market price of its debt introduces a moral hazard problem to the extent that any debt relief solution is tied to the secondary price of the debt, as debtor countries can 'engineer' a reduction in the price to obtain greater relief.

Debt–equity swap   This involves a debt denominated in a foreign currency being paid by the debtor in local currency, at an agreed discount, to the debt's face value. The bank then uses the local currency to invest in the debtor country, thereby acquiring a claim on a real asset, with the potential of capital gain as well as income return. For example, Midland Bank in 1989 swapped $63 million of debt owed by Chile into a $53 million investment in a chilean copper mine. The discount in the swap was 16 per cent, which is better than the 35 per cent discount which would have resulted from selling through the secondary market.

Debt–debt swap   This involves a bank exchanging the debt for bonds issued by the debtor country's government, where the bonds are issued either at a discount on the par value but with a market rate of interest or at par value with a lower than market rate of interest.

It has been estimated that, by 1989, the fifteen countries targeted in the Baker plan had reduced their bank debt by 13 per cent using these and other methods. Despite some success in reducing debt burdens it was accepted that the debt burdens of debtor countries remained too high. A further initiative came in March 1989 in the form of a set of proposals announced by US Treasury Secretary Nicholas Brady. These proposals represented a shift from the earlier approaches to the debt problem in that they recognise the need for official backing of schemes designed to achieve voluntary market-based debt or debt service reduction. However, the proposals also represent a continuation of the Baker approach in that participation is based on the pursuit of an IMF-approved economic adjustment programme and that new money is to be provided by the banks. Under these proposals debt relief is to be provided by the methods described above. Official money to back the initiative is to be provided primarily from the IMF and World Bank but also from developed country governments such as Japan.

At the time of writing (1990) only three deals have been completed, although others are pending. The main deal completed to date is with Mexico, covering $48.5 billion of its debt, where 88 per cent of the banks with exposure to Mexico opted for debt reduction (roughly half for bonds at a discount and half for bonds at par with a reduced interest rate) with only 12 per cent of banks opting to provide new money. The amount of new money provided fell well short of the amount targeted. This deal though has provided some help to Mexico, both directly in terms of a $1 billion reduction in interest payments per year (out of $8 billion in total) and more indirectly with the reduction in debt overhang increasing investor confidence, reducing domestic interest rates and increasing foreign direct investment and capital repatriation. The banks have also obtained some benefit from the deal as the secondary price of Mexico debt has increased (see table 4.10 above), effectively boosting the value of the residual debt left on the balance sheets of banks.

However, the positive developments provided by the Brady initiative need to be set against a deteriorating picture more generally amongst debtor countries, with interest arrears amongst the fifteen major debtors reaching $18 billion at the end of March 1990, some three times their end-1988 level. Brazil and Argentina account for nearly two-thirds of this total. This increase in interest arrears is partly explained by the reduction in the number of rescheduling and concerted lending deals achieved in recent years which previously provided debtors with sufficient funds to pay most of the interest falling due. Furthermore, recent deals between multilateral agencies and debtor countries have not followed the previous practice of making the elimination of interest arrears on commercial bank debt a prerequisite for agreement.

A number of weaknesses have been identified with the Brady initiative. Firstly, the initial impressions of the amount of debt relief that could be achieved under this initiative created exaggerated expectations on the part of debtor countries, which has generally soured the negotiating environment. Secondly, banks have objected to the use of secondary market prices as a reference point for debt discounts – see above. Thirdly, there is an inherent contradiction in the plan as it envisages banks confronting losses on their existing debt whilst at the same time providing new money. Such a situation is unlikely to occur unless the concessions on existing debt are sufficient to restore debtor countries' creditworthiness. Finally, the Brady initiative does not consider official debt, yet for some debtor countries, such as Bolivia and Peru, the debt to official creditors exceeds the debt to commercial banks. In relation to this last point however, two bilateral schemes involving partial reductions of official debt have been announced recently, namely the 'Enterprise for the Americas' initiative from the United States and the decision of the French government to halve the rate of interest on loans made to four African countries.

UK banks are now in a much healthier position in the event of default by one or more major debtors or if further debt reduction is encouraged, following a second round of provisions against the debt in 1989 – see table 4.9 above. The four largest clearing banks now have exposures to developing countries' debt, after allowing for provisions, which are below 100 per cent of the core capital of the bank – see table 4.11.

The establishment of provisions against debt to a problem debtor is now required by the Bank of England. This clearly further erodes the incentive for new lending by UK banks, as any new loans to problem debtor countries require the establishment of an equivalent percentage provision to that on existing debt.

The long-term solution to restoring countries' debt-servicing capacity

Table 4.11   *UK banks: effects of provisions on exposure to LDC debt*

	Provisions as a % of			Exposure to debt in 1989 (after deduction of provisions) as a % of shareholders' funds
	1987	*1988*	*1989*	
Midland	29	33	50	80
Lloyds	34	34	72	50
Barclays	35	40	70	8
National Westminster	33	35	75	7

Source: published accounts.

clearly requires policies to promote growth in the debtor countries. It is widely recognised that the current initiatives are unlikely to yield sufficient funds to debtor countries to adequately provide for such policies. Therefore further new lending to debtor countries will be required, although, given the reluctance of banks to provide new loans and also given that it is not clear that further loans at market rates of interest are in the debtor countries' best interest, it could be argued that officially sponsored debt relief packages should in the future provide for greater symmetry between the treatment of debt relief and the provision of new loans.

4.6 Conclusion

In this chapter we have examined the nature of wholesale banking in general and its international dimension in particular. Attention has also been focussed on two developments concerning the wholesale banking sector, namely off-balance sheet business and the sovereign lending problem. As we have noted in this chapter, the former development has implications for the way banks are regulated and we consider this issue further in chapter 17. The problems that have arisen out of sovereign lending appear to have been mitigated over the latter part of the 1980s in the sense that large defaults on the debt will not now threaten the solvency of the main banks involved. The problem though, particularly for the debtor countries, is still far from being resolved and will undoubtedly remain so for many years to come.

Chapter 5

Other deposit-taking institutions

5.1 **Introduction**

In this chapter we examine two other deposit-taking institutions, namely, building societies and finance houses. In view of their greater importance in the financial system and the recent significant changes affecting them, the major proportion of this chapter will be directed towards the building societies.

The building societies have traditionally been mutually owned, specialist financial institutions, borrowing from the personal sector and lending back to the personal sector in the form of a mortgage to finance house purchase. Up until the beginning of the 1980s the building societies enjoyed a virtual monopoly in the mortgage market. On the borrowing side, although experiencing some external competition for personal sector deposits from banks and national savings, there was little internal competition between different building societies owing to a cartel arrangement on the setting of interest rates. Over the 1980s however, building societies experienced a considerable degree of change as various liberalisation measures stimulated competition in the mortgage and personal savings markets. In the second half of the 1980s the Building Societies Act (1986) allowed for progressive deregulation of the products that building societies can offer on both sides of the balance sheet. The specialist institutions which began the decade are, as a consequence of these changes, more able to emulate banks as general providers of financial services. However, if any of the larger building societies feels that too many restrictions remain then the Building Societies Act also provides a procedure for a society to transfer from mutual to company (i.e. bank) status, and the Abbey National followed this path in 1989.

In this chapter, after providing a brief history of building societies (section 5.2), we concentrate on an examination of the pressures for change and the actual changes that have taken place in building society activity over the 1980s (sections 5.3 to 5.6), Finally, in section 5.7 we provide a brief survey of finance houses.

5.2   History of the building society movement

The first building societies were founded in the late eighteenth century. These early societies were set up by groups of around twenty to thirty people who contributed on a weekly basis to a fund which financed the purchase of land and the building of houses. These early societies were known as terminating societies because, when all the contributing members had been housed, the society terminated. The next stage came with the development of permanent societies, which increasingly borrowed from those who did not wish to buy a house and lent to those who both financed the construction of new homes and purchased existing homes. By 1912 approximately half the building societies were of this permanent type and no new terminating societies have been formed since 1953.

Up until the early 1980s there was little change in the activities of building societies, which had a specialist role involving intermediation within the personal sector, borrowing in the form of deposits and lending in the form of a mortgage to finance house purchase. Nevertheless the structure of the industry has significantly changed in two respects. First, the branch networks of the societies have expanded and, second, the

Table 5.1   *Expansion of building societies, 1900–89*

Year	Number of societies	Number of branches
1900	2,286	
1920	1,271	
1940	952	640[a]
1960	726	985[a]
1980	273	5,684
1982	227	6,480
1984	190	6,816
1986	151	6,954
1988	131	6,912
1989	126	6,236

Note:
[a] Estimates.
Source: BSA, *Building Society Fact Book*, 1988; Council of Mortgage Lenders, *Housing Finance*, 1990.

concentration of building societies has increased. This is illustrated in table 5.1.

The 2,286 building societies in existence at the beginning of this century were in the main small in size and operated over a limited local area. The interwar period saw the beginning of branching as societies sought to expand their catchment area for personal savings. Expansion of the building societies' branch networks appears, though, to have come to an end over the last half of the 1980s. Concentration of the building society sector has proceeded at a rapid pace in the period since 1960, with the majority of mergers between societies taking the form of a smaller society transferring its engagement to a larger society. The largest ten societies now account for 79 per cent of total assets compared with 71 per cent in 1980. These developments were accompanied by a large expansion of the business of building societies, as evidenced by the figures shown in table 5.2 for the level of personal sector deposits with the banking sector and total shares and deposits of building societies. The figures terminate at the end of 1988 to exclude the complications caused by the transfer of Abbey National from building society to bank status.

The figures in table 5.2 illustrate the success of building societies in the competition for personal sector deposits compared with banks. We consider this competition in more detail in the next section. What we are concerned with here is the controversy which has arisen as to whether the growth of building society deposits adversely affected the banks to any extent. The traditional argument followed the rationale that, since building societies maintain their own deposits with the banking sector, the growth of building society deposits did not entail deposit losses for the banking sector, but rather involved a change in ownership. A second argument

Table 5.2 *Stocks of personal sector savings held with banks and building societies, 1963–88 (£m)*

Year	Bank deposits (1)	Building society shares and deposits (2)	Ratio of (2) to (1)
1963	6,232	4,057	0.65
1965	7,210	5,211	0.72
1970	10,036	10,194	1.02
1975	19,206	22,748	1.18
1980	36,598	50,002	1.37
1985	61,488	104,922	1.71
1988	94,129	152,700	1.62

Source: CSO, *Financial Statistics*, various issues.

put forward noted that the societies lent exclusively on mortgage whereas banks conducted little mortgage lending and hence there was little competition between these two classes of institution on the assets side of the balance sheet.

The first argument is of an extremely dubious nature. To the extent that building societies keep reserves in the form of public sector debt (see table 5.8 below for further details), funds are lost to the banks in precisely the same manner as any other open market sale of government securities. The second argument is certainly no longer true. As we will discuss in the next section, banks became extremely active lenders in the mortgage market over the 1980s. Even more significant is the fact that this traditional argument ignored the effect of competition on the terms under which banks raised deposits. Increased competition for retail deposits must have raised to some extent the cost to banks of obtaining such deposits. These costs could arise, apart from the direct impact on interest rates, in a variety of ways, including reversion to Saturday opening, innovative time deposit schemes and reduction of charges on the operation of current accounts. Building societies' entry into the wholesale money markets – discussed in the next section – has also increased the demand for wholesale funds and must have again raised to some extent the cost of funds for banks in this market. Finally there is the evidence in table 5.7 below, which shows the withdrawal of equity from house ownership. In effect this provided indirect finance from building societies for the purchase of consumer goods at the expense of other financial institutions would normally have provided such finance.

5.3 Competitive pressures on building societies

Building societies have experienced greater competition in both their funding and lending activities since the end of the 1970s. As noted above, the main competitors to building societies in the personal sector savings market have been banks in particular and, to a lesser extent, national savings, although over the latter half of the 1980s building society deposits also came under competition from equity instruments following a number of privatisation issues, the growth of unit trusts and the growth in equity prices (temporarily reversed by the stock market crash of 1987). Table 5.3 illustrates the competition for personal sector liquid assets since 1977.

Over much of the 1970s the building societies faced little competition from other institutions for personal sector deposits. As we saw in chapter 3, the banks changed the balance of their funding from the retail market towards the wholesale market over the 1970s. Banks, however, did make an adjustment to this balance at the end of the 1970s and targeted

Table 5.3   *Competition for personal sector deposits, 1977–88*

| Year | Additions to liquid assets as a % of the total | | |
	Building society deposits	*Bank deposits*[a]	*National Savings*[b]
1977	70.7	10.1	19.1
1978	47.8	35.9	16.3
1979	41.3	47.6	11.1
1980	45.1	43.9	10.9
1981	44.9	28.4	26.8
1982	57.8	22.2	19.9
1983	61.2	20.9	17.9
1984	64.9	18.8	16.3
1985	64.8	23.0	14.4
1986	52.5	37.4	10.0
1987	57.9	32.6	9.5
1988	52.7	43.6	3.7

Notes:
[a] Includes Trustee Savings Banks deposits.
[b] Includes National Savings investment account.
Source: CSO, *Financial Statistics*, various issues, Table 14.5.

personal savings for a few years. Further competitive pressures to building societies' funding came from the government when from 1979 greater emphasis was placed on funding the PSBR through national savings. At this time the government introduced an index-linked retirement issue of national savings certificate and, with an inflation rate of around 18 per cent in 1979/80, this issue proved very popular. Also in 1980 the rate of interest on the national savings investment account was raised to a very competitive rate of 15 per cent. The competitiveness of this rate was maintained throughout 1981 and a new issue of index-linked national savings certificates without an age restriction was introduced at the end of this year. From mid-1982, however, national savings have provided less competition to building societies as inflation, and hence the popularity of index-linked certificates, has fallen, and because the government has placed less emphasis on funding through national savings.

However, over the last few years of the 1980s building societies also faced greater competition from banks in the personal sector savings market. Reasons for this is are (i) that banks increasingly viewed retail funding as a base for selling other retail financial services and (ii) perhaps by this time banks had realised that competition from building societies did impose costs on themselves. Another more specific reason for the greater competition though was the decision to put banks and building societies on the same footing in terms of deducting tax from depositors' interest at source at a composite rate of 25.25 per cent from April 1985 (abolished for both banks and building societies from April 1991). It was believed that the effect of quoting bank interest rates on a net of tax rather than gross basis would be to make their uncompetitiveness more obvious. In response to these pressures banks introduced high-interest deposit accounts similar to the building societies' short notice and instant access accounts. Later in the 1980s banks offered high-interest cheque accounts and more recently cheque accounts free of bank charges. As a consequence banks have regained some of the share of personal sector liquid asset holdings they had lost to building societies.

Up until the early 1970s the majority of the building societies' funding came from the ordinary share account. Then in 1973 building societies introduced term accounts, which offered a guaranteed differential over the ordinary share rate in exchange for the depositor leaving the deposit untouched for a certain length of time. Term accounts were generally for two years up to five years. These accounts grew very rapidly over the 1970s and by 1982 accounted for just over 23 per cent of building society personal sector funding. The next main innovation from building societies came in the early 1980s. In response to the greater competition described above, the short notice account was introduced and later the instant access account, where a higher rate of interest than the ordinary share rate is paid in exchange for a short period of notice or some minimum level of deposit. By the end of 1989, these short notice or instant access deposits accounted for just over 83 per cent of the total of personal sector deposits with building societies.

Another major development in building society funding over the 1980s was the greater volume of funds raised from wholesale sources. A series of changes in the taxation position of building societies since 1983 has allowed them to pay interest gross of tax on various wholesale instruments, thereby making the issue of such instruments more appealing to investors and hence making wholesale funding a more viable proposition for building societies. The 1986 Building Societies Act placed an upper limit on wholesale funding of 20 per cent, although this was raised to 40 per cent from the beginning of 1988 following representations from building societies. The percentage breakdown of retail and wholesale funding for building societies is shown in table 5.4.

The three main wholesale instruments issued by societies are Certificates of Deposit (CDs), eurobonds and bank borrowing. The largely floating-rate assets (mortgages) of societies mean that they would prefer to hold floating-rate liabilities. Therefore the most attractive eurobond for societies (in cost terms as well) has been the floating-rate note (see chapter 12 for further discussion). These issues have largely been euro-

Table 5.4 *Breakdown of building society funding, 1982–89 (%)*

Year	Retail funds	Wholesale funds
1982	100	0
1983	99	1
1984	98	2
1985	93	7
1986	90	10
1987	88	12
1988	86	14
1989	84	16

Source: Council of Mortgage Lenders, *Housing Finance*, various issues.

sterling floating-rate notes. Since March 1986, though, societies have been able to enter into interest rate swaps (see chaper 14) and so have started raising funds through the fixed-rate note market. The ability of societies to enter into currency swaps since the beginning of 1987 has added further flexibility, allowing societies to raise wholesale funds in a variety of currencies.

Access to the wholesale markets has allowed societies to practise liability management (see chapter 3). As with banks, which switched to liability management over the 1970s, societies have been able to reduce the level of liquid assets they hold – see section 5.5 below.

On the lending side, the building societies had a virtual monopoly on mortgage lending over the 1970s and accounted for some 82 per cent of the outstanding stock of mortgages at the end of 1979. Over the 1970s banks, although involved to a limited extent in mortgage lending, were restricted by direct controls on their lending which impinged most directly on the personal sector. Building societies, as mutual organisations, were not profit maximisers but instead attempted to reconcile the conflicting demands of borrowers for low interest rates and of savers for high interest rates by maintaining a relatively stable path for interest rates over time. This was made possible by the cartel arrangement whereby the Building Societies Association (BSA) recommended rates of interest to be charged to borrowers and savers. Such an institutional structure minimised the role played by interest rates in equilibrating supply and demand for mortgages. The stickiness of rates offered by building societies on shares and deposits meant that at times the rates were uncompetitive thus reducing inflows (figure 5.1 illustrates this stickiness for mortgage interest rates). This shortage of funds for lending that occurred at times could be

Source: CSO, *Financial Statistics*, various issues.

Figure 5.1   BSA mortgage rate and three-month LIBOR (quarterly averages), 1970–90

made up by the societies running down liquid asset stocks. However this provided only a temporary solution and, given that societies would not raise interest rates to reduce the demand for mortgages, then other means of rationing were pursued. These included queues and changes in lending arrangements. The latter generally took the form of lowering (i) the ratio of loan to borrower's income or (ii) the ratio of loan to the value of the associated property. Another criticism of the cartel arrangement was that the rates of interest set were designed to protect the smaller, less efficient, societies. This had the effect of allowing the larger societies to operate on margins which would not occur in a competitive environment and there-fore provided no incentive for them to cut costs so that the industry as a whole operated at a higher cost. However, a defence of the cartel that was often made was that, because the mortgage rate was often kept below market rates, then the cartel kept the cost of borrowing low (although at the expense of savers).

The market structure just described began to break down shortly after the start of the 1980s. In mid-1980 direct controls on bank lending (known as the 'Corset') were lifted and the banks immediately strove to

Table 5.5   *Shares of new mortgage lending, 1979–89 (%)*

Year	Building societies	Banks	Miscellaneous institutions[a]	Others[b]
1979	82	9		9
1980	78	8		14
1981	67	26		7
1982	58	36		6
1983	75	24	1	0
1984	85	12	3	0
1985	77	22	2	0
1986	72	19	9	0
1987	50	35	14	1
1988	59	27	12	2
1989	71	21	8	0

Notes:
[a] Refers to specialised mortgage lenders funded exclusively from wholesale source.
[b] Refers to insurance companies and pension funds, local authorities and other public sectors.
Source: Council of Mortgage Lenders, *Housing Finance*, various issues.

develop new areas of business. In particular they entered the mortgage market (see table 5.5) and by 1982 they had achieved a market share of new mortgage lending of 36 per cent. After this initial expansion, bank mortgage lending has generally slowed down and is now more related to demand.

5.4   Consequences of the competitive pressures

Greater competition in the mortgage market following the entry of banks and in the retail deposit markets has had a number of consequences. First of all it made societies more sensitive to interest rate changes, which in turn led to the breakdown in the cartel arrangement between societies, precipitated by the decision of Abbey National to leave the cartel in September 1983. The BSA recommendation of rates came to an end in Octorber 1983, although the BSA continued to advise rates until November 1984. The greater competition in the mortgage market and the breakdown in the cartel have led to both a greater availability of mortgage funds and price clearing in the market and therefore to an end to non-price rationing. Mortgage rates now move

Table 5.6   *The stock of dwellings in GB: distribution by tenure as a % of total, 1960–87*

	1960	1970	1980	1987
Owner-occupied	42.0	50.0	56.1	64.1
Rented from local authority or new town corporation	26.6	30.4	31.1	25.9
Rented from private owners and others	31.4	19.6	12.7	10.0

Source: *Bank of England Quarterly Bulletin*, February 1989.

more in line with money market interest rates and for much of the 1980s were above them (see figure 5.1). This has induced into the market specialised mortgage lenders which are funded completely from wholesale sources (the miscellaneous institutions in table 5.5 above). A rapid expansion in mortgage lending therefore occurred over the 1980s and this is reflected in the growth of home ownership as illustrated in table 5.6.

Whilst the main explanation of the growth in home ownership, particularly over the 1980s, is likely to be the greater availability of mortgage funding, other factors include the policy of tax relief earned on mortgage interest payments, the sale of council houses and the decline of the private rented housing stock (a long-run trend which the government is attempting to reverse by allowing market rents to be charged – see the 1987 government White Paper, *Housing: the government's proposals*, Cmnd 214).

The buoyancy in the mortgage market has also led to lending institutions, particularly building societies, extending the type of lending. Traditionally, mortgages have been predominantly in the form of first advances for the purchase of a house. In the latter part of the 1980s, second mortgages and further advances not directly connected with home improvements have been available. It is now possible for owner-occupiers to withdraw cash from the equity built up in their property, without moving house, simply by increasing the debt on the property. This has led to a rapid growth in equity withdrawal, defined as the difference between the net increase in the stock of loans for house purchase and the private sector's net expenditure on additions to the stock of owner-occupied housing, including improvements. Estimates of equity withdrawal are provided in table 5.7.

Whilst the estimates of equity withdrawal provided in table 5.7 may exaggerate the position because of the likely under-recording of housing

Table 5.7   *Equity withdrawal by the personal sector, 1980–88 (£m)*

Year	Net loans for house purchase	Private sector net investment in housing[a]	Equity withdrawal
1980	7,368	5,952	1,416
1981	9,483	6,353	3,130
1982	14,127	7,606	6,520
1983	14,520	6,887	7,633
1984	17,030	7,888	9,142
1985	19,032	8,926	10,106
1986	26,979	10,640	16,339
1987	29,521	12,456	17,065
1988	40,834	16,171	24,663

Note:
[a] Private sector residential fixed investment + council house sales – government capital grants to the private sector for housing purposes.
Source: Miles [1989].

improvement expenditure, there is still likely to have been a growing leakage of funds from housing into consumption expenditure over the 1980s contributing to the consumption boom in the latter half of that decade. As noted above in section 5.2, this imples that societies have been indirectly providing finance for consumption expenditure.

The greater competition faced by building societies led the government to recognise that new legislation was required to enable building societies to compete with other financial institutions on a more equal basis. In 1981 the BSA established the 'Nature of a building society' working group under the chairmanship of John Spalding, who was the chief general manager of the Halifax Building Society. This led to a report in 1983 entitled *The future constitution and powers of building societies*. The two key proposals of this report were (i) that the mutual status of building societies should continue but that a procedure be established whereby a society could convert to public limited company (plc) status, and (ii) that societies should be permitted to undertake a wider range of business which should be related to the mainstream business. After a period of consultation the BSA published its final proposals in February 1984 in a report entitled *New legislation for building societies*. In July 1984, the government published its proposals in a Green Paper, *Building Societies: a new framework*. This largely followed the proposals put forward by the BSA. This finally led to the publication of the Building Societies Bill, which received Royal Assent in 1986 with most of its provisions taking effect from 1 January 1987.

Under the Building Societies Act and subsequent revisions societies are permitted to offer additional services which fall into the categories of 'financial services' or 'land related'. Under the former category are:

(1) Banking services
    – money transmission (including providing cheque book accounts)
    – credit cards
    – unsecured lending (up to a maximum – see below)
    – foreign currency services
(2) Investment services
    – manage investments
    – establish personal equity plans
    – operate a stockbroking service
    – provide investment advice
(3) Insurance services
    – underwrite insurance
    – provide insurance

Under the category of land services are services relating to the acquisition, development, management or disposal of land primarily for residential purposes; in particular, the provision of estate agency services, conveyancing and estates management.

A further provision under the Act allows a society to convert from mutual status to public limited company status. A society following this route ceases to be a building society and effectively becomes a bank. Therefore as part of the conversion procedure the society would have to obtain approval from the Bank of England. The Act also allows societies to operate in the other member states of the EC. Finally the Act introduced a new supervisory body for building societies, namely, the Building Societies Commission, which took over the majority of the functions of the Registrar of Friendly Societies.

5.5 After the Act

The new services which societies have most actively taken up are in the category of banking services. In general, though, it is only the larger societies which have the capital and the size of operations to enter into competition with banks. The Nationwide Anglia was the first society to offer, in the spring of 1987, an interest-bearing current account with chequing facilities called the 'FlexAccount'. The other large building societies now also offer similar current account services. Most of the larger societies have also introduced a credit card, although the credit card market at the end of the 1980s was saturated and so most societies that have introduced credit cards have lost money on their operations so far. Many societies offer an ATM service through the Link network. The Link network of machines (which includes the machines that formerly belonged to the Halifax and the rival Matrix network) is, however, still outstripped by the combined networks of the banks. A further development in 1990 was the expansion into banking services by the Alliance and Leicester Building Society through the acquisition of Girobank.

A second area of expansion by the larger building societies is into estate agency operations. These societies saw estate agencies as an additional channel for the distribution of their mortgages. However, this expansion occurred in the final stages of a housing boom so that when the market went into depression in 1989 and 1990 an excess capacity in estate agency operations has been revealed and most agency chains have made substantial losses. This prompted the Prudential Assurance company to sell its large chain of estate agencies at a predicted substantial loss at the end of 1990. Those societies which have built up estate agency chains, however, appear to be holding on to their investment as they see them as closely tied to their principal operation of mortgage lending in the long term.

A third area of expansion for the large societies has been with the selling of insurance. Under the polarisation rules of the Financial Services Act, an institution selling insurance had to opt for either tied or independent status. The majority of the larger societies have opted for tied status, so, for example, the Halifax Building Society has tied with Standard Life. It is possible that these tied relationships may, in the longer term, lead to some mergers producing larger financial services groups. Some societies, whilst opting for tied status, have tied with their own insurance subsidiary. The Britannia Building Society, for example, took over the Glasgow-based insurance group FS and converted it into a subsidiary. The National and Provincial Building Society has taken a different route and set up its own insurance subsidiary in partnership with General Accident.

The smaller societies, not having sufficient capital to diversify into banking services, have in the main concentrated on their traditional business of savings and mortgages. Merger activity continues as some societies have attempted to achieve a size which allows them to take advantage of more of the diversification possibilities provided by the Act. Some smaller societies have diversified into specialist services allowed under the Act that don't require such a large amount of capital. For example, the Skipton Building Society and the Birmingham Midshires Building Society have each set up a subsidiary to handle mortgage administration for other new lenders such as foreign banks.

For one building society, the Abbey National, the Building Societies Act was perceived as not going far enough in removing restrictions. In

July 1989 it became the first building society to take advantage of the relevant provision in the Act and convert to plc status. The advantages of converting to plc status are, firstly, that it provides an escape from restrictions imposed on building societies. For example, building societies are not permitted to undertake corporate banking and there are limits on the extent of unsecured lending they can carry out – see below. Also, international operations for building societies are still limited to the UK and other EC countries. Secondly, it is argued that societies need to convert in order to obtain additional capital which they may use to diversify more quickly. The act of conversion itself leads to an injection of capital from the new shareholders and would, by increasing the primary capital of the company, enable other forms of capital to be increased commensurately. To indicate the differences in capital bases between building societies and the main clearing banks, the Halifax, the largest of the building societies, had core capital of £1.5 billion in 1989 compared to £3.2 billion for Lloyds Bank, the smallest of the big four clearing banks. The main disadvantage of conversion to plc status is that the newly formed company becomes more open to takeover, although it is protected from this for five years after conversion. To date, no other building society has indicated that it intends to follow the path of the Abbey National.

5.6 The balance sheet of building societies

We now turn to examine some of the effects of the changes previously described as revealed by the aggregate balance sheet position of building societies at the end of 1989.

The balance between wholesale and retail funding for building societies has been discussed in an earlier section. The other part of liabilities is made up of the societies' capital, which is mainly reserves. As building societies are mutual organisations, owned by their depositors and borrowers, they do not make profits on their operations, in the sense of an amount available for distribution for shareholders. Any surplus that is made on their operations is added to reserves. Specific capital adequacy requirements for building societies were introduced by the Building Societies Commission in 1987. These requirements set down a separate capital ratio for each category of asset as well as for off-balance sheet items (see chapter 4 for further discussion). The capital ratios for each category held by a society are then aggregated and the desired capital ratio is this aggregate plus a margin of at least 0.5 per cent. It is also expected that building societies will eventually have to operate under similar minimum capital ratios to those set by the Convergence Accord for banks (see chapter 17 for more details).

Table 5.8 *Building societies' balance sheet as at end 1989 (£m)*

Liabilities		Assets	
Retail shares and deposits	142,629	Notes and coin	281
Wholesale funds:		Sterling bank deposits	19,490
CDs	5,582	(including CDs)	
Term deposits and	11,308	Bank bills	1,265
commercial paper		Building society CDs	1,917
Syndicated borrowing	1,203	British Govt stocks	4,440
Bonds	9,905	Other public sector debt	1,432
	27,728		
		Commerical assets:	
Other liabilities and	18,214	Class 1	149,817
reserves		Class 2	4,565
		Class 3	1,816
		Other assets	3,548
Total liabilities	188,571	Total assets	188,571

Source: *Bank of England Quarterly Bulletin*, August 1990, Table 6.2.

On the assets side of the balance sheet, the first six items make up societies' liquid assets. Up until the Building Societies Act, societies were required to operate with a minimum of 7½ per cent of their assets in liquid form. The Act abolished this minimum requirement and instead stated that societies should keep sufficient assets in a form which enables them to meet liabilities as they fall due. However, a maximum level of liquid assets was set by the Act at 33⅓ per cent. With the ability to raise up to 40 per cent of deposits from wholesale sources, building societies are now able to practise liability management – see chapter 3 for a discussion of this concept – and as a consequence there is less need to hold a large cushion of liquid assets. An adjustment has therefore occurred so that, whereas in 1982 building societies' liquid assets amounted to approximately 20 per cent of total assets, at the end of 1989 – see table 5.8 above – this had declined to just over 15 per cent. The composition of building societies' liquid assets portfolio has also changed over the 1980s. In particular there has been a decline in holdings of government securities and an increase in holdings of short-term deposits and CDs. Part of the explanation for this is a change in the interpretation of the law regarding capital gains in 1984 which led to societies being taxed at the normal corporate rate whereas previously gains had generally been tax free. A further reason is that the greater volatility of socieites' retail inflows in the latter half of the 1980s as a result of greater competition from banks and equities has led societies to prefer short- rather than long-term assets.

Building societies commercial assets are divided into three categories by the Act, Broadly speaking, class 1 assets are first mortgage loans to owner-occupiers of residential property, class 2 are other loans secured on property, and class 3 are unsecured loans, investment in residential property and investments in subsidiaries and associates. Initially the limits for these three classes of commercial assets were set so that not less than 90 per cent of assets must be in class 1 and not more than 5 per cent in class 3. In addition, smaller societies are prohibited from owning certain class 3 assets. Following representations from societies, these limits were reviewed and the limits are now to be progressively relaxed as follows:

	Limit on class 2 and class 3 combined	*Limit on class 3*
Initial	10%	5%
1/1/90	17½%	7½%
1/1/91	20%	10%
1/1/93	25%	15%

The introduction of class 3 unsecured lending allows societies to offer credit cards and cheque accounts with overdraft facilities. At the end of 1989 building societies in aggregate are well below the prescribed limits, with class 2 lending at 3 per cent and class 3 lending at just over 1 per cent. This modest expansion in new types of lending is likely to be explained by the buoyancy of the mortgage market in the latter half of the 1980s and building societies' rising share of new lending in that market since 1987 (see table 5.5 above).

5.7 The finance houses

Finance houses (or non-bank credit companies) comprise a rather hetero-geneous group of financial institutions including subsidiaries of UK banks and overseas financial institutions and several independent institutions. Their activities are specialised and they account for a very small propor-tion of total lending by financial institutions. At the end of 1989 they had total assets of £9 billion, compared with £188 billion for building societies and £409 billion for retail banks. The combined balance sheet for finance houses at the end of 1989 is shown in table 5.9.

Table 5.9 reveals the nature of the business of these institutions. Nearly 70 per cent of their funds are raised by way of loans from banks and other financial institutions. On the asset side, their main business is the pro-vision of instalment credit, with the majority of this going to the personal sector. Finance companies also provide a significant amount of finance to companies in terms of instalment loans as well as through leasing and factoring. Leasing involves the finance company (the lessor) purchasing a

Table 5.9 *Non-bank credit companies' balance sheet as at end 1989 (£m)*

Liabilities		Assets	
Commercial bills	802	Cash and balances with	212
Bank loans	5,950	banks	
Loans from other financial	218	CDs	3
institutions		Other current assets	660
Other UK loans	215	Block discounts	1
Loans from overseas	21	Finance leases	1,011
Sundry current liabilities	757	Loans and advances to:	
Capital	986	UK companies	1,547
		UK persons	5,226
		Other financial assets	76
		Physical assets (own use)	78
		Physical assets (for hiring)	135
Total liabilities	8,949	Total assets	8,949

Source: CSO, *Financial Statistics*, various issues.

physical asset which is subsequently leased out to a firm (the lessee) in return for a series of rental payments over a term which usually approximates its economic life. As the lessee is in the same position as if the asset had been purchased outright, then finance leases are equivalent to raising a loan. Factoring involves a finance company taking over all or some of the debts of a company. The purchase price will be less than the book value of the debts and the gap represents the profit, including a risk element, for the finance company. As far as the company whose debts have been taken over is concerned, the gap is equivalent to the interest on an equivalent loan, with the benefit being an immediate acquisition of funds as compared with the delay before debts are normally paid.

This brief survey illustrates the nature of finance houses acting as financial intermediaries by obtaining funds mainly from banks, and therefore ultimately individuals and companies, and lending to individuals and companies. These institutions undertake a transformation of the characteristics of the funds as they pass through the institution. The transformation of risk is evident from the risky nature of their main lending activity, i.e. consumer credit, as compared with the perceived nature of their liabilities. This transformation is, of course, reflected in the relatively high interest charges on their instalment loans.

5.8 Conclusion

In this chapter we have concentrated our attention on the significant changes that have taken place in building society activity over the 1980s.

These changes were brought about largely by deregulation of the banking sector in 1980, which led to greater compectition between banks and building societies on both sides of the balance sheet. This led to the breakdown in the building society cartel on interest rate setting and a virtual end to non-price rationing in the mortgage market. The Building Societies Act of 1986 enabled building societies to undertake many more activities and so compete more effectively in the new environment, subject however to severe restraints on the quantity of non-mortgage lending. To date, only one society has felt these restrictions are severe enough to warrant giving up mutual status and converting to a bank. The slow take-up of new activities allowed under the Act also suggests that societies at present are not unduly constrained. Whilst some blurring of the roles between banks and the larger building societies has occurred, the distinctive nature of building societies still remains to a large extent. Whether this distinction remains in the future is an open question. As we have noted, building societies are facing a significant degree of competition in their traditional business of mortgage lending. Furthermore, some doubt has been expressed as to whether the rate of home ownership, illustrated in table 5.6, will continue to grow as rapidly as it has done in recent years, with the consequence that the demand for mortgages may not grow as rapidly. However, although population growth is expected to slow down in the late 1990s, the slowdown in the rate of house ownership is likely to be much less marked, assuming incomes and rents continue to grow at recent rates. The long-run outlook for home ownership and hence mortgage demand may therefore not be as gloomy as some have predicted.

Chapter 6

Investment institutions

6.1 Introduction

The investment institutions are a class of financial intermediary which enables small investors to participate in collective investment funds. These institutions pool a large number of small-value contributions into a fund which is used to finance the acquisition of a diversified portfolio of assets. The small investor thus obtains the benefit of the lower risks that come from a large diversified portfolio at a lower outlay than would be required if investing directly. Such indirect investment in capital market instruments has long since replaced direct investment by individuals, so that investment institutions now dominate the capital markets. This type of financial institution contrasts with deposit-taking institutions such as banks and building societies principally in the nature of their liabilities. Investment institutions, unlike deposit-taking institutions, have long-term liabilities and this is reflected in the nature of their asset portfolios. In the next section we examine the different types of investment institutions and the growth of these institutions in recent years. The remainder of this chapter is concerned with the nature of the activities of the different types of investment institutions.

6.2 Types of investment institutions

There are four main types of investment institution, namely:

(i)   pension funds
(ii) life assurance companies
(iii) investment trusts
(iv) unit trusts.

Table 6.1   *Assets of investment institutions, selected years 1976–88 (£bn)*

	1976	1980	1982	1984	1986	1988	% growth 1980–88
Pension funds	16.9	52.6	83.6	130.3	190.5	214.5	308
Life assurance companies	29.9	53.7	79.9	114.2	158.6	198.3	269
Investment trusts	6.1	8.4	10.1	15.2	20.5	19.3	130
Unit trusts	2.5	5.0	7.8	15.1	32.1	41.6	732
Total assets	55.4	119.7	181.4	274.8	401.7	473.7	296

Source: CSO, *Financial Statistics*, various issues, Tables 7.8, 7.9, 7.10, 7.11.

We do not include the category of general insurance companies in the class of investment institutions for reasons which we outline in the next section. At the end of 1988 the combined assets of these four types of institution were £473.7 billion. This compares with total assets for building societies of £189.8 billion and for all British-owned banks of £401.8 billion. As we noted in chapter 2, investment institutions have shown rapid growth in recent years and this is illustrated in table 6.1.

Of the investment institutions, unit trusts have shown the most rapid growth over the 1980s, albeit from a low base. Of the two largest investment institutions, namely pension funds and life assurance companies, it is the pension funds which have achieved the greatest growth over the 1980s. We will examine the reasons for the growth of these different institutions in later sections. First of all we discuss the nature of general insurance and in particular the reasons why we do not consider it to be an investment intermediary.

6.3   General insurance

The 1982 Insurance Companies Act separates the business of insurance companies into two categories; general insurance and long-term business. The former category encompasses a wide variety of business all of which is concerned with providing insurance against specific contingencies, for example, fire, accident, theft, etc. Such insurance is provided over a fixed period of time, generally one year. The general insurance companies hold funds, or reserves, to enable them to meet claims on the insurance policies they have issued. As most of these policies are effective for one year and claims are usually made very soon after the event giving rise to the claim, general insurance companies' liabilities are mostly short term. Even where claims take a number of years to settle, a reserve is maintained to cover possible payments. The short-term nature of their liabilities

Table 6.2   *Assets of general insurance companies as at end 1988 (£m)*

Asset	£m
Short term (net)	2,818
British Govt securities	6,483
UK ordinary shares	7,014
UK other company securities	1,429
Overseas securities	5,281
Loans and mortgages	1,101
Property	2,638
Other	15,008
Total assets	41,772

Source: CSO, *Financial Statistics*, 1990, Table 7.10.

is partly reflected in the assets making up the funds of general insurance companies – see table 6.2.

The majority of the long-term assets of general insurance companies are also marketable, and so can be called on at short notice, but they also provide a return to compensate for any underwriting loss – a common situation in the competitive general insurance industry where premium income is less than claims and the shortfall has to be found out of earnings on the investments. However, we are concerned in this chapter (and this book) with financial intermediaries which, as we described in chapter 2, channel funds from savers through to investors. The premium income which flows into general insurance companies is essentially a payment for a consumption service (indemnity against loss) and therefore cannot really be classified as savings. Also, whilst general insurance companies hold financial assets, these are more a by-product than a central feature of their business. We therefore conclude that general insurance companies are not strictly financial intermediaries and we do not consider them further in this chapter.

6.4   Nature of the liabilities of pension funds and life assurance companies

Life assurance companies
The long-term, or life assurance, business of insurance companies can be separated into three broad categories.

Term assurance   A term assurance policy provides insurance cover, for a specified period, against the risk of death during that period. If the insured survives the specified period then no payment is made. These term policies, which can be characterised as pure insurance policies, do not provide large sums for investment.

Whole of life policies and endowment policies   With a whole of life type of policy, the insurance company pays a capital sum on the death of the person assured, whenever that event occurs. With an endowment policy, a capital sum is paid out at the end of some specified term or earlier if the assured dies within the term. Both these types of policies provide cover against premature death and provide a vehicle for savings. The premiums for both these types of policy will be higher than for term assurance because the company is committed to paying out a capital sum at some point in time. As a consequence, the life insurance company has to accumulate a substantial fund out of which payments can be made as they fall due. Both these types of policies may be 'without profits', in which case the money value of the benefit is fixed in advance, or 'with profits', where a minimum sum assured may be augmented by bonuses declared by the company. These bonuses will be related to the performance of the fund over the life of the policy and so the 'with profits' policies have the effect of transferring some of the risk of building up sufficient benefits to the policy holder when compared with 'without profits' policies. In some cases a policy may be 'unit linked', where the premiums paid are used to purchase units in a chosen unit trust and the final payment is then dependent on the performance of that trust.

Annuities   Annuities generally involve a policy holder paying an initial lump sum which is used by the insurance company to provide an agreed income until death. In this case the insurance company will immediately create a fund which is then run down as payments are made to the policy holder.

Pension fund liabilities

Pension provision in the UK comes from three basic sources, namely (i) the state scheme, (ii) an occupational scheme and (iii) a personal pension. The state scheme consists of a first tier of a flat-rate pension, paid since 1925, and a second tier which is earnings related. We will examine recent developments in state pension provision later in this section. Occupational pensions are provided by employers in both the public and private sector. It is these pension schemes which involve the build-up of an investment fund and which form the pension funds we refer to in this chapter. Personal pensions are pensions tailored to an individual's requirements and until recently were provided only by life assurance companies. As a consequence such pensions are counted as part of life assurance business.

Recent reforms, outlined later in this section, have however widened the range of institutions which can provide personal pensions.

There are two basic types of pension scheme; the unfunded or pay-as-you-go scheme and the funded scheme. Many of the public sector schemes are unfunded schemes whereby the costs of providing benefits are met out of current contributions. In such schemes therefore there is no build-up of an investment fund and therefore little impact on the capital markets. All the state pensions are run on an unfunded basis, with benefits provided out of the general revenue of the government. The occupational schemes of the Civil Service, the NHS, teachers, police and other parts of the public sector are also unfunded, although in some instances a notional fund is maintained. The public sector industries and local authorities however run funded schemes. The disadvantage of unfunded schemes is that if the number of contributing members declines or the number of people receiving benefits increases relative to contributors (owing, for example, to medical advances etc. leading to longevity, decline in birth rate, etc.) then the burden on contributors can become excessive. There is also a risk with occupational unfunded schemes that the company may be wound up, thus making the pensions provided by the company insecure. In the private sector it is therefore the funded pension scheme which is the norm. With the funded scheme, the contributions of working members, along with in most cases the contributions of employers, are paid into a fund which is invested to yield income and capital gain out of which benefits are paid. With most funded schemes, benefits are determined by a contributing member's length of service and final salary upon retirement.

Growth of pension funds and life assurance companies
We noted in section 6.2 above that the assets of pension funds and life assurance companies increased in value at a rapid rate over the 1980s. In this section we examine the reasons for this growth. First of all we analyse the nature of the growth of these institutions by separating their growth into two categories, namely (i) net receipts and (ii) changes in price of the assets held (revaluations).

It is clear from table 6.3 that revaluations of assets held by the funds have accounted for just over half of the growth in funds over the whole period. This is explained by the strong growth in equity prices (company shares making up a substantial part of the funds' total asset portfolio, as we shall discover in the next section) both in the UK and overseas over this period. This revaluation effect is strongest in 1986 but almost disappears in 1987 as a result of the stock market crash. The growth in net receipts also reflects the strong performance of the assets held by the

Table 6.3   *Growth of life assurance and pension funds, 1980–88 (£bn)*

	1980	1981	1982	1983	1984	1985	1986	1987	1988	Total
Net receipts[a]	12.2	14.2	14.9	15.9	17.5	18.4	18.7	20.2	20.6	152.6
Revaluations[b]	12.7	2.6	23.5	22.8	23.3	19.5	39.2	3.7	19.3	166.6

Notes:

[a] Contributions of employers and employees + life assurance premiums + investment income of funds + current grants from government − pensions and other benefits − transfers to other pension schemes − administration costs. These are the net receipts of funded schemes only.

[b] Change in holding of personal sector equity in life assurance and pension funds − net receipts. The figure for revaluations may therefore also included any unidentified transactions.

Source: CSO, *UK National Accounts*, 1989, Table 4.10 (for net receipts); *Financial Statistics*, 1990, Table 14.5 (for personal sector holdings of equity in life assurance and pension funds).

funds feeding through into investment income in the form of dividends, interest and rent.

The contractual nature of premiums for life policies and contributions for pension schemes provides stability for the funds. Contributions to most life policies and pension schemes are made over a period of many years and there are penalties involved in cashing in life policies in the first few years after commencement. Life policies as a vehicle for long-term savings were encouraged up to 1984 by the existence of tax relief on premiums at 15 per cent. A further development was the introduction of Mortgage Interest Relief at Source (MIRAS) in 1982, which gave a boost to endowment policies linked to mortgages (i.e. only the interest is paid on the mortgage over the term it is taken out for, with the maturing endowment policy used to pay back the capital sum at the end of the term). Building societies have been active in selling endowment mortgages, in order to earn commissions, and the strong marketing of endowment mortgages continued after 1984 when the ending of tax relief increased the costs of this type of mortgage relative to the straight repayment mortgage. Another boost for insurance companies has come from the recent changes in the state pension system (described below) which have made personal pensions more attractive. As noted above, insurance companies had a monopoly in this type of pension scheme until recently and, despite attempts to broaden the range of providers, are still the main source.

The important factors explaining the growth of pension funds over the last twenty years are related to government policies. The first of these is the taxation treatment of 'approved' occupational pension schemes. The contributions of both employers and employees are deductible from taxable income. The investment returns achieved by a fund are also exempt from taxation. Finally the benefits payable by a fund are subject to the pensioner's rate of personal income tax, except for any lump sum paid up to a set limit which is tax exempt. Such fiscal privilege has undoubtedly had a positive impact on the growth of occupational funds.

Government policies with regard to the state pension have also had an effect on occupational schemes. In 1978 the government introduced the State Earnings Related Pension Scheme (SERPS), which provided greater benefits than the second tier state earnings-related scheme it replaced. At the same time, tougher minimum requirements on benefits paid out by occupational schemes were laid down if employers were to contract out of the state scheme. Most schemes in fact chose to contract out, which in many cases meant that benefits had to be raised. It has been estimated, though, that in 1988 approximately 13 million people were contracted into the SERPS scheme and were not in an occupational scheme. After a review of social policy in the mid-1980s the government argued that with increasing longevity and a declining birth rate the burden on the working population in supporting pensioners when the SERPS scheme matured early in the twenty-first century would become intolerable. As a consequence the SERPS scheme was reformed and the central feature of the new pension arrangements, which came into force in April 1988, was to transfer the responsibility for pension provision from the state to the private sector. To achieve such a transfer, firstly benefits available from SERPS were curtailed in order to provide an incentive to take out a private pension or join an occupational scheme and, secondly, the procedures for contracting out of SERPS were made easier and financial incentives were provided to individuals to take up a personal pension and to employers to start up occupational schemes. The monopoly on provision of personal pensions held by insurance companies was also removed to allow other financial institutions such as banks and building societies to become providers. The aim here was to encourage competition in provision. Such developments are likely to lead to an expansion of both personal pensions and occupational funds.

6.5 Portfolio investment of pension funds and life assurance companies

The portfolio investment of both life assurance companies and pension funds is determined by the nature of their liabilities and the return and availability of the various types of financial asset. In the previous section we have noted that the liabilities of both life assurance companies and pension funds are long term. In evidence to the Wilson Committee in

1977, the insurance companies stated the objectives of their investment strategy as being to maximise return, subject to risk, within an asset structure that takes the term structure of their liabilities into account.

A particular risk faced by life assurance companies is that, when a contract is written, certain sums are guaranteed to be paid in the future and these sums exceed the value of the premiums over the life of the contract. For example, in the case of an endowment policy, a guaranteed sum is assured at the outset. This sum will have been determined by reference to actuarial calculations about mortality and a prediction of likely returns on investment of the premiums. There is therefore a risk that outcomes of mortality, investment returns, etc. may prove worse than the life assurance company's assumptions. In order to protect itself against such a risk, the life assurance company can 'match' the term structure of its assets and liabilities. In this situation the assets should have a given yield which should be at least equal to the investment returns assumed in the calculation of the sum assured. The ideal type of asset for matching purposes is the British government (gilt-edged) security. As we saw in chapter 1, this asset possesses the characteristics of safety, known term to maturity, fixed interest rate and known redemption value if held to maturity. By carefully selecting gilts with terms to maturity which match the term to maturity of its liabilities, a life assurance company can immunise itself against changes in investment returns and so be in a position to meet its contractual requirements. However, there are several disadvantages with this strategy of matching. First, life assurance companies also write 'with profits' policies and the holders of these policies will expect bonuses to paid. To achieve the returns necessary to pay bonuses, life assurance companies will need to hold some proportion of their asset portfolio in assets which yield higher returns than gilts. Indeed, competition between life assurance companies will encourage them to hold high-yielding assets such as equities. Second, there is a practical constraint to life assurance companies holding portfolios constructed only of gilts. There are insufficient quantities of gilts across the range of maturities required for matching – a situation that has worsened since the authorities began buying back gilts in the late 1980s. However, the matching strategy provides a benchmark for life assurance companies in that the further away the fund is from a fully matched position, the greater the risk for the life assurance company of not meeting its contractual requirements.

The liabilities of pension funds, whilst being long term, are also different in nature from those of life assurance companies as in most cases benefits to be paid out are not known with certainty. As we noted in the last section, the benefits of most occupational pension schemes are related to the final salary of the contributor, which is not known in advance. Wage inflation complicates matters further as it increases the benefits to be paid by the fund, which has been accumulated from lower contributions over past periods. Index linking of final benefits, which occurs with some schemes, provides an additional uncertainty. As a consequence, the concept of matching is less relevant to pension funds. A greater consideration is to achieve returns in excess of the rate of inflation. Hence pension funds will look to hold assets which yield positive real returns over the long term. Examples of such assets are equities and property. Index-linked gilts, introduced in the early 1980s, provide a benchmark in this regard.

We now turn to examine the actual investments made by life assurance companies and pension funds over the 1980s. We consider first the actual holdings of the main categories of assets for the two institutions at the end of 1988. We then examine the investment strategies of the institutions over the 1980s as revealed by net investment of cash flows, which represent the conscious investment decisions of the institutions.

The figures in table 6.4 reveal that life assurance companies held a greater proportion of UK government securities in their portfolio compared to pension funds. This follows from the discussion above where we noted that the principle of matching is more relevant to life assurance companies. Life assurance companies also hold a greater proportion of other fixed-interest securities, which are mainly UK company debentures and represent an alternative (albeit more risky) investment to gilts for the purpose of matching. Pension funds have placed greater attention on index-linked gilts, which make up a larger proportion of their total holdings of gilts compared to life assurance companies. Index-linked gilts

Table 6.4 *Asset portfolio of life assurance companies and pension funds as at end 1988 (%)*

	Life assurance companies	Pension funds
Short term	3.0	5.4
UK govt securities	17.3	12.6
(of which index linked)	(10.2)	(22.0)
Other fixed interest	4.9	1.7
UK ordinary shares	42.8	55.4
Overseas securities	9.5	13.9
Property	17.0	8.5
Loans	3.1	0.0
Other	2.4	2.4

Source: CSO, *Financial Statistics*, 1990, Tables 7.10, 7.11.

Table 6.5

(a) *Investment of life assurance companies' net receipts, 1980–88 (% of total)*

	1980	1981	1982	1983	1984	1985	1986	1987	1988
Short term	2.3	8.9	6.0	4.1	13.5	2.3	6.5	13.9	8.0
UK govt securities	43.6	36.1	28.6	30.8	32.2	22.4	7.2	10.0	9.4
Other fixed interest	1.3	0.1	4.0	5.2	5.5	4.8	9.4	10.7	16.4
UK ordinary shares	17.4	19.3	25.1	21.8	25.9	41.6	48.0	46.0	36.9
Overseas securities	11.3	13.1	19.3	20.1	8.2	14.2	9.7	0.4	8.5
Property	15.8	15.9	15.2	11.8	9.2	9.5	7.8	7.3	10.8
Loans	6.1	3.5	0.2	4.1	4.2	3.3	4.1	7.1	9.0
Other	2.2	2.7	1.6	2.0	1.3	1.8	7.2	4.5	1.1

(b) *Investment of pension funds' net receipts, 1980–88 (% of total)*

	1980	1981	1982	1983	1984	1985	1986	1987	1988
Short term	−5.3	4.5	4.2	15.0	16.2	0.1	16.5	36.9	14.6
UK govt securities	32.9	27.0	17.0	35.5	31.1	28.9	13.6	−21.3	−13.7
Other fixed interest	0.0	0.5	1.3	1.2	2.3	2.2	4.5	4.5	5.9
UK ordinary shares	35.8	28.4	29.9	21.6	35.9	40.8	34.9	81.0	50.5
Overseas securities	23.1	23.8	31.7	17.4	4.5	26.9	26.7	−0.7	28.7
Property	14.0	11.3	11.0	7.3	9.0	5.1	3.8	1.5	2.8
Other	1.9	4.2	4.8	1.9	0.8	−3.7	0.0	4.5	11.4

Source: CSO, *Financial Statistics*, various issues, Tables, 7.10, 7.11.

are perhaps more relevant to pension funds as we noted above. Whilst equities are the main asset held by both life assurance companies and pension funds, they make up a greater proportion of the portfolio of pension funds. This reflects the greater requirement on the part of pension funds to achieve positive real returns. When we take into account over-seas securities, which are mainly ordinary shares of overseas listed companies, then the proportion of equities held by pension funds is approximately two-thirds of the portfolio. Another asset which generally yields positive real returns over the long term is property. Surprisingly, life assurance companies have been more active investors in property than pension funds, with the latter concentrating their investment atten-tions mainly on equities in recent years. We can observe this more clearly by examination of each institution's cash flow investment over the 1980s, which is summarised in table 6.5.

The figures in table 6.5 reveal a growth in UK equity investment over the 1980s, for both types of institution, taking advantage of the rising equity market over this period (see figure 8.1). The stock market crash of

1987 has brought about a slowdown in equity investment, although the proportion of investment directed towards equities in the year after the crash is greater than the proportion in the first five years of the decade. The popularity of equities for institutions over the 1980s is mainly explained by the fact that the real return (i.e. nominal return less the rate of inflation) on UK equities averaged approximately 13 per cent per year (compared to minus 1 per cent over the 1970s). The attractiveness of equities also partly explains the decline in investment in UK government securities by both types of institution over the 1980s. The real return on gilts averaged about 8 per cent per year over this period. The dramatic fall in investment in gilts in 1986–88 also reflects the decision by the authorities to buy back gilts following budget surpluses (see chapter 9 for further discussion). Property investment by both types of institution also declined over the 1980s as property returns slowed over this period. The real return on property was, on average, approximately 4 per cent per year over the 1980s. The slump in property values towards the end of the decade resulted in property investment virtually ceasing for pension funds.

Investment in overseas securities was high in the early 1980s as the institutions sought to restructure their portfolios following the removal of exchange controls in 1979. A second increase in investment in overseas securities also occurred in the middle of the decade as institutions sought to take advantage of the world-wide boom in equity prices. As was the case for domestic equities, the stock market crash of 1987 led to a dramatic slowdown in investment in overseas securities and some repatriation of funds by UK institutions. Following a recovery in world stock markets in 1988, investment in overseas securities has picked up again. Investment in other fixed-interest securities rose steadily for both types of institutions (faster for life assurance companies for reasons noted above) over the 1980s. This reflects the growth in issues of this type of security by companies over the decade following a collapse in issues in the 1970s as a result of prolonged high interest rates.

A final comment on investment strategies over the 1980s concerns the variable inflows into short-term assets. Investment institutions have relatively low liquidity requirements and, although short-term assets provide some return, this is generally lower than the main assets held by these institutions. Short-term assets therefore represent a depository for funds awaiting investment in the main earning assets. High investment in short-term assets generally implies uncertainty about the future returns on the main earning assets. Thus we note high investment in short-term assets in 1987, particularly by pension funds, reflecting a slowdown in equity investment in the final quarter following the stock market crash and an increase in receipts following the buy-back of gilts by the authorities.

6.6   Unit trusts and investment trusts

Unit trusts and investment trusts are institutions which allow individuals
or companies to purchase a stake in a larger and more diversified portfolio than they would normally be able to hold directly and at the same
time to obtain the benefits of a sophisticated portfolio management
service.

A unit trust is a fund to which individuals and companies may con-
tribute in order to obtain a share in the returns generated by the fund.
The institution is legally constituted as a trust where a trustee acts as
guardian of the assets on behalf of the beneficial owners and a separate
management company is responsible for investment decisions. The terms
and conditions governing these investment decisions are specified in the
trust deed under which the institution operates. The trustee company is
generally a bank or insurance company. The industry of fund management has been one of diversification over the 1980s and many institutions,
including retail banks, merchant banks, stockbrokers and insurance
companies, have become more involved. At the end of the decade,
insurance companies accounted for the largest share of ownership of unit
trust management companies.

A contributor to a unit trust purchases 'units' at a price which reflects
the aggregate value of the trust's net assets divided by the number of
units outstanding. The funds are termed 'open-ended' which means that
the fund can expand, by issuing new units at the same value as existing
units at that point in time, or it may contract, through unit holders selling
back their units to the fund at the prevailing price. There is no secondary
market in units, with all sales and purchases of units being made with the
trust managers, although another intermediary may act as agent to the
transaction. The price at which an investor purchases units is known as
the offer price, and the price at which he sells them back to the trust is
known as the bid price. To determine these prices the trustee will request
the investment manager to value the assets held at bid or offer price. The
price of units is then calculated by adding to the offer price stamp duty,
stockbrokers' commission, VAT and managers' charges. With managers'
charges typically in the region of 5 per cent and a dealing spread (the
difference between the bid and offer prices on the underlying assets)
of 2 per cent, the difference between unit offer and bid prices can be
around 9 per cent. The prices of most units are calculated on a daily basis
and the changing prices therefore reflect the changing prices of the underlying assets. The calculation of bid and offer prices just described represents a maximum spread. The quoted spread is normally much lower,
as fund managers do not always have to buy or sell the underlying
securities when they are buying and selling units but match a certain

proportion of buying and selling orders. The quoted price will therefore lie within the maximum calculated spread, so that during periods of net sales of units the quoted offer price will be at the calculated offer price with the quoted bid price at a higher price than the calculated bid price. Conversely, during periods of net redemption of units, the quoted bid price will be equal to the calculated bid price with the quoted offer price lower than the calculated offer price.

Traditionally the price at which the unit trust managers have transacted with investors has been the price related to the last valuation – known as historic or backward pricing. An alternative method, known as forward pricing, means that units are sold at prices that prevail at the valuation (a few hours after the order is processed). The Department of Trade and Industry has recently implemented new rules that give unit trust managers the choice of pricing on a forward or backward basis, with the investor being informed of the chosen method. The advantage of forward pricing is that investors are sold units at (almost) current rather than historic prices. The disadvantage is that investors do not know the transaction price when the order is made.

We noted in section 6.2 that unit trusts grew rapidly over the 1980s and at the end of 1988 had assets of just over £41 billion. They can invest in a wide variety of assets including bank deposits, UK and overseas company shares and government securities. As we can observe from table 6.6, the main asset held is company shares, both UK and overseas.

In contrast to unit trusts, investment trusts are public limit companies whose business is the investment of funds in financial assets. Investment trusts raise their finance like any other company, through the issue of shares and debentures, by retaining income, etc. Therefore if an investor wishes to acquire an interest in an investment trust it must acquire its shares either by subscribing to a new issue or by purchasing the shares on the stock market. These shares can be sold on to a third party through the stock market.

The investments held by the investment trust industry are summarised

Table 6.6 *Investments held by unit trusts as at end 1988 (%)*

Short term securities	4.5
British govt securities	1.1
UK other fixed interest	4.0
UK ordinary shares	55.3
Overseas ordinary shares	32.6
Other overseas securities	1.7

Source: CSO, *Financial Statistics*, 1990, Table 7.8.

Table 6.7   *Investments held by investment trusts as at end 1988 (%)*

Short-term securities	3.3
British govt securities	2.0
UK other fixed interest	1.8
UK ordinary shares	46.8
Overseas ordinary shares	41.1
Other securities	5.0

Source: CSO, *Financial Statistics*, 1990, Table 7.9.

in table 6.7. Ordinary shares make up the overwhelming majority of securities held, with a more even split between UK and overseas shares compared to unit trusts.

The existence of borrowed funds, as opposed to equity, in the capital structure of an investment trust means that if the value of the underlying securities fluctuates there is a 'gearing' effect on the value of the shares issued by the trust. To illustrate this effect we will consider a simple example of an investment trust which has a capital structure consisting of £2 million in outstanding debt and £8 million in shareholders' equity claims, attributable to 4 million issued shares. The total value of funds invested by the trust is therefore £10 million, which we assume is invested only in ordinary shares. The net asset value (NAV) per share (the value of assets less debt divided by the number of issued shares) is thus £2. Now if the value of the investment trust asset portfolio were to double to £20 million then the NAV per share would increase to £4.5. Therefore a 100 per cent increase in the value of assets held has led to an increase in the NAV per share of 125 per cent. The gearing effect of course can work to the detriment of shareholders when the assets of the investment trust fall in value. There is also a gearing effect on the income to be distributed to shareholders resulting from a change in the net income (before interest) derived from the investment trust's asset portfolio. Whilst the gearing effect is always of benefit to shareholders, in terms of the NAV of their shares, in a rising stock market the effect from income generation will only be of benefit if the return from utilising the borrowed funds is greater than the interest cost. The actual gearing of investment trusts in aggregate in recent years has been relatively modest, averaging around 8 per cent.

A particular curiosity of investment trusts is that the share price of most of them is at a significant discount to the net asset value per share. The price of shares is of course determined by demand, and so the existence of a discount would imply that demand for the investment trust's shares is lower than the demand for its portfolio of shares bought independently. We noted in section 6.2 that investment trusts did not grow as rapidly as unit trusts over the 1980s. This lower demand for the services of investment trusts may be due to the fact that, unlike unit trusts, investment trusts cannot advertise themselves through the media. Another factor which discourages investors may be the greater risk of the investment coming from the gearing effect. The existence of a discount makes investment trusts vulnerable to takeover, especially when a trust owns an appreciable stake in a target company. The potential bidder can acquire up to 30 per cent of the trust and therefore the shares owned by it at a discount. The full bid for the remainder will have to reflect the net asset value. An example of such a process is the 1979 Lonhro agreed acquisition of the Scottish and Universal Trust, which held 10.29 per cent of the shares in House of Fraser, which Lonhro went on to bid for.

6.7 The performance of institutional investors

Rising equity markets around the world over most of the 1980s resulted in historically high performances, with regard to returns, by UK fund managers. The discussion that follows, which examines the nature of this performance over the 1980s and some recent developments in fund management techniques, relates specifically to pension funds but the main points broadly apply to other parts of the UK fund management business.

Average annual returns on pension fund investments over the 1980s were 19.5 per cent, which compares favourably with average inflation and wage inflation, over the same period, of 6.9 per cent and 9.5 per cent respectively. The figure for wage inflation represents a form of target return for those pension funds whose benefits are linked to final salary. This performance over the 1980s contrasts strongly with performance over the 1970s where pension fund investment returns underperformed wage inflation by, on average, approximately 6 per cent per year. The consequence of this was that pension fund actuarial deficits had to be met by higher contributions from employers. The considerably higher investment income over the 1980s resulted in actuarial surpluses for many funds, which has allowed companies to take 'contribution holidays'.

The investment performance by pension funds over the 1980s was largely a consequence of rising equity markets, which was as we noted in section 6.4, were tapped by funds which invested most of their cash flows into equities. The diversification into overseas equities, where growth has at times been stronger in particular markets than in the UK, was also a contributory factor. However the diversification into overseas equities has not been as successful as it could have been, as evidenced by a failure of funds to closely match the index in overseas equity markets. The return on UK equities was on average 23.2 per cent per year over the 1980s, compared to 23.6 per cent return on the FT index – a close match after taking costs into account. In contrast there was underperformance of the indexes in the US by, on average, 3.6 per cent and in Japan by, on average, 2.5 per cent. This underperformance has led to consideration by fund managers of index-tracking funds. These are funds which are constructed according to a chosen index, with the shares making up that index included in the fund according to the weightings in the index. Such an index has the advantage of low transaction costs as shares are bought and sold only to keep the fund in line with the index. Depending on how well the index has been tracked, this type of passive management yields returns in line with returns on the index. Index funds were first established in the US and have only been slowly taken up in the UK. However, it has been estimated that about 8 per cent of UK pension funds are now of the index-tracking type (reported in a *Financial Times* survey of pension funds, 3 May 1990).

A recent development affecting the investment strategy of pension funds and unit trusts was the removal in 1990 of a tax restriction on trading derivative products such as futures and options – see chapters 13 and 14 for further discussion of these instruments. Prior to this, futures trading which was not for hedging purposes was liable to corporation tax. This allows fund managers to use derivative products to adjust exposure to the market without having to buy or sell the underlying securities. The recent introduction of new rules also makes it easier for fund managers to create futures funds.

A final comment concerning fund management relates to the way the performance of managers is assessed. Performance of fund management is conventionally assessed on a quarterly basis. This is not to say that managers are hired and fired on such a timescale – but it is argued that subtle pressures may be introduced. Such pressures may lead managers to focus on short-term objectives. If a hostile takeover attempt is made and a fund manager holds shares in the target company in his portfolio, then it is argued that the manager may accept the offer to boost short-term performance. We consider the general debate about 'short termism' in more detail in chapter 16.

6.8 Conclusion

In chapter 2 we noted the significant growth of assets held by investment institutions in recent years when compared to the growth of assets held by the deposit-taking institutions. In this chapter we have shown that the principal reason for this is that the main assets held by investment institutions are equities, which achieved substantial returns, in terms of both income and capital gain, over the 1980s. Other reasons suggested to explain the growth of investment institutions relate to government policy and include tax-privileged contributions to pension funds and changes in the state pension scheme which have encouraged private provision.

We have now completed our discussion of financial institutions and so in chapters 7 to 14 we turn our attention to financial markets.

Chapter 7

Financial markets: introduction

7.1 London as an international financial centre

Three international centres dominate the financial scene: New York, London and Tokyo. The main exception to the dominance of the so-called golden triangle of London, New York and Tokyo lies within the sphere of futures and options trading where Chicago dominates. During 1989 the three major markets in Chicago (the Chicago Board of Trade (CBT), the Chicago Mercantile (CMT) and the Chicago Board of Exchange (CBOE)) accounted for 65 per cent of total world trade in these increasingly used financial instruments. During the same period London and the rest of Europe attracted 6.25 per cent and 7.14 per cent respectively. It is, however, pertinent to note that the US share has decreased over the last decade since, in 1984, the relevant figure was 94.4 per cent of world transactions. Since London occupies a position mid-way between the eastern and western time zones, it is no surprise, therefore, to find a large number of financial institutions and markets present in London.

With reference to banking, London has long been a major international banking centre and has developed since the 1960s as a eurocurrency banking centre. At the beginning of the 1980s, London was by far the largest international banking centre in the world, accounting for 27 per cent of total international lending. Table 7.1 shows that, by the end of the 1980s, the figure had declined to just over 19 per cent and London had lost its dominance to Japan, which accounted for 21.5 per cent. London nevertheless remains the dominant international banking centre in Europe, with France at 6.4 per cent (also declined since 1980) being its nearest rival.

Whilst London's share of international lending has declined and Japan's has increased, particularly over the latter half of the 1980s, if we

Table 7.1 *International banking: share of total interna-tional claims outstanding by centre, 1980–89 (%)*

Centre	December 1980	December 1985	September 1989
Belgium	4.2	3.8	3.2
Luxembourg	6.7	4.1	4.0
France	10.8	7.1	6.4
Germany	5.5	3.2	3.7
Italy	2.3	2.2	1.7
Netherlands	4.7	2.6	2.7
Switzerland	4.5	2.6	2.1
Swiss trustee accounts	–	3.8	3.4
UK	27.0	25.4	19.3
Canada	2.7	2.3	1.2
Japan	5.0	10.8	21.5
of which:			
offshore banking	–	–	7.9
other	–	–	13.6
United States	13.4	13.3	9.4
of which:			
IBFs	–	6.5	5.5
other	–	6.8	3.9
Offshore banking centres	10.7	18.5	17.6

Note: figures unavailable.
Source: *Bank of England Quarterly Bulletin*, November 1989, May 1990.

look more closely at the make-up of this lending (see table 7.2) we see that Japanese international lending is heavily based on lending in foreign currencies to residents. In terms of cross-border eurocurrency banking, which is the part of eurocurrency banking which distinguishes an interna-tional centre from a regional centre, London accounts for 23.4 per cent of the total whilst Japan accounts for 13.4 per cent.

Table 7.2 *Breakdown of international lending for Japan and the UK as at end September 1989 ($bn)*

| | Foreign currency lending | | Cross-border domestic |
	Residents	Non-residents	currency lending
UK	282	822	72
Japan	481	471	359

Source: *Bank of England Quarterly Bulletin*, May 1990.

The 1980s saw a marked increase in Japanese international banking conducted through both Tokyo and its overseas establishments in London, United States and elsewhere. This growth largely reflects the growth in Japanese international trade and investment. London, in fact, is the most important centre for Japanese banks outside of Japan. The other major foreign banking presence in London is the US banks, which were the dominant international banks in London over the 1960s and 1970s (see table 7.3). However, over the 1980s the US banks experienced a decline in their share of total international lending both generally and through London. This partly reflects a retrenchment by US banks to concentrate on domestic business, following the sovereign debt crisis which broke in 1982. However, whilst the on-balance sheet business of US banks operating in London has declined, these banks continue to be the main players in international off-balance sheet activities such as foreign exchange dealing and swaps. The other main source of growth of international banks based in London is other European banks.

The markets located in London include (i) the sterling money markets, (ii) the capital markets both primary and secondary, (iii) the foreign exchange market, (iv) financial futures, (v) the commodity markets and (vi) the eurocurrency and eurobond markets. In fact it is more than a case of existence of these markets in London because, as we shall see, London occupies a dominant position as an international financial centre. The London foreign exchange market is the largest in the world. As far as equities are concerned, whilst only the third largest equity market, London's importance as an international centre for equity dealing is evidenced by the fact that there are more foreign companies listed on the London stock exchange and turnover in foreign company equities is larger than on any other world equity market.

Table 7.3 *International banks in London: share of international lending through London, 1975 and 1989 (%)*

	end 1975	end 1989
US	38	13
Japan	13	35
UK	22	17
Other European	6	22
Other overseas	22	13

Source: *Bank of England Quarterly Bulletin*, November 1989, August 1990.

Given its importance in international banking business and foreign exchange dealing, it is not surprising that London is one of the major centres for dealing in eurocurrencies and eurobonds. An indication of London's dominance of the secondary trading of eurobonds is given by the fact that 80 out of 114 dealers reporting daily or weekly prices to the Association of International Bond Dealers (AIBB) were located in London. London is also one of the two primary centres (the other being New York) for dealing in swaps, which are a rapidly growing market closely linked to eurobonds. The various markets are discussed in more detail in chapters 8 to 13.

The emergence of London as an international financial centre can be explained with reference to a number of factors apart from the time-zone factor briefly noted above. London has a long tradition of international business arising from the development of the empire and the accompanying international trade. International financial institutions have been attracted to London because of the existence of a number of features. These include a suitable pool of experienced and skilled labour, relatively light restrictions on access to financial markets, a tax regime which is not hostile to financial innovation, the absence of exchange controls since 1979, relatively light reserve requirements, a stable political regime and the English language. This last factor is an important consideration for US institutions setting up a European base. A more detailed discussion is provided by Davis and Latter [1989] and Davis [1990], with the latter paper examining the development of international financial centres from a more theoretical perspective. The growing concentration of financial firms in London owing to these factors will have attracted to London new firms which are likely to have been the more innovative financial institutions at the forefront of the development of new instruments and techniques. This in turn will have reinforced the importance of London as a financial centre.

All the markets mentioned above are both global and 'wholesale' markets and deal only in large-value transactions between both domestic and foreign institutions. The retail markets are linked to these markets via banks and other financial institutions. Thus, for example, a private individual buying foreign currency for his holiday would go along to his high street bank which would have obtained the currency originally on the London foreign exchange market. The markets are also organised in the sense that trading there requires operators to conform to rules specified within a 'rule' book and/or those imposed by the supervisory authority. These markets together with the financial institutions which use the markets are known colloquially as 'The City'. In the next section we examine in more detail the nature of markets.

7.2 The nature of markets

In the past, it was easy to define a market according to the geographical location where deals were made; for example the stock exchange was a building where interested traders could meet and strike bargains. In many cases the growth of screen-based information systems has changed all of this. This has removed the need to meet fellow traders and deals can be made over the telephone or the screen itself. Up to now this has not been true of all markets since, for example, financial futures have tended to maintain the 'open-outcry' system of trading, but the CBT and CMT are currently taking the first steps towards the introduction of screen-based trading. The London International Financial Futures Exchange (LIFFE) also provides a system of automated trading outside normal trading hours.

This raises the question of how to define an organised market, since asset prices are now publicly available via the payment of a subscription to an information system (the pricing function is said to be 'transparent'). Three core functions can be identified. First, there is the price discovery system whereby demand for and supply of the particular asset are brought together to determine the equilibrium price. The trading rules of the market determine how this function is to be carried out. The second core function is the surveillance function through which the public can be guaranteed as far as possible that any deal is fair. The market is, in effect, giving its stamp of approval. This function is also ensured through the trading rules by such means as regulations concerning disclosure, settlement, etc. Third, an organised market either provides a meeting place where, or a network through which, interested parties can be brought into contact with each other. The problem for the organised market is that both the first two functions are in the nature of public goods. Consequently there is little to stop individuals extracting the information and dealing on their own account, i.e. 'piggy-backing'.

Markets can be characterised in a number of ways. First, a distinction can be drawn between continuous and batch markets. In a continuous market, as the name suggests, buyers and sellers are in continuous contact with each other throughout the period the market is open and deals can be concluded at any time. In a batch market on the other hand, orders for purchases and sales are accumulated and are executed together at particular points of time. A second distinction can be made between auction and dealers' markets (sometimes these two market types are called 'order'- and 'quote'- driven markets respectively). An example of an auction market is the markets for futures where an 'open outcry' system is used for dealers to strike individual bargains between each other. It is also possible for the bargains to be struck via a computer network. In the case of the dealers' markets, market makers exist and they guarantee to operate throughout the time the market is open. They publicise two prices for an asset throughout the market. The first is known as the 'bid' price and refers to the price at which the market maker is prepared to buy the asset. The second and higher price is termed the 'ask' price and is the price at which the market maker is prepared to sell the relevant asset. The gap between the two prices is known as the 'bid – ask spread' (or more simply the 'spread') and provides funds to meet the market maker's operating costs and the provision of profits. Normally there is some slight variation between quotes by different market makers, and the spread between the highest bid price and the lowest ask price is termed the 'market touch'. This provides an indication of the liquidity of the market. A market is said to be 'tight' if prices are close to the true market value for small transactions and 'deep' if this applies to large transactions. Thus, for example, a market for which the bid – ask spread is small for large and medium-size transactions but widens substantially for small transactions would be said to be deep but not tight. A final attribute of a market is termed immediacy, i.e. the speed with which a proposed transaction can be completed. In the case of continuous dealers' markets, immediacy is present provided the dealers do not suspend trading for any reason.

Financial markets provide opportunities for many different types of activity and we now consider three specialist activities, namely hedging, speculation and arbitrage.

7.3 Hedging, speculation and arbitrage

These techniques originally developed in the commodity markets and we shall use a hypothetical example of the sale/purchase of grain in the following discussion to illustrate their role.

The term 'hedging' refers to the purchase of a financial instrument or portfolio of instruments in order to insure against a possible reduction in wealth caused by unforeseen economic fluctuations. For example, a producer of grain may wish to hedge against a fall in the price of grain over some future period. One method of achieving such a hedge is to find a party who wishes to hedge against the opposite risk, i.e. that of a price rise. One example of such a person would be a bread producer who wishes to avoid a rise in price of his future purchases of grain. The two parties can then agree on the price of grain for future delivery and this removes the risk of adverse price changes for both parties. This type of transaction would take place in a futures market where trade is highly organised. Such markets exist for all major commodities traded and for many financial assets including foreign currency, short-term deposits, bonds and equities. At this stage it is worth emphasising that both traders have gained certainty of price rather than made a profit. For example, if the price of grain does fall the purchaser has forgone profits which would have been obtained if he had deferred purchasing grain until later. The converse would apply in the case of a price rise.

A second hedging possibility for the grain producer is to transfer the risk to a party who is less risk-averse than the hedger. Such a party is a speculator who would purchase (or sell goods) for later resale (or purchase) in the hope of profiting from any intervening price changes. In this example, the speculator would purchase the grain at a set price for delivery in the future (the 'futures' price) in the expectation that the market price at that time (the future 'spot' price) would have risen above the purchase price. If speculators make accurate forecasts they improve the efficiency of markets. They buy when prices are perceived to be low and sell when prices are perceived to be high, thus evening out price fluctuations. However, inexpert speculators (and in some instances rational speculators) can destabilise markets – for further discussion see Newbery [1989]. Speculative activity is prevalent in all the major commodity and financial markets.

An arbitrage opportunity is an investment strategy that, in a particular situation, guarantees a positive payoff with no possibility of a negative payoff occurring. Thus arbitrage takes advantage of price or yield differentials in different markets (geographically or over time) in a riskless transaction. A simple example of an arbitrage transaction would be to borrow at one rate and lend at a higher fixed rate of interest when there was virtually no risk of default. Given the growth of informational technology, such differentials would not be expected to exist for any significant period of time since the action of arbitrageurs serves to eliminate them.

7.4 The efficient markets hypothesis

At this stage it is also useful to examine in general terms the nature of the term 'efficiency' as applied to markets. Efficiency can take three meanings: operational efficiency, allocative efficiency and informational efficiency. The first type of efficiency is concerned with whether the market operates at the lowest level of cost or whether excessive resources are allocated to the operation of the market. In this connection it is likely that absence of price competition and presence of cartels will lead to economic inefficiency. This is one of the motives behind the drive to liberalise financial markets seen in recent years. The second facet refers to the role of the market in the allocation of resources. The third aspect deals with the question of whether market prices reflect all available information. The 'efficient markets hypothesis' is restricted to this narrow and technical meaning of the term efficiency, but it is, however, worth noting that it would be difficult to conceive how allocative efficiency is possible if informational efficiency is not present.

If market efficiency is present anywhere, it is likely to be in the context of some financial markets. This is so for a number of reasons. First, financial assets are akin to durable assets in the sense that they are not purchased for immediate consumption. In fact, as we noted in chapter 1, they are purchased because of both the running yield or return they offer and, probably what is more important, the expectation of a capital gain which may occur due to price change. Second, continuous trading is a feature of financial markets and in many cases this is international rather than just national continuous trading. Consequently prices are free to move to eliminate any imbalance between demand and supply. It may be expected that, given these two features, dealing between sophisticated traders would force financial asset prices to reflect all available information. There will be clearly some dispersion in the interpretation of information, but, on average, the market will arrive at the 'correct' view.

The idea of market efficiency embodies two components: first, the belief that an equilibrium market price exists; second that the actual observed market price of the asset will adjust to this equilibrium price quickly. Two predictions follow from these observations: (i) that prices will alter only if new information is received on the market – this is technically known as 'news' and (ii) since all information within the designated information set is reflected in the price, all knowable above-normal profits will have been eliminated by trading or arbitrage in the technical jargon. This second prediction carries with it the belief that trying to outperform the market by forecasting is not worthwhile because the market price will contain an accurate prediction in the light of current conditions. The qualification concerning above-normal profits is particularly important. Trading to financial markets is risky and, unless it is assumed that operators are risk-neutral or indifferent to the degree of risk, it is natural to assume that a relatively high level of profit is necessary to induce them to enter the market. However it is very difficult to quantify a precise numerical value for the element of profit necessary to compensate for the high degree of risk (or 'risk premium' as it is called in the literature) so that the 'efficiency' of the financial markets is still a controversial issue.

A formal definition of the 'efficient markets hypothesis' is that a specific market may be termed efficient if the prices of the assets traded on that market instantaneously reflect all available information. Fama [1970] neatly defines three types of empirical tests of market efficiency according to the extent of the information set available:

(a) Weak efficiency – in this category the asset price is tested to see that it reflects fully the information concerned in the past history of both the price and volume of trading of that asset.
(b) Semi-strong efficiency – in this instance the asset price is required to reflect fully all publicly available information. The information set here would include all reports and statistics available in the media.
(c) Strong efficiency – this embodies the requirement that the asset price should reflect all information whether publicly available or not. This category would include all privileged (inside) information.

Clearly these categories are interdependent. Thus a market which is strongly efficient must also satisfy the semi-strong and weak tests. Similarly, a market which satisfies the semi-strong test must also satisfy the weak test. It is unlikely that any market will fully satisfy the requirements of efficiency on all occasions but, conversely, it is difficult to perceive of a market which is perfectly inefficient – i.e. a market in which asset prices never reflect any available information! Consequently the important question is whether markets approximate efficiency for all practical purposes.

Empirical testing of the efficient markets hypothesis is fraught with problems. Normally, at least two hypotheses coexist in any efficient markets test: first, that expectations are formed in the manner prescribed in the particular test and are used to arrive at the information set; second, that the market uses these expectations in an efficient way in the price-setting process. Thus failure to find support for the efficient markets hypothesis may be due to failure of either (or both) of the sub-hypotheses. A further difficulty arises because we observe price data at discrete periods, generally at the end of the day, which is the trading price reported most often in the media. The assumption underlying most empirical work is that the process of arbitrage has been completed during the trading period so that the end-of-trading period price reflects all the information in the prescribed test.

The plan of the next seven chapters on financial markets is as follows. In chapters 8 and 9 we discuss the equity and bond markets before proceeding in chapter 10 to examine the money markets. In chapters 11 to 13 we examine the foreign exchange market, the international financial markets based in London and the traded options and financial futures market respectively. In chapter 14 we finish our look at financial markets with a discussion of how these markets may be used to manage risk. Generally in each chapter we will consider not only the institutional detail but also the extent to which the market concerned conforms to the efficient markets hypothesis.

Chapter 8

The market for equities

8.1 Introduction

The market for equities is part of the capital market, which refers to the market for long-term finance as distinct from the money markets, which are markets for short-term funds, Clearly this distinction is difficult to draw at the margin as there is no clearcut time rule to differentiate between the two classes of market. In principle the capital market can be divided into two segments: (i) the primary market where new capital is raised and (ii) and secondary market where existing securities are sold and bought. Again this distinction is blurred since new capital can be raised via the stock exchange and existing securities sold on the same market. Furthermore the existence of a secondary market is necessary to support the primary market since an essential prop to the market for long-term capital is the existence of a market where these long-term claims can be sold if the holder requires to obtain liquidity. A further distinction can be made between private sector finance and public sector finance. We can also distinguish between fixed-interest securities and equities. In this chapter we discuss the equity market and in chapter 9 the market for fixed-interest securities. We commence by examining in section 8.2 the raising of finance by private firms and in section 8.3 the secondary market for private sector finance. In section 8.4 we examine the degree to which the stock market conforms to the efficient markets hypothesis.

8.2 The primary market

At the outset of this section it is worth examining the ways in which private firms can raise long-term finance. The main methods in recent years have been the following:

(i)   long-term bank loans
(ii)   equipment Leasing
(iii)   issues of fixed-interest securities
(iv)   issues of equities
(v)   retained profits
(vi)   finance obtained from official sources.

We have discussed the nature of bank loans in chapter 1, so no further comment will be made in this section other than to draw the reader's attention to the importance of this source of finance. Equipment leasing is a substitute for firms' raising finance in as much as they lease the equipment instead of raising finance themselves for the purchase. Categories (iii) and (iv) arc discussed below. An important source of finance to firms comes from the profits they have attained from trading but have not distributed to shareholders in the form of dividends. Finally it is possible for firms to obtain government assistance, for example the award of investment grants in connection with the regional selective assistance policy of the UK government.

Table 8.1 shows the pattern of finance raised by British firms over the period 1963 to 1984. A few explanatory remarks concerning table 8.1 are necessary. First, a negative figure indicates a repayment of the debt. Second, the item marked 'sundries' comprises three items: accruals, capital transfer and import and other credit. Accruals refer to items where the change of ownership has occurred but payment has not been made. Third, 'other loans and mortgages' refers to instalment credit received, loans from financial institutions other than banks and from the public sector.

The statistics contained in table 8.1 show differences in the relative importance of the various components over time. Over the whole period, however, the importance of internal funds as opposed to external funds is patently obvious, with just over 59 per cent of total funds raised being generated from within the companies. Of the external bank funds, loans are the most important component. Issues of ordinary shares contributed only 6 per cent of total funds over the period, although this figure was significantly higher in the 1980s compared to the 1970s as firms took advantage of the rising equities market. Debentures showed a large drop for a time after 1973, due no doubt to the rises in the rate of interest to levels not experienced before. As firms became accustomed to these levels, issues of debentures and preference shares picked up again. Note also the rising importance of overseas funding towards the end of the period.

We now turn to the main subject of the this section, which is new issues, New issues can be made by firms whose shares are already quoted

Table 8.1 *Identified sources of capital funds of industrial and commercial companies, 1963–89 (£m current prices)*

Year	Internal funds	Bank loans	Other loans & mortgages	Ordinary shares	Debentures & preference shares	Sundries	Overseas funds
1963	2,522	554	121	123	212	51	165
1964	2,887	745	158	158	254	50	106
1965	2,978	514	228	63	345	23	115
1966	2,659	197	124	124	452	22	172
1967	2,655	411	108	65	350	212	236
1968	3,194	672	159	303	183	472	261
1969	3,733	749	213	177	362	716	140
1970	3,813	1,183	302	39	193	652	377
1971	4,724	888	236	149	285	741	342
1972	5,859	3,032	113	296	267	785	17
1973	8,710	4,688	429	98	87	971	538
1974	9,330	3,126	375	38	27	1,058	1,285
1975	9,609	504	505	954	257	678	1,016
1976	12,325	2,700	213	770	56	1,271	1,188
1977	16,280	2,460	404	710	−46	876	1,159
1978	18,750	2,402	500	797	−41	991	533
1979	25,339	3,962	780	879	5	2,030	397
1980	18,938	6,321	176	896	152	463	1,865
1981	20,794	5,672	715	1,660	739	2,056	1,025
1982	18,310	6,635	857	1,033	243	1,137	1,223
1983	25,932	1,619	750	1,872	610	1,204	1,630
1984	30,323	7,082	575	1,127	248	451	−2,826
1985	32,250	7,454	876	3,522	816	695	572
1986	27,903	9,096	1,450	5,608	490	563	3,627
1987	36,642	12,141	2,720	13,338	534	606	5,434
1988	36,959	31,064	3,771	4,817	1,207	1,147	5,475
1989	30,810	33,945	7,964	2,694	2,980	832	10,353
Total	414,228	149,816	24,822	42,210	11,267	20,753	36,425
%	59.2	21.4	3.5	6.0	1.6	3.0	5.2

Source: CSO, *Financial Statistics*, various issues, Table 8.2, and ESRC Data Bank.

on the stock exchange or by those companies seeking a listing on the exchange. In this latter case the company must meet a list of requirements concerning its financial status and past trading record. In 1980 these requirements were relaxed for small and growing companies which could then seek access to the Unlisted Securities Market (USM). When the USM opened, twelve companies had their shares quoted. By the end of 1986 this figure had risen to 368. In 1987, a third tier was provided for small untested companies to have access to a 'third' market. This three-tier structure changed at the end of 1990 in response to European Community directives to harmonise listing requirements. These are summarised in the *Bank of England Quarterly Bulletin* (May 1990) and effectively lower the requirements for the main market, which, in turn, has led to lower requirements for the USM. At the same time, the requirements for the third market would have to be tightened, making the difference between this market and the USM minimal. Consequently the third market closed down at the end of 1990.

Every new issue will involve a stockbroking concern and is generally managed by an issuing house which, in these days of financial conglomerates, may be part of the same company. The main issuing houses are members of the Issuing Houses Association and are generally merchant banks. Their function is to manage the new issue by (i) offering advice concerning the timing and the terms attached and (ii) handling the publicity and administration involved. The issuing house may act as a principle by buying the shares from the company and then disposing of them on its own account or it may act as an agent. Even in the latter case some risk is involved since the issuing house normally provides a guarantee that a specified sum will be raise. In order to spread this risk of a failure to sell the whole issue to the public, the issuing house will normally arrange for the issue to be 'underwritten'. This involves an institution guaranteeing that the whole issue will be sold at the price indicated. If the issue is taken up by the public, the underwriter has no further liability. If, on the other hand, only part of the issue is sold to the public (i.e. 'partly subscribed'), the underwriter will purchase the remainder of the issue himself. In return for this service the underwriter will obtain a commission on the issue in the region of 1¼ per cent of the value. The main underwriters of new issues are the long-term investment institutions, i.e. the insurance companies, the pension funds and investment trusts.

The main methods for new issues are the following:

(i)   *Placings*. The issuing house purchases the securities from the issuer and places the shares with investors. Normal prudence dictates that the major proportion of these placings will be preplaced with the investors, who are generally the long-term investment institutions. In addition to the quantity preplaced, one-quarter of the new issue must be made available for the general public. This method of new issue is restricted to issues up to £15 million. These restrictions were modified with effect from January 1991. Initial public offerings up to £15 million may now be placed entirely with clients of the sponsor, subject to a minimum of 5 per cent being placed with at least one independent market maker. For offers between £15 million and £30 million (defined as medium-size offers), up to 75 per cent of the offer (or £15 million, whichever is the less) may be placed with the sponsoring broker's clients. At least 5 per cent of the shares being placed direct must be offered to two independent market makers of the shares concerned. All offers greater than £30 million must be made by way of an offer for sale. In this case, a sponsor will be permitted to place or underwrite 50 per cent of the issue wth its clients. As in the case of medium-size offers, there must be at least two independent market makers and they must be offered at least 5 per cent of the shares placed or underwritten.

(ii) *Offers for sale by tender.* In this case the public is invited to purchase shares at any price over a publicised minimum price. A single so-called striking price is established at which it is believed that the issue will be fully subscribed and all tenders at that or a higher price will receive an allotment at this striking price, irrespective of whether their tender was at a higher price or not. This system of allocation is called a 'common price tender'.

(iii) *Offers of sale.* Here is the issuing house purchases the whole issue at a specified price and then offers the issue for sale to the general public.

(iv) *Offers for sale by subscription.* This method is a variation of (iii) above whereby the company rather than the issuing house offers the shares to the public.

(v) *Rights issue.* This method is restricted to companies whose shares are already quoted on the stock exchange (i.e. a secondary issue). Existing shareholders have the right to purchase additional shares in proportion to their existing holdings at a fixed price. The price is normally at a discount to that currently quoted on the stock exchange so that the issuing price is unlikely to be higher than the price quoted on the stock exchange at the time of the issue due to price fluctuations. The shareholder does not have to take up the rights issue and may, in fact, sell the right. If it so wishes, the issuing company may avoid the necessity for the issue to be under-written by making the right at a large discount compared to the current market price (at a 'deep' discount) so as to make the offer attractive. Such rights issues must be approved by the shareholders and protection for existing shareholders against dilution of their holdings is afforded by the Companies Act 1985 and stock exchange rules. These are termed pre-emption requirements. As part of the reorganisation following 'Big Bang' (discussed later in this chapter), the stock exchange decided to withdraw the pre-emptive rights requirement for listed companies. Other methods of raising equity finance are now more common for secondary issues, as funds are more speedily obtained than for rights issues. The stock exchange has followed this path mainly because it wished to reduce the possibility that new member firms would by-pass the London market and issue securities through other world capital markets.

The method of issue adopted by an individual firm will depend on the costs involved relative to the total of the funds being raised. These costs include administrative expenses, advertising and, in the case of an issue by a company new to the stock exchange, any discount on the nominal price of the share. In the case of a secondary issue, this cost is not applicable since the total value of outstanding stock will remain the same. The Bank of England carried out a survey of new issues for the period 1983 to 1986 (*BEQB*, December 1986) which was updated to 1989 (*BEQB*, May 1990).

Since 1985, £24 billion of equity has been raised in initial public offerings in the main stock market. The number and sizes of the various methods of initial public offerings are shown in table 8.2. The most common method of initial public offering over the last half of the 1980s was placing, although the table shows the importance of offers for sale in large value issues. There has not been a tender issue since 1986 and offers

Table 8.2   *New issues of equity, 1985–89*

Method[a]	*Sums raised (£m)*	*Number*
Offers for sale	5,855	94
Tenders	361	11
Placings	725	120
Privatisations[b]	16,661	15
Total	23,603	240

Notes:
[a] Initial public offerings does not include rights issues.
[b] The large sizes of issues associated with the privatisation of nationalised industries has meant that slightly different methods of issuing techniques have been used. Most of the privatisation offers have contained elements of placing and offers for sale.
Source: 'New equity issues in the UK', *Bank of England Quarterly Bulletin*, May 1990.

for sale have been a declining method over these last five years. This trend follows the raising of the limit on placings to £15 million in 1986.

The broad conclusions of the early survey carried out by the Bank of England were that, for initial offerings for small amounts, placing is the cheapest method and is invariably followed in the USM and third market. Costs of issue were lower on the USM than the listed market. Substantial economies of scale were evident and issue expenses (excluding the under-pricing cost) were in the region of 11 per cent for placings and 17.8 per cent for offers for sale for amounts up to £3 million but faling to 4.7 per cent for amounts over £10 million in the case of offers for sale. Com-parative figures on the unlisted market were 10 per cent for placings and 16.6 per cent down to 2.3 per cent for offers for sale. Rights issues were cheaper than initial issues on the listed market and were estimated to be in the region of 3.9 per cent for issues during 1985. Deep discount issues were cheaper again because of the absence of the need for the issue to be underwritten. This method of raising new capital is rarely used (only 5 issues during 1985 as compared with 82 other issues) and the average cost was estimated to be 1.5 per cent. The later survey, restricted to the main market, found that the proportionate costs of placings and offers for sale changed little over the last half of the 1980s except for small issues (under £5 million), which have risen since the Big Bang in 1986.

As a final comment in this section we wish to draw the reader's attention to a new method recently adopted by firms to raise finance. This has a variety of names including 'auction market preferred stock' (AMPS) and 'variable dividend preference shares'. The idea behind AMPS is quite simple. The issued securities count as preference shares in the issuing company's capital. They are perpetual and can, therefore, be redeemed only at the issuer's option. The novelty is that their dividend is reset by a periodic auction process. Clearly demand and supply conditions at the auction will reflect market perceptions about the future prospects of the issuing company. Loss of confidence will push the dividend rate up. In the event of insufficient buyers at an auction, then the existing holders con-tinue to hold the shares at a prescribed fall-back rate – the upper limit to the dividend. Experience in the US suggests that auction failure rarely occurs in practice and, in any case, the company can redeem the shares if it feels that the rate has been pushed too high. The advantages of AMPS accrue to both the issuer and the purchaser. Because of the frequent auctions, the lender has the advantage of liquidity in that the investment is basically short term but earns a higher rate of return than say treasury bills because of the greater degree of risk. For his part, the borrower has obtained long-term finance which has the appearance of equity capital but at a lower cost.

The use of AMPS is more pronounced in the US where it is estimated that the market is worth more than $25 billion, but it is spreading to Europe including the UK.

8.3 The secondary market for private securities

Nature of the market
Stock exchanges are subject to ever-increasing internationalisation. For example, according to the Deutsche Bundesbank, non-residents own more than 20 per cent of all shares issued by German companies. Similarly, dealing in non-domestic shares is an important component of trading on the London exchange. Currently negotiations are proceeding over the establishment of some form of a standard European share trading system, i.e. The Price Information Project Europe (PIPE). The outcome of these negotiations is unclear at the time of writing (1990) but their very existence demonstrates both the internationalisation of security dealing and the fear of potential competition from existing exchanges, particularly the National Association of Securities Dealers Automated Quotations (NASDAQ) and also Reuters has plans to enter the share-trading field. In comparison with other European stock exchanges, the International Stock Exchange in London (ISE) is the largest in terms of total turnover (i.e. domestic and foreign) but smaller than the New York or Tokyo exchanges. On the other hand, the non-domestic business is larger than any of the other exchanges. Details are shown in table 8.3.

The International Stock Exchange in London is a market for private sector securities and public sector debt. Table 8.4 shows that, in terms of turnover, trading in gilt-edged securities is the main component. The

Table 8.3   *Comparison of major stock exchanges at end 1989*

	Market value of domestic equity (£bn)	No. of companies Domestic	Foreign	Turnover (£bn) Domestic	Foreign
Tokyo	2,639	1,597	119	1,436	12
New York	1,800	1,634	87	957	n/a
London	507	2,015	544	198	85
NASDAQ	241	4,026	267	249	14
German Federation of exchanges	227	628	535	218	11
Paris	227	462	223	69	3
Zurich	107	117	229	n/a	n/a
Milan	106	211	0	27	0

Source: Internation Stock Exchange, *Quality of Markets Quarterly*, Spring 1990.

Table 8.4 *Transactions on the London Stock Exchange, 1974–89*

Year	Value (£m)		Number of bargains (thousands)	
	Total	Gilts	Total	Gilts
1974	56,753	38,263	5,026	538
1975	94,037	67,246	6,030	688
1976	106,435	81,925	4,868	766
1977	173,334	135,759	6,085	978
1978	138,770	103,678	5,489	751
1979	168,941	128,950	5,457	883
1980	192,687	151,699	5,708	996
1981	190,665	146,057	5,287	951
1982	260,045	203,389	5,385	1,073
1983	287,587	210,754	6,007	867
1984	364,675	268,679	6,049	822
1985	390,472	261,527	6,711	758
1986	646,263	424,416	8,847	797
1987	1,757,493	1,148,358	15,399	1,098
1988	1,602,804	1,129,112	9,191	909
1989	1,627,265	975,211	10,680	683
Total	8,061,826	5,475,023	112,219	13,558
%		67.9		12.1

Source: CSO, *Financial Statistics*, various issues.

figures also show that, whilst the percentage of turnover attributable to gilt trading is nearly 68 per cent for the whole period, that for the number of transactions is only 12.1 per cent. This implies that the average size of order is much larger for gilts than for equities.

The ISE is a continuous dealers' market using VDUs to display prices but not for actual trading. At the moment, actual deals are made by telephone, though there are plans to extend the facilities to a paperless trading system by 1993 through the Taurus computer system, with the consequent elimination from share trading of paper certificates. This will lead to a reduction in costs and an improvement in settlement arrangements. The price information is distributed through the Stock Exchange Automated Quotations System (SEAQ) which supports two market segments: domestic and international.

The former categorisation of domestic shares (alpha, beta, gamma and delta) has been abolished and, since January 1991, shares are allocated to bands according to their 'normal market size' (NMS) based on market turnover. There are twelve levels, varying from 500 to 200,000 shares.

Deals for all shares with an NMS greater than 2,000 shares must be reported to the system within 3 minutes of the trade taking place unless the transaction is a very large transaction. The latter is defined with reference to a 'maximum publication level' (MPL), which is linked to the equity's NMS – currently three times the NMS. In this latter case, notification must be carried out within 90 minutes of the transaction. All 'agency crosses' (in-house deals) must be reported irrespective of the NMS of the equity concerned. Greater liquidity is ensured for shares with an NMS less than 2,000 by a commitment that there will be at least two market makers displaying firm quotations.

SEAQ International is the analogous system for leading international stocks which are traded by international market makers operating in London. In the manner described above for domestic markets, quotations for each stock are brought together on the screen with the 'yellow strip' providing the best available bid and ask prices at any one time.

The system is backed up by the SEAQ Automatic Execution Facility (SAEF) enabling member firms to buy and sell, automatically matching the order against the best bid or ask quote within the system. This facility is used mainly for small orders and enables the avoidance of telephone calls to execute orders. For each share, the maximum size of order which can be executed via SAEF (MSS) is currently fixed at 10 per cent of its NMS.

Changes in trading arrangements: Big Bang

The arrangements at the ISE were subject to a fundamental change on 27 October 1986, the so-called 'Big Bang'. Prior to this date the London Stock Exchange was subject to a number of restrictive practices. In particular, three practices were important. First, there was single capacity since the market makers in shares, termed jobbers, were only able to deal on their own account. All contact with the jobbers was to be conducted via stockbrokers who, in turn, were unable to deal in shares. In other words, stockbrokers were purely agents acting as intermediaries between the ultimate customer and the jobber. Second, a cartel arrangement applied whereby minimum commissions were fixed for all trades irrespective of size. Third, ownership of brokers and jobbers was restricted to private partnerships until 1969. In that year brokers and jobbers were permitted to form limited companies and further relaxation occurred in 1971 when ownership of corporate members could be held by outside members, but subject to the severe restraint that no one shareholder could hold more than 10 per cent of the capital of a single firm. Economic theory predicts that cartels have the effect of raising members' income and consequently it is certain that the minimum commission arrangement raised dealing costs. On the other hand, it was suggested that it protected the interest of the public since there was no conflict of interest because the market makers could not deal directly with the public and brokers could not deal in shares. Thus each party had no motive to act against the interests of the public.

There were two separate motives for change. First, after 1979, the Conservative government was interested in increasing the degree of competition throughout the economy. This resulted in a reference of the stock exchange rule book to the Restrictive Trade Practices Court in 1979. Within this motive was, perhaps, the feeling that the government was providing excessive commission incomes on dealings in gilts. Second, the London Stock Exchange was losing business following the abolition of controls on movements of capital for UK residents in 1979. Share dealings have become dominated to an increasing extent by the institutions. These are the agents most likely to suffer from minimum prices since their deals would be of a large size. A significant development at this time was the growth of American Deposit Receipts (ADRs). US financial institutions purchased blocks of shares in UK companies and then issued titles to the underlying shares, which were traded on the New York Stock Exchange. Costs of trading were lower in New York, which had experienced its equivalent to Big Bang ('May Day') in 1975. Consequently large dealings in UK shares tended to move to New York at the expense of London.

Agreement was reached in 1983 between the stock exchange and the government which led to the dropping of the reference to the court. Three important components of the agreement were: (i) the abolition of minimum commissions, (ii) the permission of dual capacity and (iii) relaxation of the rules of outside ownership. With regard to (ii) above, there is now a single form of institution called a broker–dealer who can operate either on his own account or as an agent for another institution/ person. Within this category there is a subset who are registered to act as market makers or dealers. These market makers may specialise in a particular group of shares. Restraints operate where the broker–dealer, who is not a market maker, is acting as an agent, in as much as he can deal only on his own account or match an order with another client if he can show that he can execute the order at a superior price than by going to a market maker. Similarly, a market maker can act as an agent only if he can deal at a price at least as good as that which could be obtained from another market maker. The three components of the agreement were closely interconnected. Abolition of minimum commissions would place income of brokers under great pressure so that they would be likely to seek alternative sources of income. One such source would be market making. Second, dealing is a high-risk industry and new sources of capital would be needed in view of the likely fall in incomes. Thus outside interests were permitted to own 100 per cent of the share capital of single-member firms as from 1 March 1986. This led to a scramble to buy up firms and to form financial conglomerates such as, for example, Barclays de Zoete Wedd.

Along with changes brought about by Big Bang, the screen information system described above was introduced, so that the old 'face-to-face' discussions between stock exchange members were quickly eliminated. What effect did these changes have on share dealing? First, the level of commissions has fallen on deals. In February 1987 the Bank of England (*BEQB*, 1987) suggested that, for an equity deal in the region of £10,000 to £1 million, commission rates fell from 0.4 per cent to 0.2 per cent. Larger falls were reported in larger deals, with the largest fall being obtained in deals carried out by the institutions which have conducted a large part of their business net of commission. It also appeared that commissions on small transactions did not rise to any great extent and might have actually fallen slightly.

The evidence also suggests that the market touch has fallen for beta and gamma shares and remained the roughly same for alpha shares. There was also anecdotal evidence that the touch does not widen significantly for larger quotes; in other words, the market is deeper than before. As would be expected from the elementary theory of demand and supply, lower prices stimulated demand and increased turnover was observed on both the listed and unlisted markets immediately after Big Bang. Increases of the order of 20 per cent were obtained and this, together with the trend increase in share prices experienced during the early months of 1987, enabled profitable trading to continue. Reference to table 8.4 demonstrates the dramatic growth in turnover in the years after 1986. However, this situation did not last for any length of time and substantial falls in share prices occurred on a global basis during October 1987. This is demonstrated in figure 8.1.

The graph reveals a steady rise in the share index from 1985 to the middle of 1987 when the dramatic fall in prices occurred. It is also noticeable that the rise in the index was particularly pronounced during the early months of 1987. As is demonstrated in table 8.4 above, this fall in prices was accompanied by a decrease in the volume of turnover, resulting in a dramatic loss in profitability for the dealer–brokers. In fact this decrease in trading was far more pronounced in the number of transactions as compared with turnover. As noted above, the larger orders were subject to falls in commission rates and this enhanced the general loss of profitability in the market. In other words, there was large-scale excess capacity, which has led to some firms giving up market making altogether. Following Big Bang there were some thirty-two domestic equity market makers but by 1990 this has fallen to twenty-six

Source: CSO, *Financial Statistics*, various issues, Table 13.7, and ESRC Data Bank.

Figure 8.1   FT-SE 100 Share Index, monthly, 1985–89

firms. Reductions in capacity also came from other firms restricting their market-making activities.

Stock market crash

There is no consensus concerning the reasons for the dramatic fall in stock market prices which began on Monday 19 October 1987 ('Black Monday') when the New York Stock Exchange suffered a drop of 22.6 per cent (its largest ever in a single day) and quickly spread to most exchanges around the world, including London. Four possible causes have been suggested. First, there was uncertainty over the international payments situation. Recent years have seen persistent balance of payments disequilibria. The USA and UK have experienced large deficits, which have been matched by large surpluses obtained by Japan and Germany. At the same time, corrective measures for the US federal budget deficit also seemed to be proving to be inadequate. Perhaps the perception of the serious nature of these problems was enhanced by the continued problem of sovereign debt (see chapter 4). It could be argued, therefore, that bad US trade figures on the Thursday before the crash provided the trigger for the fall in stock prices. Two problems remain with this approach. First, the world-wide nature of the 'crash' across a wide number of exchanges in different countries seems to be out of keeping with the weight of news. On the other hand, a look at the 'fundamentals' suggests that share prices should be sensitive to changes in expectations. By definition:

$$\text{Expected rate of return} = (E_tP_{t+1} + E_tD_t - P_t)/P_t \qquad (8.1)$$

where P refers to the share price at the beginning of the period, D to the dividend paid during the period and E to the expectation operator, so that E_tP_{t+1} refers to the forecast of the price at the beginning of the next period.

Solving equation (8.1) for the current price and noting that, in equilibrium, the required rate of return is equal to the required rate of discount:

$$P_t = \frac{E_tP_{t+1} + E_tD_t}{(1 + R)} \qquad (8.2)$$

where R is the required rate of discount.

Note that in (8.2) investors have to forecast the price of stock and future dividends, i.e. expectations of future events are important. This is often termed the intrinsic value of the stock. If it is assumed that dividends will grow at a constant annual rate (g), and also that the discount rate is constant, equation (8.2) can be solved to produce the 'Gordon' growth model:

$$\text{Current price} = \frac{E_tD_t}{(R - g)} \qquad (8.3)$$

Note that equation (8.3) requires the required discount rate to be larger than the expected growth rate of dividends (g). Given values of £0.30 for the forecast of dividends and 8 per cent and 6 per cent for the required discount rate and the expected growth rate of dividends respectively, then the share value will be £15. If the expected growth rate of dividends falls to 5 per cent, the price of each share falls to £10. This explanation would, therefore, require investors to revise downwards their expected rate of growth of dividends (or equivalently the forecast of dividends) or to revise upwards the required rate of discount in the light of uncertainty about future events due to the international financial problems. A problem with this approach is that survey evidence in the US suggested that investors regarded the equity market as being overvalued before the crash. This evidence was, however, collected after the crash and may be tainted with wisdom after the event.

The second potential cause for the crash has been identified with 'speculative bubbles'. The basis of the belief in the existence of speculative bubbles is that rises in share prices induce expectations that the price will rise even further. This has been dubbed 'the greater fool theory', in the sense that each purchaser believes that he will find an even bigger fool who will buy the equity from him at a higher price which, by definition, is not related to the 'fundamentals'. This cause implies market failure in the sense that shares become increasingly overvalued until the bubble bursts at a particular point of time for what may seem a trivial reason. Examination of the time pattern of the share price index in figure 8.1 shows the index increasing at a fast rate throughout the early months of 1987 and this might be taken as casual support for the 'speculative bubble' hypothesis. However, existence of speculative bubbles would require that sequences of price changes are related, but Santoni [1987] presents evidence that suggests that this requirement was absent from daily data for the US for the period 2 January 1986 to 25 August 1987. Two tests were applied to the Dow-Jones index for this period: (i) based on an examination of the autocorrelation coefficients and (ii) based on runs of positive and negative changes. Neither of these tests supported the rejection of the hypothesis that the data conformed to a random walk.

The third possible cause lies in the belief that there may have been a temporary market failure triggered by an initial price decline. Suggested causes of this failure include (i) value-insensitive trading due to automatic computer trading, (ii) false price signals resulting from the abnormally heavy trading observed and (iii) the absence of countervailing price-sensitive market traders acting from a viewpoint of the fundamentals. It could be argued that the heavy price falls themselves induced a change in market expectations which then validated the new lower prices. It may also be argued that the growth of high-speed communications and trading mechanisms increased the possibility of such crises, and this has led to a demand for the introduction of circuit breakers in markets. These would have the effect of suspending trading when prices fell (or rose) beyond a specific amount during the day. The idea is that a 'cooling-off' period may restore calmer conditions during the subsequent trading period. Two problems arise with such proposals. First, if traders wish to trade, they may well do so off the market. Second, is it just to suspend trading just at the time when the public has a strong desire to trade?

A fourth reason for the crash suggested by the Brady Commission concerns the use of the futures market to obtain portfolio insurance. Discussion of the futures market takes place in chapter 12, but it is possible to outline here the main thread of the argument. If it were possible to enter into a series of put options (i.e. the right to sell all the securities in the portfolio at predetermined prices) then the risks of adverse price changes would be reduced. Portfolio insurance replicates this position by taking a simultaneous position in a risky portfolio and a synthetic put option by shifting funds from the risky portfolio into a safe liquid asset on the basis of the Black/Scholes option pricing model. This involves selling shares when prices are falling and, if used by sufficient operators, will increase the volatility of prices on the market. In the USA, portfolio insurers bought and sold futures contracts on a share index rather than the shares themselves. This has the obvious advantage of lower cost since it would be difficult, and therefore costly, to carry out the alternative of entering into contracts to purchase or sell shares across the whole range of securities in a share price index. A second facet of the argument concerns the practice of arbitraging between shares making up the index and the relevant futures contract. For example, if the futures contract falls below the share price by a sufficient amount then it is possible to make a profit by purchasing the futures contract and selling the shares making up the index. Clearly the futures price discount must be sufficiently large to offset the transactions costs. During the week preceding the crash, portfolio insurers were selling futures heavily and this induced index arbitrage purchasing futures and selling shares. It appears that at certain critical times the volume of this trading accounted for up to 66 per cent of transactions. In addition, the underlying techniques of portfolio insurance are well known on the market, so that other operators could identify when insurers were likely to sell securities. This would lead them to try to sell in advance of the insurers in the hope of buying stock back later at the lower price induced by the sales of the insurers.

It is claimed that the volume of sales on the futures market was so large on the Monday and Tuesday of the crash that index arbitrageurs were unable to absorb the pressure by purchasing futures, but the falling futures price still provided a guide as to the likely price of the shares making up the market, thus inducing more sales and price falls.

In conclusion of this section, the causes of the crash are still controversial and we are unable to come to any firm conclusion. We now move on to consider the empirical evidence concerning the efficiency of the stock market.

8.4   The stock exchange and the efficient markets hypothesis

In this section we briefly survey the literature on the informational efficiency of the stock market. At this stage we would, however, like to stress the practical importance of this. If the stock market conforms to the efficient market hypothesis, then forecasting future movements in share prices is not likely to be worth the effort involved because the market price reflects all available information. Thus on *average* it will not be possible to out-perform the market consistently. The caveat applying to this statement is that of risk aversion, and it may be that the operator's degree of risk aversion is less than that ruling in the market.

Most early studies tended to support the hypothesis that the stock exchange was efficient. One interesting approach was to consider the role of filter rules. Basically a filter rule is an automatic instruction to buy a stock after it rises x per cent above a recent trough and sell again after it falls y per cent below a recent peak. The object of the rule is to identify cycles, from which it is hoped to make profits. The size of x and y (which may be the same) is determined empirically from past data. If the two filters are small, a large number of transactions will be undertaken. This increases cost but at the same time, hopefully, identifies profitable trading opportunities. Thus there is a trade-off between costs and the identification of potential for profit. An early study by Alexander [1954] suggested that filter rules did offer scope for obtaining profits above those realised from a buy and hold strategy. These conclusions were modified in the light of biases in the original study. A subsequent study by Fama and Blume [1966] investigated the profitability of a wide range of filters for the thirty individual securities in the Dow-Jones index. The period involved was between 1957 and 1962 and the total number of observations ranged between 1,200 and 1,700 per share. After taking commissions into account, filter rules failed to provide as profitable a strategy as that obtained from buying and holding the securities. Thus it appears that the market is 'weakly' efficient.

The evidence against the efficient market hypothesis as applied to the stock market comes from three different sources. These are (i) the records of some forecasters, (ii) the volatility of the prices of stocks and (iii) the so-called anomaly literature. First, regarding predictive evidence. Dimson and Marsh [1984] describe a study covering 3,364 one-year horizon forecasts for share prices by a number of brokers for a large UK investment institution during the calendar years 1981 and 1982. They found that acting on these forecasts produced profitable trading. Similarly Bjerring, Lakonishok and Vermaelen [1983] examined the profitability of the recommendations of a Canadian brokerage house for forecasts involving both US and Canadian stocks. After allowing for transaction costs, Bjerring *et al.* calculate that an investor who followed the recommended list would make 9.3 per cent more than those who bought and held the market. Finally, Value Line in the US categorises stocks according to the expected performance over the next twelve months. The prediction of Value Line is good – see for example Stickel [1985].

The second attack on the efficient market came from the observed volatility of share price changes. This work is particularly associated with Shiller (see e.g. [1981]). Shiller studied the aggregate dividends and earnings of the Standard and Poor (S&P) Index from 1871 to 1979. This information was employed to calculate what the price of the index should be if investors possessed perfect foresight. The actual value of the index was more volatile and this led Shiller to conclude that the market was excessively volatile, which could only be explained by irrational behaviour of the operators. The methodology involved may be illustrated quite easily with reference to a single share. Define the perfect foresight market value (V^*) as:

$$V_t^* = \sum \delta^{t+k} D_{t+k} \qquad (8.4)$$

where $\delta = 1/(1 + R)$ is the discount factor.

Given rational expectations, the expected value of V_t^* is equal to the observed value V_t plus a random uncorrelated error term e_t, i.e.

$$V_t^* = V_t + e_t$$

This leads to the variance bound:

$$\text{Var}(V^*) > \text{Var}(V) \qquad (8.5)$$

However, it has been argued (see Kleidon [1986]) that it is inappropriate to use time-series data from one economy to construct variance bounds and that the correct method would be to derive cross-section statistics for expectations and realisations from identical economies.

Third, the anomaly literature has discovered that prices vary according to an unusual pattern. Typical examples are the fact that returns measured from the close of Friday to the close of Monday are typically negative over a wide range of securities (see e.g. Gibbons and Hess [1980]). Blume and Friend [1974] showed that there were large differences between the returns on large firms and those on small firms and these differences were not explainable by models of security pricing. It was also noticed that the majority of these differences occurred in January (Keim [1986]). These anomalies are difficult to explain within the context of acceptance of the efficient markets hypothesis.

The efficiency of the stock market is an open question, but a growing volume of evidence may point to a refutation of this hypothesis in its extreme form. The question of whether this evidence is sufficient to claim that the stock exchange does not approximate an efficient market remains a question of judgement.

Chapter 9

Interest rates and the bond market

9.1 Introduction

In this chapter the main foci of discussion are the bond market (in particular the market for gilt-edged securities) and the term structure of interest rates. We have linked these two topics together because the discussion of the term structure of interest rates is mainly conducted in the context of government securities. As an introduction we briefly survey the differing theories of the level of interest rates in section 9.2 before discussing the market for gilt-edged securities as regards to both new issues (section 9.3) and the secondary market (section 9.4). The determinants of the term structure are considered in sections 9.5 to 9.7 before the empirical evidence is summarised in section 9.8.

Quotations of interest rates in the press take the form of publishing two rates. The lower figure represents the rate at which funds are accepted on deposit (the 'bid' rate) and the higher figure the rate at which the institution is prepared to lend out funds (the 'offer' rate). At the outset of the discussion it is necessary to emphasise that interest rates differ for a number of reasons and in particular:

(i)   the risk of default
(ii)   the cost of administering the loan
(iii) tax arrangements
(iv)   the term of the loan.

Discussion of the last factor is carried out in the main body of the chapter.

Clearly the risk of default is an important feature of the determinant of the difference between interest rates charged to different borrowers. Market arbitrage should equalise the risk-adjusted rate of return rather

Table 9.1   *Selected money market rates (offer rates) as at 26 September 1990*

Treasury bills	Discount market	Bank bills	Local authority	Company deposits
$14^5/_{16}$	$14^1/_2$	$14^{11}/_{32}$	$14^7/_8$	$14^{15}/_{16}$

Source: *Financial Times*, 'London Money Market Rates', 27 September 1990.

than the actual rate itself. The role of risk can be illustrated with reference to the structure of rates of three-month securities on the London money markets at close of trading on 26 September 1990 shown in table 9.1. It can be seen that these short rates rise slightly as the risk of default (itself almost non-existent on the first three securities) increases. The other factors are fairly easily dealt with. Very small loans at, say, pawnbrokers not only incur a high risk factor but are also costly to administer, with the result that the interest rate charges involved are also high. Tax arrangements differ between financial securities, with some being tax exempt and others bearing taxes at the normal rates. Clearly it would be anticipated that the rates charged would differ in such circumstances.

A final distinction must be made between nominal and real rates of interest. The nominal rate is the rate paid on the loan or security, whereas the real rate is the rate paid after making allowance for inflation. The relation between these two rates is as follows:

$$(1 + R) = (1 + i)(1 + E\Delta p) \tag{9.1}$$

where R is the nominal rate and i is the real rate (both rates applying to a single period) and $E\Delta p$ is the rate of inflation expected during the period to maturity.

Simplifying (9.1) produces:

$$R = i + E\Delta p + iE\Delta p \tag{9.2}$$

Since the last term on the left-hand side is the product of two decimals which are both likely to be small, the relationship may be approximated by:

$$R = i + E\Delta p \tag{9.2a}$$

(9.2a) is the normal formula used linking the real rate of interest and the nominal rate. Market efficiency suggests that short-term, nominal rates of interest for differing maturities should therefore be a function of (i) the real rate for the relevant maturity and (ii) the level of inflation expected during the maturity of the security. We shall return to this topic in section 9.8 of this chapter.

9.2 The level of interest rates

The level of interest rates can be considered to be an index or some average value around which individual interest rates vary according to the factors discussed above. This is the approach taken in basic macro-economic text books which discuss the determination of 'the' rate of interest via *IS* and *LM* curves. In this connection two distinct theories can be discerned; (i) the monetary approach and (ii) loanable funds theory.

The monetary (not monetarist) approach explains the level of interest rates in terms of the demand for and supply of money. Typically, money demand equations depend on factors such as real income, rate(s) of interest on money (this may be implicit or a convenience yield) and alternative assets, and possibly inflation and incorporate some form of dynamic adjustment to the desired long-run equilibrium. Money supply is normally specified to depend on (i) a variety rates of interest, such as those paid on deposits and earned on bank loans, and (ii) the monetary base. Non-domestic factors can be allowed for by the inclusion of foreign rates of interest in both the demand and supply functions. The equilibrium rate of interest then follows from the equality of the demand for and the supply of money. In terms of the economy as a whole these are of course only the proximate determinants of the level of interest rates because the levels of real income and other explanatory variables will themselves be determined within the context of a simultaneous model at the same time as the interest rate. Notice this explanation is in terms of stocks. Increases in the rate of interest can be due to either an increased demand for money or alternatively a reduction in the supply of money.

The loanable funds approach, in contrast, emphasises flows in the form of the demand for and supply of credit by the various sectors including the overseas sector. In turn savings come from the financial surpluses of the various sectors in the form of excess of income over expenditure. The main sources of savings are personal savings and retained profits by firms. At times, however, the overseas sector provides credit by way of balance of payments capital inflows. Borrowings are required to finance either consumption or investment expenditure. For ease of exposition in the following narrative we shall assume that borrowing to finance consumption expenditure can be considered as negative saving and that all borrowings are made for the purpose of financing investment. Links to the monetary sector are introduced via increases in the money supply being representative of an additional source of credit but provided by the banks. Similarly increases in the demand for money (technically known as hoarding) are akin to a demand for loanable funds. Hence the supply of loanable funds can be defined to be the sum of saving (S) plus increases in the money supply (ΔM) whereas the demand for loanable funds is specified as investment (I) plus increased demand for money (ΔH). Thus the equilibrium rate of interest is determined by the equality of the demand and supply schedules for loanable funds, i.e. where:

$$I + \Delta H = S + \Delta M \qquad (9.3)$$

It is argued that both investment and saving are functions of the rate of interest, with savings increasing and investment declining as the domestic rate of interest rises. The allocation of savings to and borrowings from overseas as opposed to domestic sources will depend on the relative levels of domestic and foreign rates after taking into consideration the prospects of exchange rate changes during the period of the loan. The other two components may in the main reflect changes in taste (hoarding) and government policy and so can be considered as an addition to the interest rate components. However this is not a vital assumption since, if anything, the money supply is likely to increase and hoarding to decrease as domestic interest rates rise in the same manner as savings and investment. Equilibrium in the credit market is demonstrated in figure 9.1.

Increases in the rate of interest can, according to this approach, be caused by an increase in the demand for loanable funds attributable to increased investment or hoarding or a reduction in the supply due to

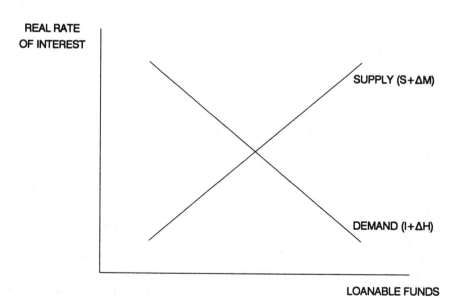

Figure 9.1 Equilibrium in the credit market

reduced saving or a reduction in the money supply. A rise in the foreign rate of interest (given expectations of future interest rate changes) would also cause a rise in domestic rates through a reduction in supply of and an increase in demand for domestic loanable funds. It should be noted that this explanation of the level of interest rates emphasises real factors such as productivity determining investment opportunities and saving as a function of thrift, so that the rate of interest is the real rate.

Although the two theories have a different rationale, they are consistent with each other to a considerable degree. First, long-run equilibrium requires that both (i) savings equals investment (using the broad definitions adopted in this section) and also (ii) changes in the money supply equal changes in the demand for money. Second, the predictions of the two theories are the same following, for example, an increase in the quantity of money. Similarly an increase in investment will raise the rate of interest directly in the case of the loanable funds theory and indirectly in the case of the liquidity preference theory via the resulting increase in income raising the demand for money. A possible reconciliation is that the liquidity preference theory applies mainly to the short run where, for example, factors in the money market are predominant, whereas the loanable funds theory is more relevant to the long run where agents have sufficient time to adjust their expenditure and financing plans.

We now turn to examining the gilt-edged market in the following two sections.

9.3   The market for gilt-edged securities: new issues

The central government requires finance to meet the surplus of its expenditure over revenue and to meet the cost of refinancing debt as it matures. Further funds may be necessary to cover the cost of intervention in the foreign exchange markets. If the government intervenes to push the exchange rate down, this entails the selling of sterling on the foreign exchange markets in return for convertible currency reserves. Thus finance has to be raised over and above that required for purely domestic purposes. In contrast, intervention to push the exchange rate up involves the loss of convertible currency reserves and a gain of sterling finance thus reducing the amount of finance necessary for purely domestic purposes. Consequently, even if the central government is in fiscal balance during any one year, new issues of debt may be necessary to refinance maturing existing debt and to finance intervention in the foreign exchange market, though, of course, this last component may be negative. Any finance that may be necessary is obtained through the issue of new securities of a variety of types and maturities including:

£million

Source: CSO, *Financial Statistics*, various issues, Table 2.6, and ESRC Data Bank.

Figure 9.2   The Public Sector Borrowing Requirement, annual, 1963–89

(i)   bonds termed 'gilt-edged' securities
(ii)   non-marketable debt such as national savings and tax reserve certificates
(iii)   treasury bills.

Figure 9.2 shows the financial position of the public sector over the period 1963 to 1989. The salient feature is the move into surplus in recent years, though, as we noted in chapter 2, this situation will be reversed in the financial years following 1991/92. Some of this surplus is due to the revenue achieved from the sale of assets through the policy of privatisation but the remainder is due to a positive fiscal balance. The surpluses shown in this figure meant that the markets have tended to be short of funds, causing upward pressure on interest rates. As we discuss in chapter 10, this has forced the Bank of England to intervene in the discount market by purchasing commercial bills of exchange, thus providing extra funds for the discount market. The other side of this coin is of course the 'bill mountain', i.e. the stock of commercial bills held by the Bank of England as a result of purchases in the market.

Turning now to the various methods of raising finance, we have already discussed the nature of treasury bills in chapter 1. Sales of non-marketable debt are achieved by varying the returns on national savings from time to time according to prevailing interest rate conditions. In addition major innovations are made, though very infrequently. Such innovations include the introduction of premium bonds and index-linked national savings.

We now consider the issue of gilt-edged securities. The procedure for the issue of gilt-edged securities is more simple than that described in chapter 8 for company debt. The underwriting function is performed by the Bank of England, which not only manages the issue but also takes any unsold debt into its own portfolio. The standard method of issuing new gilts is to offer debt by public tender. Issues are in quantities of several million pounds and in order to avoid dislocating the market the Bank of England adopts the following tactics. An advertisement is placed in the financial media advertising the terms of the issue (fixed coupon value, date of maturity, payment dates, etc) and the minimum price acceptable and inviting tenders for specified amounts of stock. If the issue is under-subscribed the stock is allocated at the minimum price with the Bank of England taking the balance into its own portfolio. If, on the other hand, the issue is oversubscribed the bids are accepted in descending order of price offered until the whole issue is allocated. A second method of issuing new stock is by way of additional supplies of existing stock known as 'tranchettes'. These are taken directly into the portfolio of the Bank of England.

Both these methods involve the Bank of England subsequently selling stock via the market. The Bank of England is also involved in the purchase of short-dated stock as it nears maturity. We shall discuss the methods of purchase and sale in our examination of the secondary market for government debt (section 9.4). In recent years the Bank of England has also used on a trial basis the method of auctioning government stock without indicating a minimum price. In this case all stock would be sold according to the highest bids without the Bank of England performing an underwriting function. The Bank has, however, reserved the right to intervene in the case of extreme abnormal market conditions although, in fact, has not found it necessary to do so. Finally, in this connection, the Bank has also carried out what are called 'reverse auctions'. The central government surplus implies a reduction in the total stock of gilt-edged securities and so the Bank has invited tenders to sell to it specific quantities of gilts.

9.4   The market for gilt-edged securities: the secondary market

Changes in the market for gilts mirrored those occurring in the market for
private securities discussed in chapter 8. Prior to 'Big Bang' there were
eight gilt-edged jobbers of whom two accounted for 75 per cent of the
turnover. The new system of trading created an institution known as a
'gilt edged market maker' (GEMM) who acted in a dual capacity as
market maker and agent. GEMMS have an obligation to communicate,
on demand, to other market participants continuous and effective bid–
ask prices for a wide range of gilts in any trading conditions. GEMMS
have a direct dealing arrangement with the Bank of England in gilts such
that the Bank will bid to buy gilts from the GEMMS at prices of its own
choosing and will respond to bids for gilts from the GEMMS at its
discretion. This is of course the counterpart to the arrangements for issue
of gilts discussed in section 9.3 whereby the Bank of England took into its
own portfolio any unsold stock. The GEMMS are subject to the Bank's
prudential control and, in particular, with reference to capital adequacy
which is required to be 'dedicated' to the operation in gilts. GEMMS
have also approved borrowing facilities at the Bank.

A special facility is that the GEMMS have sole access to the inter-
dealer broker mechanism, Inter-dealer brokers (IDBs) are subject also to
the Bank of England's prudential control and supervision in order to
ensure that the system works satisfactorily. The essential purpose of the
IDBs is to enable the market makers to unwind their stock positions as
and when required without trading directly with each other whenever
they wish this dealing to be anonymous. A further important support to
the market making function is provided by stock exchange money brokers
(SEMBs) who lend both stock to the GEMMs and also money generated
from their equity lending operations at rates which are competitive with
those in the money market.

The impact of these changes was similar to those described for Big
Bang, Prices of dealing fell. The Bank of England reports (*BEQB*,
February 1989) that typical spreads before the change were 2–4 ticks
(£2/32–£4/32) for shorts and 4 to 8 ticks for longs and these fell to 1 to 2
ticks and 2 to 4 ticks respectively. Similar falls were observed on index-
linked stocks. In addition, the size of deal that can be transacted at
normal prices increased. Transaction costs fell because commissions
largely disappeared on the wholesale market. These factors led to an
increase in turnover (see Table 8.4 in the previous chapter). The Bank
also reported that trading had risen from around £1¼ billion a day to
around £4¼ billion a day, out of which about half was intra-market
between GEMMS dealing primarily via IDBs. Competitive pressures on
the market operators became quite severe. The number of market makers

increased from the eight quoted above to twenty-seven GEMMs. Not unnaturally many of these firms made substantial losses given the fall in trading prices. At the time of writing, nineteen firms remain. The Bank of England also reports (*BEQB*, February 1990) that, during 1989, the financial performance of the GEMMs improved and they were close to break-even in their operations after experiencing considerable losses in the two years after Big Bang. This trend continued during 1990 so that the market makers in gilts made an operating profit for the first time since Big Bang.

This improved performance comes despite the difficult operating environment as the size of the gilt-edged market has continued to decline because no new issues of gilts were made between between October 1988 and January 1991. Over this period the authorities purchased stock. Consequently, the total gilt-edged stock available in the market fell by 9 per cent from £142 billion to £129 billion during 1989.

The service provided by the IDBs was new to the gilt market and six firms started, but four have now withdrawn leaving two at the end of 1989. The number of SEMBs increased at the time of Big Bang from six to nine. A tenth firm subsequently joined the list but this was matched by one firm withdrawing, leaving the total at nine.

This completes the discussion of the gilt-edged market and we now turn to discuss the determinants of the term structure of interest rates.

9.5   The expectations theory of the term structure

First of all we need to define the term 'yield to maturity' as the return on securities which are held to maturity. Thus if we take as an example a three-year bond, redeemable at par (£100) and returning a coupon of £X paid once a year and with a current market price of £V, then solving the following equation for R provides the yield to maturity on that bond:

$$V = x/(1 + R) + X/(1 + R)^2 + X/(1 + R)^3 + 100/(1 + R)^3 \qquad (9.4)$$

Notice in this example that we are assuming that the interest received is immediately re-invested in the security. The term structure then refers to the differences in yields to maturity on securities which are identical except for the outstanding (not initial) maturity. The yield curve itself is a representation of the term structure in a graphical form.

It is difficult to find examples of securities identical in all respects save for the outstanding term to maturity, with one major exception. This is for government securities where the risk of default is virtually zero but more crucially the same on all issues. For example, the UK government has just over ninety different issues of gilt-edged securities with similar terms, although differences do occur e.g. index-linked, undated stock,

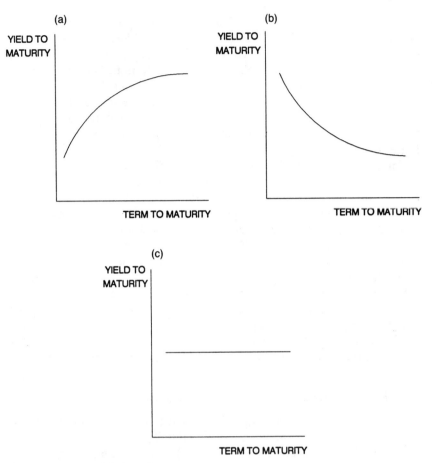

Figure 9.3   Observed yield curve shapes
(a)   Upward-sloping curve
(b)   Downward-sloping curve
(c)   Horizontal curve

etc. Thus the quantity of different stocks issued is sufficient to derive yield curves. This contrasts with the issue of bonds by companies although, in principle, their debt issues would be subject to the same term structure plus a risk premium, which might vary over time and between different companies. Figure 9.3 depicts the patterns of yield curves which have been observed over time. In addition, combinations of the general patterns illustrated can be seen from time to time. Consequently any credible theory of the term structure must be able to explain a wide variety of patterns of yield curves observed over time.

So far our discussion has been in terms of yields but it should be noticed that quotations in the market or media refer to security prices. There are intrinsically no differences between these two approaches since, given a coupon value and outstanding term to maturity, a yield to maturity on a bond implies the market price and, similarly, the market price implies the yield to maturity.

The expectations theory explains the term structure of interest rates as being a function of the rates of interest expected to exist in the future. Thus, for example, if short-term interest rates were expected to rise in the future, it would be reasonable to assume that long-term rates encompassing the period of those future short-term rates would be higher than current short-term rates. According to this theory, arbitrage ensures that the return for holding different securities for a specific period will be the same irrespective of their outstanding maturity. This is the basis of the expectations theory and in the following paragraphs we critically examine this theory. We make the following preliminary assumptions:

1. Agents possess perfect foresight so that they know all current and future interest rates.
2. A perfect capital market exists.
3. Interest is paid once a year and is immediately re-invested in the same bonds.
4. Two classes of bonds only are available:
   (a) a one-year bond
   (b) a three-year bond.
   Both types of bond are issued at par.
5. The investor has a holding period of three years, that is, he wishes to invest funds for three years.

Assumptions 3 to 5 are merely simplifying assumptions to facilitate the exposition, Assumption 1 is clearly unrealistic and is made as a temporary aid to the explanation and will be relaxed later in this section. The second assumption is one normally made in the analysis and implies the absence of transaction costs, a spread between buying and selling prices, etc. It is a useful approximation to the truth as long as it is realised that the resulting predictions are likely to be less precise in practice.

The investor then has a choice of investment strategies. He can either buy a three-year bond or alternatively buy a sequence of one-year bonds, re-investing the proceeds as the first two bonds mature. The choice of which strategy to follow will depend on which offers the higher return. Consequently arbitrage and market clearing will force the yields on the two strategies to be equal. For example, if the yield on the three-year bond is higher, then agents will buy three-year bonds at the expense of one-year bonds. This raises the yield on one-year bonds (lowers the price) and lowers the yield (raises the price) on three-year bonds. The converse would apply if the yield on one-year bonds was higher than that on three-year bonds. Thus, given the assumptions made, market clearing ensures that:

$$(1 + {}_tR_3)^3 = (1 + {}_tR_1)(1 + {}_{t+1}R_1)(1 + {}_{t+2}R_1) \qquad (9.5)$$

where the first subscript applied to R refers to the time the interest rate pertains, i.e. t represents year 1, $t + 1$ represents year 2, etc. and the second subscript represents the time period of the rate, e.g. 1 is the one-year rate and 3 the three-year rate.

The term on the left-hand side represents the return from purchasing a three-year bond at time t and that on the right-hand side the return from investing in a succession of one-year bonds for three years. Consequently the three-year rate can be expressed as the geometric average of the current and subsequent one-year rates. Note also we have ignored the redemption of the bonds at the end of year three because the sum obtained would be the same in both cases.

Patently the assumption of perfect foresight is absurd if applied to the real world and must therefore be relaxed. This entails replacing the known future rates with their expected values, denoted as $E_{t\ t+1}R_1$, etc. The first subscript t refers to the time period at which expectations are formed and the second subscript to the time period at which the rate is to hold.

At this stage we introduce another assumption at the same time as relaxing that of perfect foresight. This is the assumption that the agents are risk-neutral, i.e. they are indifferent to risk due to the uncertainty of the future (not default) and motivated solely by the return on the security. In this case, market equilibrium would for all practical purposes be the same as that given perfect certainty, but with the expected values replacing the perfect foresight variables, and would therefore be represented by:

$$(1 + {}_tR_3)^3 = (1 + {}_tR_1)(1 + E_{t\ t+1}R_1)(1 + E_{t\ t+2}R_1) \qquad (9.5a)$$

So now the three-year rate is the geometric average of the known one-year rate and the expected future one-year rates. More generally, any long-term rate can be decomposed into a series of short-term rates and for the one period rates (R) the equilibrium condition can be shown as:

$$(1 + {}_tR_n)^n = (1 + {}_tR_1)(1 + E_{t\ t+1}R_1)(1 + E_{t\ t+2}R_1) \ldots (1 + E_{t\ t+n-1}R_1) \quad (9.6)$$

Solving for R_n gives:

$$R_n = [(1 + {}_tR_1)(1 + E_{t\ t+1}R_1)(1 + E_{t\ t+2}R_1) \ldots (1 + E_{t\ t+n-1}R_1)]^{1/n} - 1 \quad (9.7)$$

showing that the long-term rate will be the geometric average of the current known and future expected short-term rates into which it can be decomposed. This result is perfectly general and is not restricted to the one-period rates used for the above demonstration.

We now look at the predictions of the expectations theory. First, the shape of the yield curve reflects expectations of future interest rates. Thus, if interest rates are expected to rise in the future, the yield curve will slope upwards, whereas if they are expected to fall a downward-sloping yield curve will be observed. The second prediction follows from this dependence on expectations of future interest rate movements. The relative supply of securities with different maturities will not affect the yield curve. This has implications for government policy. If the expectations theory is correct, it is irrelevant for the impact on the economy whether the authorities intervene at the short or long end of the market. Arbitrage will cause the shape of the yield curve to remain the same in either case since the long rates will retain the same relationship to short-term rates given by expectations. Arbitrage will also ensure that inflation expectations are incorporated into the term structure via their impact on current and expected short-term rates. Finally, external effects would also be included via the interest rate parity condition applying to the various term rates.

The expectations theory is open to a number of objections. First, there is the stylised fact that over long periods of time upward-sloping yield curves are more commonly observed in the markets than other shapes. Whilst it is certainly true that interest rates have trended upwards since the 1950s, this is unlikely to be sufficient to account for the general preponderance of upward-sloping yield curves. It is likely that some other factor has also been at work. The second source of criticism is that the degree of forecasting ability credited to market operators is, to say the least, excessive. Is it really credible to assume the existence of agents able to forecast future movements of interest rates for a large number of years ahead? The third objection arises in connection with forecasting difficulties. The existence of uncertainty regarding future movements in interest rates casts doubts on the appropriateness of the assumption of risk neutrality. Casual observation of portfolios suggests diversification rather than concentration of asset holdings in areas where the highest expected mean returns exist as would be suggested by the dominance of risk-neutral operators. Similar to the third objection is the problem of the potential existence of diverse expectations, which, according to the expectations theory, would suggest an infinite amount of dealing between operators. The problem of the existence of diverse expectations can be accommodated by appealing to pragmatic considerations such as transaction costs or limitations on borrowing which, in practice, prevent unlimited dealing between operators.

We now turn to an examination of the preferred market habitat theory, which meets these objections to some extent.

9.6 The preferred market habitat theory of the term structure

The preferred market habitat theory assumes that market operators are in fact risk-averse, that is, they are unwilling to incur extra risk without some extra reward in the form of a premium. Given that the risks on long-term securities are greater than those on short-term securities, it would be expected that long-term rates would be higher than short-term rates; that is, the yield curve would normally slope upwards. This does not imply that expectations of future rates are irrelevant and, as we shall see in the following explanation, these expectations will be incorporated into the yield curve.

It is believed that there is a difference between the preferences of lenders and borrowers. Lenders will prefer to hold short-term securities so that they can liquidate their loans more easily in the event of cash shortages. In contrast, borrowers prefer to borrow long term so as to obtain greater security of funding. This is another illustration of the conflicting requirements of lenders and borrowers encountered generally in direct financing (see the discussion on this in chapter 2). This divergence of preferences is reinforced as far as the lenders are concerned because long-term lending involves a greater degree of risk since the future is uncertain and the market prices of long-term securities fluctuate more than those of short-term securities. Note that the risk that we are considering is not one of default since the securities are identical in this respect by assumption. The logical consequence of these points is that lenders demand, and borrowers are prepared to pay, a risk premium for long-term lending over the rates for short-term lending. The risk premium is also likely to rise as the term of lending increases and may vary over time according to the degree of uncertainty present. The important point is that the risk premium is unlikely to be constant. Hence a risk premium (L) is introduced into the market clearing equilibrium discussed earlier so that agents will enter arbitrage arrangements only if the gain is greater than the risk premium. This means that the long-term rate will be greater than the geometric average of the current actual and future expected short-term rates. More formally, the equilibrium condition described by (9.6) has to be replaced by:

$$(1 + {}_tR_n)^n = (1 + {}_tR_1 + L_1)(1 + E_{t\ t+1}R_1 + L_2)(1 + E_{t\ t+2}R_1 + L_3) \ldots$$
$$(1 + E_{t\ t+n-1}R_1 + L_n) \tag{9.8}$$

where $L_n > L_{n-1} > \ldots > L_1$.

Similarly, solving for R_n, it is necessary to replace (9.7) with

$$R_n = [(1 + {}_tR_1 + L_1)(1 + E_{t\ t+1}R_1 + L_2)(1 + E_{t\ t+2}R_1 + L_2) \ldots$$
$$(1 + E_{t\ t+n-1}R_1 + L_n)]^{1/n} - 1 \tag{9.9}$$

Note that in this theory expectations still play an important role but their impact is modified by the existence of a risk premium. This leads to the prediction that the normal shape of the yield curve will be upward sloping owing to the existence of the risk premiun but that downward-sloping yield curves will be observed in instances when the expected fall in interest rates is sufficient to offset the risk premium. Debts of the various maturities are no longer perfect substitutes for each other so that changing the relative supply of debt with different maturities will, according to this theory, alter the term structure and the shape of the yield curve.

Moving from postulating that debts with different maturities are imperfect substitutes to the belief that no substitution at all is possible leads to the market segmentation theory.

9.7 The market segmentation theory of the term structure

The essence of this approach to the explanation of the term structure is that there are completely separate markets for debt of different maturities. Substitution between these markets is not possible, which explains the title of market segmentation. This leads to the prediction that the shape of the yield curve reflects the differing demand and supply conditions in the various markets. Hence it would be expected that the yield on long-term debt would exceed that on short-term debt since supply will be less and demand greater at the long end of the market.

In this extreme form it is easy to be critical of the view that no substitution is possible. For example, if it is felt that long-term rates are more attractive than short-term returns, it is not necessary for, say, five-year bonds to be substituted for three-month treasury bills, All that is necessary is that portfolios go longer so that, say, five-year debt is substituted for four-year bonds in one portfolio and, say, two-year bonds for one-year bonds in another. Subsitution over small but overlapping segments of the maturity spectrum means substitution over the whole spectrum. A ripple effect will occur so that in the end the more attractive (in terms of yield) longer-term debt has been substituted for shorter-term debt across portfolios in total until equilibrium is restored.

We have now completed our review of the theory of the term structure and move on to examine briefly the relevant empirical evidence.

9.8 Empirical evidence

Early empirical studies tended to favour the expectations theory. For example, Modigliani and Shiller [1973], building on earlier work by Modigliani and Sutch [1966], approached the problem of testing the role of expectations in the term structure by obtaining forecasts of short-term rates and then examining how well these forecasts explained the term structure in conjunction with a risk premium. Forecasts of future rates were based on averages of post observed nominal rates and inflation on the grounds that the expected nominal rate could be considered to be the sum of the expected real rate and the expected rate of inflation. The estimating equations were quite satisfactory, with a high degree of explanatory power and well-determined coefficients. Further support for the role of expectations was obtained by Meiselman [1962] who, using an error correction model, found firm evidence of correlation between forecasting errors and the changes in the expected one-year rates implied by the expectations hypothesis. The way these are derived can easily be seen by assuming a two-year holding period and the existence of only one-year and two-year bonds. In this case, according to the expectations hypothesis, market clearing would require that:

$$(1 + {}_tR_2)^2 = (1 + {}_tR_1)(1 + E_{t\ t+1}R_1) \tag{9.10}$$

The expected short rate implied by the expectations theory can then be obtained by solving for $E_{t\ t+1}R_1$ from (9.10) above to obtain:

$$1 + E_{t\ t+1}R_1 = [(1 + {}_tR_2)^2/(1 + {}_tR_1)] \tag{9.11}$$

Further evidence supporting the role of expectation in the determination of the term structure came indirectly from the difficulty in identifying any role for supply-side effects in the form of alterations in the available quantities of securities with differing maturities (see, for example, Malkiel [1966] for the US and Goodhart and Gowland [1977] for the UK). Possibly the apparent absence of these effects can be attributed to the authorities supplying debt with maturities which compensate for any changes in relative yields.

Subsequently, however, the role of expectations in the determination of the term structure has come under attack from two sources. First, similar to our discussion of excess volatility in section 7.4 with reference to the stock exchange, the volatility of long rates seems excessive (see, for example, Shiller [1979]. The second line of attack concerns the behaviour of short-term rates. Sargent [1972] noted that short rates exhibit a high degree of first-order correlation, so that estimation of equations of the form:

$$R_t = \alpha + \beta R_{t-1} \tag{9.12}$$

produces estimates of β greater than 0.8 and often not significantly different from unity, thus implying a random walk. This information should be incorporated into expectations of future short-term interest rates, but evidence by Sargent [1972] for the US and Goodhart and Gowland [1977] for the UK suggests that the revision of expected rates is less than implied by the observed historical auto-regressive properties. This characteristic has more destructive implications for the expectations-based theory of the term structure. Since long rates under-predict changes in short rates, any movement in short rates would alter the slope of the yield curve, Thus, for example, an upward change in short-term rates would produce less than appropriate changes in long rates, so that the slope of the yield curve would tend to decrease (assuming that it was upward sloping for purposes of exposition) or even become negative if the change in short rates was sufficiently large. Goodhart [1989] points out that on balance the long rate has tended to fall when the yield curve is upward sloping and rise when it is downward sloping. In the case of a major fall in short rates this also has the implication that operators could profit from selling long-term bonds since it is likely that long rates will rise (i.e. bond prices fall) in the future. Evidence by Mankiw and Summers [1984] suggests that this directional failure is also matched by an inability of the term structure to predict future short-term rates of interest.

This survey of the empirical evidence has of necessity been brief and we have merely tried to identify the important strands of the literature. For further detail the reader is referred to Goodhart [1989] and the original studies., Nevertheless we have covered sufficient ground to indicate the main areas of controversy and to draw the conclusion yet again that the efficiency of yet another financial market, in this case the bond market, is an open question.

Chapter 10

The sterling money markets

10.1 Introduction

The sterling money markets located in London are markets for short-term funds and consequently provide facilities for economic units to adjust their cash position quickly. The rationale for their existence is that receipts of and payments in cash are not generally synchronised. This would entail the holding of quite large quantities of cash balances if these variations in payments made and received are to be accommodated. The problem here is that cash holdings provide either no or a very low return, so that the opportunity cost of holding large working balances is quite high. If on the other hand markets exist which can, at short notice and with low transaction costs, absorb surplus cash and also provide facilities for borrowing, then agents can economise on cash holdings and earn a higher rate of return on the deposits made in the money markets. Thus cash positions can be adjusted by placing funds on deposit in the money markets when cash balances are temporarily too high and withdrawing or borrowing funds when the balance is too low. The success of this strategy depends on the existence of wide markets which can offer facilities for such transactions by catering for short-term deposits or lending without large fluctuations in rates of interest.

The London money markets are 'wholesale' markets with transactions typically for amounts of £500,000 or more. There are no particular central locations where members meet face to face and most of the business is conducted via the telephone (or telex) or even by personal visits. In many cases brokers act as intermediaries bringing depositors and borrowers together. We show in table 10.1 the main London money markets, together with an estimate of their size at the end of 1989.

The size of a market is not an unambiguous concept and the statistics have been derived as follows:

Table 10.1 *London sterling money markets, as at end 1989*

	£bn
The traditional discount market	15
The local authority market	2
The inter-bank market	77
Certificate of deposit market	48
Finance houses deposit market	4
Commercial paper	1

Source: see text.

(i)   discount market – total borrowed funds by the discount houses as shown in *Financial Statistics*, June 1990, table 6.5

(ii) local authority market – total stock of temporary money (source: *Financial Statistics*, June 1990, Table 4.6)

(iii) inter-bank market – total sterling time deposits of banks held with UK banks (source: *Financial Statistics*, June 1990, table 6.4)

(iv) CD market – total of sterling CDs issued by banks plus issues by building societies (source: *Financial Statistics*, June 1990, tables 6.4 and 6.8)

(iv) commercial paper – the figure refers to end of 1986 (source: *Commercial Paper Markets: An International Survey* contained in *BEQB*, February 1987)

(vii) finance houses deposit market – total short-term funds obtained by non-bank credit companies from the banks (source: *Financial Statistics*, June 1990, table 7.4).

The longest-established market is the traditional discount market, with the other markets developing alongside the discount market over the last thirty years being termed parallel or complementary money markets. Although in the above classification we have distinguished between different markets, we would like to emphasise that these are all closely interrelated, with the same institutions operating in many of the markets. Consequently interest rates in the various markets will tend to move together, reflecting the same trading environment. The basic similarity between these markets is that they all cater for short-term funds.

In the following exposition we will concentrate mainly on the traditional discount market, which is discussed in section 10.2. In section 10.3 we examine the parallel sterling money markets, before proceeding to a brief review of the extent to which short-term rates of interest incorporate inflation expectations in section 10.4. The institutional detail covering the banks is covered in chapters 3 and 4 and the reader may find it necessary to refer back to these chapters in order to appreciate the following analysis.

10.2   The traditional discount market

The main operators in the discount market are:

(i)   the Bank of England (hereafter termed the Bank)
(ii)   the commercial banks
(iii)   the discount houses.

The object of the Bank's daily money market operations is either to even out the daily flows of cash between the central bank and the commercial banks collectively and/or to enforce its interest rate policy. The commercial banks for their part use the discount market to offset daily fluctuations in their individual balances at the Bank. This is achieved by making deposits at the discount houses, with such loans being secured by collateral security in the form of asset titles. Thus the impact of any shortage of funds is, first of all, seen in the discount market as the banks withdraw funds from the discount houses. Conversely, any surplus is initially represented by an increase in funds lent to the discount houses. The discount houses operate to make the market and earn profits for themselves by purchasing assets with a yield higher than the rate of interest paid on the funds borrowed by them. We now discuss the operations of these parties in more detail.

In order to understand the nature of the Bank's operations in the discount market it is necessary to describe the background of the impact of payments to and by the central government on the commercial banks' cash position. Any payment by the central government to other sectors increases the banks' balances at the Bank of England. Conversely, any payment to the central government by any other sector has the effect of reducing the commercial banks' balances at the Bank. The daily totals of these payments are very large and also fluctuate widely on a daily basis. Part of this impact is netted out as some commercial banks will be withdrawing funds from the market whereas others will be lending additional funds, but overall it is likely to lead to market imbalances which are both large and difficult to predict. For example, the *Financial Times* (7 September 1990, money market report) noted that on 6 September 1990 a 'shortage of around £650 million was initially forecast but this was revised to £750 million at noon and to £850 million in the afternoon' – note that the higher figure represents about 5½ per cent of the total borrowed funds held by the discount houses indicated in table 10.1. The impact of any shortage/surplus is seen in the discount market as the banks withdraw/deposit funds with the discount houses. The magnitude of the figures involved suggests that instability would exist in the discount market unless the Bank intervened to even out these cash flows. It does this mainly by transactions with the discount houses but also, though more rarely, directly with the banks. In the case of shortages of funds (typically the case) in the market the Bank will buy bills (treasury bills, eligible bank bills and local authority bills) from the discount houses or make loans to them. Conversely, in the case of surpluses it would sell treasury bills. There are two trading sessions per day and by custom the banks do not withdraw funds from the discount houses after mid-day.

The bills are categorised into the following bands according to the outstanding maturity of the bill:

Band 1	1–14 days
Band 2	15–33 days
Band 3	34–63 days
Band 4	64–91 days

Intervention is mainly at the short end of the maturity spectrum, i.e. in bands 1 and 2, so that a very small variation in the price of a bill will lead to a significant change in the annual rate of interest. The Bank indicates that it is prepared to purchase/sell bills and leaves the discount houses to make the appropriate bids. The Bank then decides which bids to accept, thus allowing it either to permit interest rates to remain unchanged or alternatively to allow them to rise or fall. As an alternative the Bank may also require the discount houses to offer eligible bills for sale to the Bank with an agreement for the repurchase of the bills by the discount houses at an agreed later date. The Bank will specify terminal dates for the repurchase and the discount houses then submit offers of bills at rates of interest they are prepared to pay on the proceeds for the period indicated. The Bank responds to the bids in the manner discussed above for offers for outright purchase. Note that intervention prices are published after the transactions have been completed. In framing any bid, therefore, the discount houses will have prior knowledge of previous intervention prices and will also take into consideration the general financial environment and the likely future course of interest rates.

As an alternative to purchasing bills the Bank may decide to make loans. This practice is usually followed when the Bank wishes to give a clear signal to the market over interest rates, such as when rises are desired. For example, at the beginning of September 1990 when there was discussion over the UK joining the ERM with a subsequent reduction in interest rates being envisaged, the *Financial Times* report quoted above stated that 'The Bank of England indicated its concern about lower interest rates by refusing to operate in the bill market. The authorities did not offer to buy bills, but underlined the present interest rate structure by lending money to the discount houses for seven days at the clearing bank base lending rate of 15 per cent.'

As noted at the beginning of this chapter, the banks use the discount market to even out their cash position. In terms of the attributes discussed in chapter 1, deposits with the discount houses are liquid, short term, capital certain and virtually free of default risk. Because they earn a rate of return, they offer the perfect medium for banks to carry their first reserves against any cash shortages. Since the greater proportion of the deposits made with the discount houses originated from the banks themselves, the discount houses can themselves be considered almost as 'armslength' departments of the banks. They borrow funds from the banks, purchase short-term monetary assets and sell such assets to the banks. They operate to make a market in treasury bills and eligible bank and local authority bills. They underwrite the treasury bill tender (see chapter 9) and operate facilities to borrow and lend gilt-edged stock through money brokers. As an assistance to the provision of these facilities, the discount houses have a direct dealing relationship with the Bank which involves the purchase and sale of bills to the Bank and also borrowing facilities. The discount houses are also the subject of prudential supervision by the Bank.

In order to broaden the market, the Bank indicated, during autumn 1988, that it was prepared to consider applications from other financial institutions for the direct dealing relationship applicable to the discount houses as described above. Such institutions would be required to accept the obligations and duties at present undertaken by the discount houses. They would further be required to conduct their business through separately capitalised entities although, in the case of existing gilt-edged market makers, the Bank would consider applications without formal separation of capital.

The existence of institutions operating as intermediaries between the central and commercial banks is unique to the UK financial system. It is therefore useful to list the functions of the discount market. These are:

1.   The daily adjustment by banks of their liquidity position through the placing or recall of funds with the discount houses.
2.   Daily intervention by the Bank to offset the impact of uneven flows between the central government and the rest of the economy.
3.   The provision of a channel through which the Bank can permit, initiate or reinforce a movement in short-term interest rates.
4.   The provision of a market for treasury bills.
5.   The provision of a market for eligible local authority and commercial bills. In the case of the latter, the discount houses provide expertise

in assessing the quality of bills received for discount and the very act of discount assists the provision of finance for deficit units.

It is true that the facilities provided by the discount houses could be provided by the banks themselves and it remains an open question whether or not the existence of these institutions is strictly necessary. In 1959 the Radcliffe Report concluded that, in relation to their function at that time, 'they are doing the work effectively, and they are doing it at a trifling cost in terms of labour and other resources'. The same conclusion is probably true today.

10.3   The parallel sterling money markets

There are a number of general points about the structure of these markets that are worth making before the more detailed discussion of the various markets themselves. These are:

1. Lending is not secured in the manner discussed above for the traditional discount market.
2. There is no direct intervention by the Bank of England in these markets, so the discount market is the sole channel used by the Bank of England to enforce its short-term interest rate policy. Consequently interest rates in these markets move freely to reflect the underlying forces of supply and demand.
3. There are strong links between all the markets (both parallel and the discount). The same operators are involved to a considerable extent and arbitrage will ensure that interest rates move in a similar manner in all the markets.
4. There is no formal lender of last resort standing behind these markets in the manner that the Bank provides borrowing facilities for the discount houses. On the other hand, our discussion of prudential supervision of the banks by the Bank of England in chapter 17 suggests that the Bank would be extremely loathe to countenance the failure of any major monetary institution. This proviso suggests that this distinction between the discount and parallel money markets is superficial.
5. Much of the volume of transactions in these markets is routed via brokers who act as intermediaries between the ultimate borrowers and lenders.

We now turn to an examination of these markets. The discussion on each market will be much briefer than that of the discount market above. This does not mean that these markets are less important to the operation of the UK financial system but rather that they possess a relatively simple structure.

The first market we wish to discuss is the local authority money market. The requirement of local authorities to raise short-term finance arises from the different timing of their receipts and payment. Finance can be raised in a variety of ways. The first method is through the issue of bonds, normally for maturities of one to five years. The second method is through the issue of bills. Normally these are offered for tender and possess maturities up to six months. The third method of interest in this discussion is by way of what is called temporary money. These are deposits with local authorities for varying periods up to one year, although, in fact, the average maturity is for a much shorter time, with the greater proportion of deposits being for less than seven days. The minimum size of deposit is £100,000 and they are non-negotiable. The sources of the deposits are monetary institutions (roughly 50 per cent), large industrial and commercial companies and overseas institutions.

The inter-bank market, as its name suggests, is a market for unsecured lending between different banks. The market grew rapidly during the 1960s when the international banks, newly located in London, extended their inter-bank lending practice from foreign currencies to sterling deposit. In fact the market now is considerably broader than just between banks (both retail and wholesale) as depositors include large industrial and commercial companies, international institutions, discount houses and other financial institutions. Deposits can be made for a variety of periods from a minimum of overnight, but are mainly for maturities of less than three months. The minimum size of transaction is usually £500,000 and, as in the case of the local authoriry market, deposits are non-negotiable. Borrowing in the inter-bank market provides an indication to the banks of the marginal cost of raising new funds, so that one rate in particular, the London Inter-Bank Offer Rate (LIBOR), is widely used as a basis for calculating charges on loans with variable interest rates. In addition, their own base rates are sensitive to movements in this rate.

This market provides a means for banks to balance their inflow of deposits with the demand for loans (see discussion of liability management in chapter 3). Thus, for example, a bank with a new deposit and no foreseeable immediate demand for a loan can make a deposit in the inter-bank market and earn a rate of interest. Similarly a bank with a demand for a loan from a customer and no new deposit to hand, can raise the necessary deposit in the market. In this way the market serves a smoothing function in a manner similar to that described for the discount market. A second function provided by the market is facilities for non-banks to make deposits for short periods as part of their cash-management techniques. The third function provided by the market is that it enables banks with less well-known names to raise finance by borrowing in the inter-bank market rather than direct from customers. As a final comment it should be noted that the existence of inter-bank lending increases the connecting links between banks and raises the potential risk of systemic failure following the collapse of one institution.

A third parallel money market is the secondary market in Certificates of Deposit (CDs). CDs are negotiable certificates confirming that a deposit has been made with a UK office of a UK or foreign bank and, since 1983, with certain large building societies. Issues in London can be denominated in either dollars or sterling, with the latter market being the larger. They are issued in multiples of £10,000 from a minimum of £50,000 and are usually for a maturity of between three months and five years. The key advantage of a CD as distinct from a straight deposit for the holder is that it is negotiable, i.e. he can liquidate his loan should a need for the funds arise. Consequently the rate of interest on CDs is normally slightly lower than that on deposits for the same maturity. This advantage depends critically on the existence of a secondary market in which existing CDs can be bought and sold. The market makers in this secondary market are the discount houses.

The fourth market to be considered is the market for finance house deposits. This is smaller than the other markets considered so far and refers to the raising of funds by finance houses which, in turn, use the funds for the finance of consumer credit, leasing, block discounting and factoring. Many of the institutions concerned are now classified as banks, which tends to blur the distinction between this and the inter-bank market. Much of the deposits comes from banks and other financial institutions but deposits are also made by industrial and commercial companies.

The sterling commercial paper market represents the most recent development in the sterling money markets. In its present form it dates from 1986, though an inter-company market for short-term deposits existed in the 1970s. Because of its recent development, information on this market is rather scarce and this section draws heavily on discussions in the *Bank of England Quarterly Bulletin*, November 1987. Commercial paper is a short-term financial instrument similar to a promissory note. It is a general unsecured financial instrument with a maturity typically between seven days and three months. Commercial paper contrasts with bills of exchange since it is the liability of the issuer only, whereas bills are obligations of the drawer and the accepting house except when issued by the Treasury, banks and building societies. In terms of world markets for commercial paper, the US is the largest. The Bank of England (*BEQB*, February 1987) reported that in late 1986 outstanding issues in the US amounted to $322.7 billion compared with only $1 billion in the UK. In fact at this time it is estimated that the US market accounted for just over 80 per cent of total world outstanding issues. The recent growth in issues of commercial paper represents the general move towards securitisation. This can be attributable to a number of factors such as financial liberalisation, the move by banks and financial institutions towards fee-earning operations as distinct from direct lending.

In 1986 the powers conferred on the Treasury by the Banking Act 1986 to remove specified transactions from the definition of deposit taking were exercised. This relaxation permitted the issue of short-term sterling debt subject to three main restrictions. First, the issuing company should be listed on the International Stock Exchange and have net assets of £50 million or more. Second, the issues should have an original maturity of between 7 and 364 days. Third, issues should be in minimum denominations of £500,000. The Bank permitted the use of authorised intermediaries to manage the issue and it appears that most issues have been made via an intermediary. The functions of the intermediary include making arrangements for the issue and redemption of the debt, offering advice on the issue and, in some instances, placing the debt. Although statistics on this new market are scarce, most of the paper issued in the UK seems to have a maturity of between fifteen and forty-five days and originally to be held by other industrial and commercial companies (in the region of 60 per cent or above) and monetary institutions. At the moment there also appears to be no secondary market although, in some cases, the authorised intermediaries are prepared to buy paper back prior to its maturity. Given the short-term nature of the debt generally issued, it is probably true to say that there is little need for a secondary market for the sale of existing commercial paper.

This market offers new scope for the raising of money by industrial and commercial companies. It is difficult at this stage to comment on the cost of raising finance through the issue of commercial paper because of the wide variety of issuers. The market also offers a short-term outlet for industrial and commercial firms to place surplus funds. Problems started to emerge for this market by the beginning of 1990. It is alleged that there was less emphasis on the credit quality of the issuer in the UK than in the US. It appears that by this time much of the commercial paper, particularly for the lower-quality issuers, was being placed with banks. The development of the commercial paper market contributed to the relaxation of the formerly close relationships between banks and their customers. Business was now being conducted on a transactional basis where the paper was placed with financial institutions offering the lowest cost for the particular service. In addition, competition between institutions led to low rewards for dealers in the market. It is estimated that the spread between the bid and offer price for commercial paper had fallen to about 3 basis points a year (3/100 of 1 per cent). Given the short-term maturities for this type of instrument, this implies a large number of placings have to be achieved to earn even this return. Not unnaturally these low returns have led to dealers leaving this market; for example, S.G. Warburg in 1990 and Merrill Lynch in 1990, both important participants. Consequently the continuing growth of this market is under doubt.

10.4 Short-term interest rates and inflation

It may be considered difficult to apply tests of market efficiency to markets for short-term deposits given the degree of intervention by the authorities. However, one interesting question was raised by Fama [1975] concerning the role of inflationary expectations in the setting of short-term rates of interest. Equation (9.3a) is reproduced below for the sake of convenience:

$$R = i + E\Delta p \qquad (9.3a)$$

where R is the nominal rate of interest, i is the real rate and $E\Delta p$ refers to the expected rate of inflation. Equation (9.3a) is often termed the 'Fisher' hypothesis and has often been tested by running a regression of the general form:

$$R_t = \alpha + \beta E_t \Delta p_{t+1} \qquad (10.1)$$

Comparing (10.1) with (9.3) reveals the explicit assumption made that the real rate i is a constatnt. An estimated value for β of unity supports the existence of complete adjustment of the nominal rate to inflation expectations – often called the strong Fisher hypothesis. A value between 0 and unity supports the weak Fisher hypothesis that inflation expectations have some role to play in the determination of short-term rates of interest but are not completely anticipated. Early evidence failed to support the view that the markets were incorporating efficient forecasts of inflation in the setting of interest rates. Various reasons were suggested, including poor price data and faulty representation of the inflation series – normally carried out by a distributed lag of past price changes.

Using US data, Fama tested whether the nominal interest rate acted as a good predictor of inflation by transforming (10.1) above to obtain:

$$\Delta p_t = \beta_r' R_t - \alpha' \qquad (10.2)$$

where $\beta' = 1/\beta$ and $\alpha' = \alpha/\beta$. Fama found support for the strong Fisher hypothesis since the estimate of β' was not significantly different from unity. This result was criticised by a number of investigators. The first criticism was that it was possible to obtain alternative estimators of the future rate of inflation using time-series analysis and, when compared with the predictions from the rate of interest, it was found that these provided additional information. This suggested that the market's setting of short-term rates of interest failed to take into account all available information concerning future rates of inflation. The second approach followed the inclusion of additional variables to the right-hand side of (10.2) and it was found that these improved the fit of the equation, thus implying an improvement in the forecasts of future inflation. Fama conceded that these criticisms were correct, but argued that the improvements were very small quantitatively so that his initial result was largely intact.

Demery and Duck [1978] carried out a similar analysis based on UK data and also found support for the Fisher hypothesis, but, in this case, the weak version. They concluded that nominal rates of interest rise as expectations of inflation rise but that, even in the long run, they probably fail to adjust fully for the increase in expectations of future inflation.

Chapter 11

The foreign exchange market

11.1 Introduction

In this chapter we first of all in section 11.2 examine the nature of the foreign exchange market in London (forex) and in section 11.3 examine the nature of transactions carried out in the market. In section 11.4 we briefly summarise the empirical evidence concerning the efficiency of the forex.

It is useful as a prelude to the consideration of the foreign exchange markets to summaries current theories concerning the determination of exchange rates. It is an area of great controversy and it will not therefore be a great surprise to the reader to learn that there is no single theory which commands a wide degree of acceptance. All agree that, in the absence of intervention by the authorities, the exchange rate is determined by the demand and supply of currencies on the market, but there is little agreement on the factors underlying the forces of demand and supply. There are basically five main models, which differ from each other to a greater or lesser degree.

The first, the simple monetary model, assumes flexible prices and combines the purchasing power parity view of exchange rates with a simple quantity theory. Consequently changes in the exchange rate in the case of flexible exchange rates or in the balance of payments given fixed rates are determined by relative excess demands of/supplies of money in the two countries involved.

In contrast, the second model, commonly designated the Mundell–Fleming model, assumes fixed prices. In a regime of floating exchange rates, balance of payments equilibrium is obtained through the sum of the current and capital accounts being zero. A zero balance on the current account is not required even in the long run, and the offsetting balance on the capital account is achieved via the equilibrium rate of interest which clears the domestic goods and money markets. In the case of the fixed exchange rate regime, balance of payments equilibrium is achieved through changes in official reserves caused by intervention by the authorities in the foreign exchange markets.

The third model, the Dornbusch model, is an amalgam of both the previous two models. Financial markets are supposed to clear instantaneously, i.e. prices are perfectly flexible. This contrasts with the goods markets where prices are sticky. This results in the well-known prediction that the exchange rate overshoots the long-run equilibrium level following a shock. The long-run equilibrium level is, however, consistent with the predictions of the simple monetary theory discussed earlier.

The fourth model is the portfolio balance model, which widens the choice of assets available rather than concentrating simply on money. Consequently the exchange rate arises from the determination of equilibrium portfolios, and any shock will change the desired composition of the portfolio and therefore the equilibrium returns, including those on foreign assets which include expected exchange rate changes.

The final model considered is the currency substitution explanation of the exchange rate. This concentrates on the role of money as a store of value and assumes no restraints on the substitution of domestic for foreign currency. In these circumstances the demand for domestic money relative to foreign money will depend on the expected depreciation of the exchange rate, thus providing the basis of a theory of the exchange rate in terms of the demand for money as a store of value. It would be expected that this theory should be able to provide a satisfactory explanation of exchange rate movements within the EC given the absence of capital controls. A good detailed account of exchange rate determination is given in Copeland [1989].

In the following section we review the nature of the London foreign exchange market. Much of the quantitative detail concerning the institutional framework about the forex is derived from two Bank of England surveys of the operators within the market carried out in March 1986 and April 1989. These were carried out at the same time as other central banks' surveys and were reported in the *Bank of England Quarterly Bulletins* of September 1986 and November 1989 respectively. As a result of the information derived from the 1989 surveys, the Bank for International Settlements estimated that the total global foreign exchange turnover (net of all double counting) amounted to a staggering $640 billion per day.

11.2 Nature of the forex

The UK forex is located in London and there is no significant market for foreign exchange elsewhere in the UK. Retail transactions are of course carried out by local financial institutions, but these institutions ultimately obtain their currency mainly from transactions on the London forex. London continues to be the largest centre world wide for foreign exchange dealing and the average dealing turnover was estimated by the Bank of England to be about US$187 billion per day in 1989. This compares with a figure of US$90 billion per day in 1986. Other large centres were New York, Tokyo and Switzerland, where average daily turnover in US$ billion was 129, 115 and 57 respectively in 1989. Closely behind were the other Asian centres of Singapore ($55 billion per day) and Hong Kong ($49 billion per day). It is interesting to note that the gap between London and New York and Tokyo has reduced considerably, since the corresponding figures for the 1986 surveys for New York and Tokyo were $58 billion and $48 billion per day respectively. The magnitude of these flows indicates that the trading in currency in London is far greater than that warranted by trade flows into and from the UK, thus demonstrating the importance of London as a world financial market. A second feature revealed by the surveys is the very fast rate of growth in the volume of transactions. This far outweighs the growth of physical trade and no doubt is a reflection of the liberalisation of capital markets and, in particular, a general relaxation of capital controls.

The dollar is the main vehicle of exchange on the London forex and the bulk of the trading consisted of sterling/US$ (27 per cent) and US$/Deutschmark (22 per cent) and also US$/yen (15 per cent). Nevertheless, trading not involving the US$ (termed 'cross currency') also grew from 3 per cent in 1986 to 9 per cent in 1989 and about a third of this business involved sterling/Deutschmark transactions. The surveys also showed that the business on the London forex was more diversified than elsewhere. For example, in Tokyo 72 per cent of the business was between the yen and US$ and in New York 85 per cent of the business was between the US$ and the four major currencies (DM, yen, sterling and the Swiss franc) as compared with 74 per cent in London.

The market is a continuous dealers' market and there are four types of operators within the market:

(a) *Market makers.* These are mainly the major banks which agree to buy and sell currencies on a continuous basis. Trading is carried out via VDU screens so there is no building serving as a market meeting place. The gap between the bid and ask prices reflects the market maker's margin to cover costs and make a profit. Profits will also accrue from taking a view of the future course of exchange rates, i.e. speculation. The market maker carries a stock of currencies and he is the operator who incurs the risk of unanticipated changes in exchange rates. Business in the market is quite widely dispersed: ten of the 356 principals in the Bank of England 1989 survey covered only 35 per cent of the reported business.

(b) *Brokers*. These are institutions that act as middle men. They act as agents seeking out bargains and do not trade on their own account. The share of business passing through brokers amounted to 38 per cent of the total in the 1989 survey as against 43 per cent in 1986.

(c) *The Bank of England*. Apart from its role of supervising the market, the Bank will, as is true of other central banks, intervene in the foreign exchange markets to influence the exchange rate. Intervention is normally carried out via a broker, with the identity of the Bank being kept secret.

(d) *Customers*. Customers for foreign exchange transactions on the forex are large companies and other financial institutions. The proportion of turnover reported to have been accounted for between market makers and their customers rose from 9 per cent in 1986 to 15 per cent in 1989 (9 per cent with other financial institutions and 6 per cent with non-financial institutions). Ultimate customers are companies and individuals who require to purchase or sell foreign exchange in the normal course of their activities. Such transactions would normally be below the minimum size required for direct dealings on the forex.

11.3 Nature of business

Four types of transactions can be distinguished:

(i)   spot transactions
(ii)   forward
(iii) options
(iv)   futures.

The bulk of the transactions fell into the first two categories (99 per cent), with just 1 per cent consisting of the remaining two categories. We reserve discussion of both futures and options until chapter 13.

Spot transactions are required to be settled within two working days of the agreement. These have fallen as a proportion of total turnover since 1986 (73 per cent to 64 per cent) and the Bank suggests that this due to the growth in 'swaps' and other hedging instruments in the forward market. In the following discussion we will use the $/£ rate for illustrative purposes. Market makers quote two rates. The lower rate represents the rate or price at which they are prepared to buy sterling in exchange for US dollars (or, of course, sell dollars in return for sterling). The higher rate is the rate at which they are prepared to sell sterling in return for US dollars (or equivalently buy dollars in exchange for sterling). For example, the *Financial Times* in the currency market report section on 14 June 1990 shows, amongst other information, the following details:

'pound spot – forward against the pound'
the close of trading on 13/6/90:   1.7030 – 1.7125
One month   :   0.94 – 0.92 cpm

The spot quotation shows the best sterling buying and selling rates, indicating that the market makers concerned would buy sterling from the seller at the rate of $1.7030 for each £1. Conversely they are prepared to sell sterling at the rate of $1.7125 for each £1.

Forward transactions represent an agreement to purchase the currency at a later date but at a price agreed now. A margin may be required by the seller of the forward contract, but some market makers merely require the purchaser to hold cash in a deposit account with them. As evidenced by the Bank of England 1989 survey, the bulk of such forward contracts were for maturities up to one month (24 per cent out of the 35 per cent of turnover comprising forward contracts). Ten per cent represented maturities greater than one month but up to one year, with the remaining 1 per cent being for maturities more than one year.

Forward rates are quoted as discounts or premiums over the spot rate for the currency concerned. Thus, as shown above, on 13 June 1990 the closing one-month forward premium for the dollar was 0.94c–0.92c premium. Since the dollar is at a premium, the pound is at a discount, so that the premium has to be deducted from the spot rate quoted above to arrive at the forward rate for the pound. Hence the one-month forward rate is 1.6936 – 1.7033, with the former rate representing the buying rate for one-month forward pounds and the latter the selling rate. If the rate had been quoted as a discount, then this would have to be added to the spot rate. A number of standard maturities exist, with the most frequently quoted in the media being one and three months. In some instances the trader will not be certain when the precise payment is required and he can, in such circumstances, arrange for an option forward contract which enables the trader to purchase (or sell) the currency at an agreed rate within a specified time period rather than on a particular date. A further type of forward contract is a 'swap' whereby either (i) a spot purchase against a forward sale (or vice versa) or (ii) purchase and sale of currencies forward for different dates is undertaken.

11.4 The efficiency of the foreign exchange market

The question of whether the foreign exchange market is efficient (informationally) is one of considerable importance for the end customer of the market. If arbitrage between sophisticated traders produces prices which do reflect instantaneously all available information, then forecasting by end customers is not a worthwhile exercise since the market has already processed the available information. In this section we provide a brief survey of the current literature on market efficiency with respect to the foreign exchange markets. This research is ongoing and the interested reader is recommended to examine for himself the original literature. At the outset it should be emphasised that the absence of consensus on the appropriate theory of exchange rate determination causes difficulties in testing for market efficiency. Tests of efficiency of the foreign exchange market have therefore to be directed towards testing the implications of the efficient markets hypothesis rather than whether the market exchange rate conforms to the theoretical equilibrium rate.

Reverting to the 'Fama' classification of types of efficiency (see chapter 7), we first of all deal with the weak tests. One type of study concerning the weak efficiency of the foreign exchange markets relates to filter rules. As noted in chapter 7, the nature of a filter rule is to buy the currency if the price rises x per cent above a recent trough and sell the currency if it falls y per cent below a recent peak. The object of the rule is to identify upturns and downturns other than small fluctuations, and the values of x and y are set by the speculator in the light of previous experience of the series. Clearly, the smaller x and y, the greater the number of profitable opportunities identified but also the greater the cost of the transactions, which will offset and perhaps eliminate the profits obtained. On the other hand, large values for x and y will reduce the transaction costs but miss some profitable opportunities. Two major studies of the profitability of filter rules were carried out by Dooley and Shafer [1976] and Logue and Sweeney [1977]. Both these studies identified profits above a 'buy and hold' strategy, but losses were incurred in some periods. This raises the question whether these profits were the reward for incurring risk of exchange rate losses. S. Taylor [1986] examined time-series analysis methods of forecasting the £/$ exchange rate using daily observations for the period 1974 to 1982. He again found some improvement of the forecasts over predictions by market prices but the improvement was quite small.

One type of semi-strong test involves the forecasting ability of the forward exchange rate. If we assume that speculators are risk-neutral, so that they are indifferent to risk, then their sole motivation will be to attain profits. If the forward rate for $s per £1 is below the level they expect at the end of the period in question, then they will buy sterling forward and sell the the sterling spot on the maturity of the agreement. If their expectations are correct they will obtain a profit denominated in dollars. Conversely, if the risk-neutral speculators expect a lower spot rate as compared with the relevant forward rate, then they will sell sterling forward and buy spot later to cover the forward contract. Obviously if the exchange rate moves in the reverse direction to that expected, then the speculators will make a loss, and the assumption of risk neutrality implies that they are not deterred from their attempt to take advantage of potential profits by the chance of a loss. Hence, given the existence of risk-neutral speculators, the forward rate should provide a good prediction of the spot rate in the future. More formally:

$$F_{t-1} = E_{t-1} S_t \tag{11.1}$$

where F_{t-1} is the forward rate observed at time $t - 1$ for the delivery of currency at time t and $E_{t-1} S_t$ is the expected spot rate at time t with the expectation formed at time $t - 1$.

It is possible to test equation (11.1) by running regressions of the form:

$$S_t = \alpha + \beta F_{t-1} \tag{11.2}$$

If the forward rate is an unbiased predictor of the spot rate, it is necessary that the estimates of α and β are not statistically different from 0 and 1 respectively. It appears that this relationship is rejected by the data – for example, see Baillie, Lippens and McMahon [1983] using data for the US\$, sterling, the Deutschmark, lira and the French franc (1973–80) and the Canadian dollar (1977–80). Two explanations are possible for this rejection of the hypothesis that the forward rate is an unbiased predictor. First, the market is inefficient and is not processing all available information correctly. Second, speculators are not risk-neutral but are, in fact, risk-averse so that they require a risk premium (which may vary over time) to compensate them for the risk of a loss following an adverse movement in the exchange rate. Whatever the reason, it seems apparent that the *dual* hypothesis of risk neutrality and market efficiency is rejected by the data.

A second type of semi-strong test of market efficiency arises from covered interest arbitrage. Starting from sterling, the one-period return from assets denoted in foreign currency (say dollars for illustrative purposes) may be defined as:

$$\Pi_\$ = S_t (1 + R_\$)/(E_t S_{t+1}) \tag{11.3}$$

where the time periods are consistent and $R_\$$ represents the one-period nominal rate of interest on dollar securities and $E_t S_{t+1}$ is the spot rate (\$ per £1) expected to exist at the end of the single period. Thus the equation represents a spot purchase of dollars at the rate of S_t, the subsequent purchase of a dollar security yielding a rate of interest equal to $R_\$$ during the period t to $t + 1$ and the subsequent repurchase of sterling at period $t + 1$ expected to be at the spot rate S_{t+1}. Equality of the return in the domestic market with that in the foreign market as depicted by equation (11.3) represents a situation of uncovered interest rate parity, i.e. the returns in the two centres are equal but the transaction is not covered in the forward market. However, equation (11.3) can be modified by substituting the forward rate (F_t) for the expected spot rate so that all rates (both interest and exchange rates) are known with certainty at time t. Similarly the return on sterling assets is given by $(1 + R_£)$.

The efficient markets hypothesis implies that the returns in the two centres should be equal. This condition is called covered interest rate parity because the transaction is covered in the forward market. This hypothesis has been tested by a number of researchers including Frenkel and Levich [1975 and 1977] and M. Taylor [1987]. In general, Frenkel and Levich, using end-of-day data, found that profits were not available from covered interest arbitrage in the eurocurrency markets after taking into consideration transaction costs. In the case of domestic centres, some profits were available but these could perhaps be accounted for by the greater risks involved such as actual or potential controls on capital movements. Taylor, using high-frequency data, i.e. observations of actual rates during the day, found some departures from interest rate parity during times of turbulence on the foreign exchange markets but in general interest rate parity held.

Finally in this section we look at the performance of professional forecasting agencies. The test examines whether forecasting agencies can consistently outperform the market, i.e. a 'strong' test in the Fama terminology. It is, of course, difficult to obtain information on forecasts sold to clients. However, a limited number of tests have been carried out by researchers including Goodman [1979], Levich [1979], Bilson [1983] and Blake, Beenstock and Brasse [1986]. The studies by Goodman, Levich and Blake *et al.* suggested that the forward rate was at least as good a predictor as that provided by the forecasting agency. Bilson found that the gain from combining forecasts, including those of a forecasting agency, and adopting a portfolio approach involving more than just one currency offered the prospect of gaining substantial profits.

The question of whether the foreign exchange market conforms to the efficient markets hypothesis remains open. It seems clear that the evidence points to the rejection of the dual hypothesis of risk neutrality and efficiency.

Chapter 12

Euro-securities markets

12.1 **Introduction**

In chapter 7 we established that London is one of the main international financial centres in the world. Three main areas of international financial activity can be distinguished: (i) banking, (ii) bonds and similar types of securities and (iii) equities. We have already discussed the nature and extent of international (mainly eurocurrency) banking in chapter 4 and the extent of international equities trading through London in chapter 8. In this chapter we will examine the euro-securities markets which have developed out of the eurocurrency markets and then discuss some of the wider developments in international financing. The euro-securities markets we consider, in sections 12.2 to 12.5, are those of eurobonds, euronotes and euro-equities. These markets have been the subject of a great deal of financial innovation over the past decade and the new financial instruments which have emerged have tended to blur the distinction between traditional international banking and securities trading. We finish this chapter therefore with a discussion of securitisation. This process describes how changes in the financial environment and the changing preferences of borrowers and international banks have led to a move away from international financial intermediation through banks to direct financing through greater use of international capital markets.

12.2 **Eurobonds**

Nature
A large borrower wishing to raise long-term funds through bond issues can turn to either the domestic bond market as we saw in chapter 9, or, alternatively, to the international bond markets. We can distinguish

between two types of international bonds. A foreign bond is one issued by a non-resident borrower on the market of a single country and denominated in that country's currency. For example, foreign bonds issued in New York in dollars, London in sterling or Tokyo in yen are known respectively as yankee, bulldog and samurai issues. The other type of international bond is the eurobond, which are bonds issued in markets other than that of the currency of issue and sold internationally. Thus a German company which issues a US dollar bond in New York is issuing a foreign (yankee) bond, whereas if the company issues the bond in a number of national markets, other than the US, then it is classed as a eurobond.

Eurobonds are generally issued 'off-shore', which means that the issue of such bonds is not subject to the rules and regulations which govern the issue of foreign bonds in that currency, such as obligations to issue detailed prospectuses and any interest-withholding taxes, i.e. taxes deducted at source before interest is paid for non-resident holders of bonds. This is not to say that there are no restrictions on eurobond issues and trading, since the Association of International Bond Dealers (AIBD), founded in 1969, is a self-regulatory body which has introduced trading rules and standardised procedures in the eurobond market.

Growth of the eurobond market
The first eurobond was issued in 1963 and their use grew at a slow rate throughout the 1960s and early 1970s, and then explosively over the 1980s. Table 12.1 shows the characteristics of international bonds issued over the 1980s.

There are a number of reasons which explain the rapid growth of eurobond activity over the 1980s. Over this period international interest rates fell steadily, making the issue of both equities and fixed-interest bonds more attractive to borrowers. Banks have generally been reluctant to lend at fixed rates of interest over the long term. In addition, the problems of banks over the 1980s and the greater cost of borrowing through banks, described in section 12.6 on securitisation, have led borrowers to look more to the international capital markets as a source of funds. Whilst international bond issues grew rapidly over the 1980s, it is clear from table 12.1 that eurobond issues, starting from a roughly equal share with foreign bonds at the beginning of the 1980s, accounted for the majority of this growth. One reason for this is the lower cost of eurobond issues compared to domestic or foreign bond issues. The ability of buyers of bonds to escape withholding tax and income tax on interest receipts enables borrowers to issue at lower yields. Eurobonds are generally issued in bearer form, eliminating the need for registration of ownership, so that ownership is vested in the holder. The anonymity this brings

Table 12.1 *Growth of international bond issues, 1979–89*

	1979	1980	1981	1982	1983	1984	1985	1986	1987	1988	1989
Total international bonds ($bn)	39.0	38.3	51.8	75.5	77.1	109.5	167.7	226.4	180.8	229.7	254.0
of which:											
Eurobonds (%)	47.9	53.2	60.4	66.6	64.9	74.6	81.5	83.0	77.7	77.9	83.5
Foreign bonds (%)	52.1	46.8	39.6	33.4	35.1	25.4	18.5	17.0	22.3	22.1	16.5
Currencies (%):											
US dollar	37.8	42.7	63.0	63.9	57.0	63.5	61.1	54.9	36.2	36.8	49.8
Japanese yen	7.3	4.9	6.0	5.2	5.3	5.5	7.7	10.4	14.7	9.8	9.4
Swiss franc	24.9	19.5	15.7	15.0	17.5	12.0	8.9	10.3	3.14	11.5	7.5
Deutschmark	22.0	21.9	5.0	7.1	8.6	6.2	6.7	7.5	8.3	10.3	6.5
Sterling	0.7	3.0	2.8	2.6	3.9	5.1	4.1	4.8	8.4	10.4	7.4
ECU	0.8	0.2	0.8	2.6	2.6	2.8	4.2	3.1	4.1	4.9	5.2
Other	6.5	7.8	6.7	3.6	5.1	4.9	7.3	9.0	14.9	16.3	14.3

Source: OECD, *Financial Statistics*, monthly, various issues.

allows owners to avoid tax on interest. The repeal of withholding tax on interest paid to foreign purchasers of domestic bonds in the US in 1984 together with changes to allow US residents to issue bearer bonds to non-resident borrowers may have been expected to make eurobonds less attractive. However, there are other advantages to issuing eurobonds which account for the continued growth. The lack of restrictions on eurobond trading makes it easier and therefore speedier to make issues and thus take advantage of a favourable 'window' in interest rate movements or other economic changes. Also the liberalisation of domestic capital markets in the US, Germany and Japan and the general globalisation of capital markets that took place over the 1980s have encouraged borrowers and investors to look more to international capital markets.

International bond issues are denominated in currencies which are important for national trade. This explains the importance of dollar-denominated eurobonds. However, the dollar-denominated dominance of the eurobond market is not quite as great as the dollar dominance of the eurocurrency loans market. This is because borrowers have also tended to issue bonds to tap the savings of countries which have a high savings ratio, in particular over the 1980s the economies of Germany and Japan. Furthermore, investors look for securities denominated in strong currencies. As we shall see in a later section, the use of swap contracts allows the currency denomination of the funds raised to be swapped into a different currency if required.

It should be noted that the Swiss authorities have acted to prevent the emergence of a eurobond market in Swiss francs so as to control the international use of its currency. Swiss franc issues of international bonds are therefore solely issues of foreign bonds. The prevention of Swiss franc-denominated eurobonds together with the growth of eurobonds vis-à-vis foreign bonds partly accounts for the decline in Swiss franc-denominated international bonds. One feature of recent eurobond issues, partly revealed in table 12.1, is the growth in ECU-denominated bonds. ECU stands for European currency unit, which is a composite currency unit made up of the currencies of the members of the European Community (see chapter 15 for further details). Issues of ECU-denominated eurobonds grew steadily over the 1980s but in 1990 rose to around 10 per cent of new issues, making it the fourth largest currency sector. The growth rate appears to have increased in 1991 with almost 11 billion ECU of eurobonds issued in the first two months, which is over two-thirds of the ECU issues in the whole of 1990. The reason for the growth in ECU bond activity is clearly not commercial activity when only 2 per cent of EC trade is denominated in ECUs. Most issues in recent years have in fact come from European governments and supranational bodies. Thus the motivation behind the recent growth is likely to be mainly political,

Table 12.2 *Main issuers of international bonds by country of origin 1987–89 (%)*

	1987	1988	1989
Japan	25	22	37
US	12	7	6
UK	7	12	8
Canada	5	6	5
France	5	7	5
Germany	6	5	4

Source: OECD, *Financial Statistics*, various issues.

with European governments showing their commitment to European monetary union. Some issues have had other motives, for example the 2.5 billion ECU bond issue by the UK government early in 1991 which was designed to encourage trade in the ECU bond futures contract on LIFFE – see chapter 13.

The geographical location of borrowers in the international bond markets in recent years is shown in table 12.2. This shows the dominance of Japanese borrowers, both banks and non-banks, over the last three years of the 1980s. The growth in Japanese-based issues of bonds largely reflects the strength of the Japanese stock market since the mid-1980s with most of these issues being equity-related bonds (discussed below).

Types of eurobonds
The eurobond market was the subject of a great deal of financial innovation over the 1980s and many different types of eurobonds have been created. It is possible though to classify eurobonds as belonging to one of three basic types:

(a) *Straight fixed rate*
     These are the traditional type of bond with a fixed coupon payment.
(b) *Floating-rate notes (FRNs)*
     These are bonds issued with coupon payments made on a floating-rate basis. The coupon, which usually consists of a margin over a reference rate such as LIBOR, is paid at the end of each interest period, usually six months, and then reset in line with the reference rate for the next interest period. FRNs are generally medium-term bonds, that is, with maturities from five to fifteen years.
(c) *Equity-related bonds*
     There are two types of equity related bonds:
     (i)   Convertibles
           These give the holder the right to convert the bond into

ordinary shares, with the terms and conditions of the conversion set at the time of issue.

(ii) Bonds with equity warrants attached

Warrants are options which give the holder the right to buy shares in a company at a given price in the future. Warrants are attached to the bonds but are securities in their own right and so can be stripped from the bond and sold separately. This distinguishes them from convertibles where the conversion rights are an integral part of the issue.

A breakdown of issue volumes by type is shown in table 12.3. Floating-rate notes were the fastest-growing section of the eurobond markets in 1983, 1984 and 1985 and the first half of 1986. There were various innovations on the standard FRN, and issues by UK building societies and other UK financial institutions pushed sterling into the second largest currency for FRNs. The floating-rate note market is dominated by financial institutions, banks in particular, which both issue and invest. A particular form of floating-rate note, the perpetual floating-rate note, so called because it is never redeemed, was popular with banks as it qualified as primary capital. All these developments receded with the virtual collapse of the FRN market at the end of 1986. This was due to a variety of reasons, including (i) excess competition in the issue side of the market driving down yields on some issues to unattractive levels and (ii) concern from central bankers that perpetual FRNs both issued and held by banks did not properly spread risk outside the banking system. A further contributing factor to the demise of the FRN market, namely growing interest in the euro-commercial paper market, is discussed below. The floating-rate note market, though, was beginning to show signs of recovery in 1990.

The equity-related issues of international bonds have seen rapid growth since the end of 1986. These issues have been predominantly of bonds with attached warrants, issued mainly by Japanese investors and denominated in US dollars. As noted above, this was related to the strength of

Table 12.3   *Eurobond issues classified by type, 1980–89 (%)*

Type	1980	1981	1982	1983	1984	1985	1986	1987	1988	1989
Straight fixed rate	67	64	72	59	51	52	65	68	72	60
Floating rate notes	21	27	24	31	39	40	25	8	11	10
Equity related	9	4	9	10	8	10	8	24	17	30

Source: Bank for International Settlements, annual report, various years.

Table 12.4 *Euronote issues classified by type, 1982–89 ($bn)*

	1982	1983	1984	1985	1986	1987	1988	1989
Euronotes	2.4	3.3	18.8	50.3	71.1	73.4	79.0	66.4
of which:								
Note issuance facilities	2.4	3.3	18.2	33.6	15.1	3.9	3.7	1.6
Euro-commercial paper	–	–	0.6	16.7	50.5	57.5	59.2	52.8
Medium-term notes	–	–	–	–	5.5	12.0	16.1	12.0

Source: *Bank of England Quarterly Bulletin*, annual article on 'Developments in international banking and capital markets', from 1985 on; Bank for International Settlements, annual report, various years.

the Japanese stock market in the late 1980s which made the issues attractive to investors.

12.3 Euronotes

In contrast to the longer-term eurobonds, the euronote markets encompass the various types of short-term securities issued to tap the eurocurrency markets. There are three basic types of euronotes, although there are many variations on these types. The original euronotes were note issuance facilities, which first appeared in 1978. The other types of euronote instruments, namely euro-commercial paper and medium-term notes, were based on the note issuance facilities and made a significant appearance in the mid 1980s. The issue volumes of euronotes and the relative volumes of the various types of euronotes over the 1980s are shown in table 12.4.

Note issuance facilities (NIFs)
The original euronotes were note issuance facilities, which are formalised, syndicated underwritten medium-term loans which enable borrowers to issue a stream of short-term bearer notes, usually of one, three or six months' maturity, on a rollover basis. These are generally issued through a tender panel and, if the borrowers are unable to sell the notes at a given spread over LIBOR to investors in the market, then the underwriting banks guarantee to purchase the notes themselves. Thus borrowers obtain medium-term funds, generally seven to ten years, financed by successive issues of short-term notes. NIFs are therefore transforming short-term funds into long-term funds, a transformation which is normally carried out through banks in their role as financial intermediaries. In this situation banks are, however, simply earning fee income for arranging and underwriting the facility and, as long as the notes are placed at the maturity dates without problems, then the business is off-balance sheet.

NIFs were developed as an alternative to syndicated loans and partly performed that role in 1984 and 1985 as issues of these facilities increased at a rapid rate. Their decline from the peak of 1985 is largely explained by the action of central banks which sought to ensure that banks increase their capital when underwriting NIFs for borrowers with low credit standing. This led to banks limiting NIFs to borrowers with high credit standing and, partly in response to this, new types of short-term credits have emerged, in particular euro-commercial paper.

Euro-commercial paper (ECP) and euro medium-term notes (EMTNs)
The issue of euro-commercial paper is a recent development in the euromarkets, making a significant appearance in late 1984, although the issuance of commercial paper dates from the mid-nineteenth century in the US (see chapter 10 on domestic money markets for a description of commercial paper). ECP programmes differ from NIFs in two important respects: first, they are not underwritten and, second, borrowers use a small group of appointed banks and dealers to distribute the notes on a 'best efforts' basis. In addition, the paper generally has more flexible maturities than NIFs, which can be tailored to investors' preferences. Dealers impart marketability to the paper by agreeing to repurchase them from holders before maturity. An important difference between US commercial paper and euro-commercial paper is that the former is always credit rated. When euro-commercial paper first appeared, very few of the issues were credit rated, although by 1989 approximately 45 per cent of issues had credit ratings and recent announcements (see *BEQB*, August 1990, 'International financial developments') suggest that around 90 per cent of new issues have a credit rating. This trend towards a fully credit-rated market appears to have been accelerated by defaults by some ECP issuers in 1988 and 1989. As shown in table 12.4, the greater emphasis on credit ratings appears to have had a slowing effect on the market for ECP in 1989, as lesser rated borrowers which were originally attracted to the market in 1986–1988 found it difficult to establish facilities. Despite the convergence of the US and euro-commercial paper markets on this feature, there are still important differences remaining which are discussed in Jeanneau [1989] and McCauley and Hargraves [1987].

The deepening market in ECP has enabled highly credit-rated borrowers to obtain funding at a lower all-in cost than would have been possible in the US commercial paper market. The emergence of the ECP market has provided a security which approximates an international money market instrument. It has had a significant impact on the floating-rate note market since it has largely replaced FRNs as a short-term instrument.

Euro medium-term notes are borrowing facilities backed by issues of paper where the paper has a maturity over nine months. The maturity of the paper can in theory be any length of time up to infinity, but in practice is limited to around ten years as a maximum. The market has shown steady growth since its emergence on a significant scale in 1986, although there was a turndown in 1989 reflecting the turndown in non-underwritten notes generally. EMTNs though were less affected than ECP by default in the late 1980s. There are a number of reasons to suggest that the EMTN market will expand in the future and in particular will take business away from the international bond markets. First, medium-term notes are a more flexible instrument than a bond. The maturity of the note issues, together with the characteristics of the drawings under an EMTN facility, can be varied to meet the needs of investor and borrower. Second, the liquidity of a bond issue is to a large extent determined by its size, and investors may require some minimum issue size in order to attract them to hold the bond. In contrast, the liquidity of EMTNs is provided by the guarantee of dealers to buy and sell the security. Finally, recent developments in the US domestic market, where corporate borrowing appears to have shifted from bonds to EMTNs, suggest that this may carry over to the international capital markets.

12.4 Euro-equities

Euro-equities or international equities are equities issued for sale outside the issuer's home country. The term 'international equity issues' is used to refer to both primary issues of shares and secondary placements of existing shares. The equity instrument is the same as that issued in domestic markets, so the only difference between domestic and international issues of equities is the method of distribution. One method of international equity issue is to obtain a simultaneous listing on more than one national exchange. This method has become less popular as it can be costly owing to widely different listing procedures across the various exchanges. A method that is increasingly used is the two tranche issue, where all the issue is listed on a domestic exchange, but one tranche is targeted at foreign investors. The distribution of the foreign tranche is increasingly organised through a syndicate made up of one financial institution in each country where the issue is targeted.

There are no reliable data available on international equity issues but table 12.5 shows approximate figures for the volume of international equity issues since the mid 1980s. Up until 1987 growth of international equity issues was rapid, owing to rising world stock markets and an increasing tendency towards international portfolio diversification following both liberalisation of financial markets and the abolition of capital controls in many countries. This growth was reversed following the world

Table 12.5   *Volume of international equity issues, 1984–89 ($bn)*

	1984	1985	1986	1987	1988	1989
International equity issues	0.2	3.5	15.5	20.0	9.0	14.9

Source: *Bank of England Quarterly Bulletin*, annual article on 'Developments in international banking and capital markets', various years.

stock markets crash of 1987. It appears, however, that the earlier growth was resumed in 1989 and appears likely to continue, fuelled by the continuing trend towards international portfolio diversification.

There are a number of advantages to a company from an international issue of its equity. Firstly, it has the effect of widening the ownership of the company beyond that of the domestic market. Secondly, it may be possible to issue at lower cost in foreign markets. Finally, it provides an escape from the size constraint of the domestic market. This is particularly the case for companies in some European countries with small stock markets. At present, the management of international equity issues can be more profitable for a bank than an international bond issue. Greater competition in the future, however, is likely to reduce margins and therefore issue costs.

12.5   Use of swaps in Euro-securities markets

The nature of swaps is discussed in chapter 13 on derivative instruments. Swaps are widely used in international capital market transactions and have been one of the forces behind the rapid growth of the eurobond markets over the 1980s. Swaps enable a borrower to raise funds in the market in which it has a comparative advantage and then swap into a liability with preferred characteristics. For example, a borrower X may a have a competitive advantage in the fixed-interest bond market but a preference for floating-rate funds to match its floating-rate assets. Thus the borrower can raise funds at a competitive cost through the issue of a fixed-rate bond but swap for a floating-rate obligation with borrower Y which has a competitive advantage in the floating-rate market but is looking for low-cost fixed-rate funds. As long as the interest rates swapped into by the two parties are lower than the interest rates obtainable from direct borrowing through the markets where they do not have a competitive advantage, then the swap is worthwhile. This fixed/floating-rate swap is a classic type of interest rate swap and, if the floating rate is one linked to LIBOR, is known as a 'plain vanilla'.

A second type of swap transaction used in the international capital markets is the currency swap. Here the swap involves an exchange of interest payments and principal denominated in one currency for payments in another. Again borrowers will borrow in the currency in which they have a comparative advantage and then swap into the preferred currency. There are two main types of currency swap in the capital markets; fixed/fixed currency swaps and fixed/floating currency swaps. The latter, referred to as cross-currency interest rate swaps, involve both a currency and an interest rate swap. More complex swaps have been developed in recent years and the interested reader is referred to Walmsley [1988].

Tables 12.6 and 12.7 indicate the size of the interest rate and currency swap markets at the end of 1988. We see that the US dollar market accounted for approximately 70 per cent of the interest rate swap market and that 85 per cent of activity in the currency swap market involved the US dollar on one side of the transaction. There are no up-to-date estimates of the number of eurobond issues which involved currency and/or interest swaps, although the Bank of England (see *BEQB*, February 1987) has estimated that around 75 per cent of fixed-rate international bonds issued in 1986 involved a currency swap.

Table 12.6   *Interest rate swaps in 1988 ($bn)*

	US$	Yen	DM	UK£	Other	Total
Interest rate swaps	728.2	78.5	56.5	52.3	94.7	1010.2

Source: Bank for International Settlements, annual report, 1990.

Table 12.7   *Currency swaps in 1988 ($bn)*

Currencies	Against US$	Against other	Total
Japanese yen	103.5	27.5	131.0
Swiss franc	39.5	34.5	74.0
Deutschmark	25.1	8.9	34.0
Other	101.4	23.7	125.1
Minus double-counting on non-$ swaps		−47.3	−47.3
Total	269.5	47.3	316.8

Source: Bank for International Settlements, annual report, 1990.

12.6 Securitisation

Major borrowers can raise funds in the international markets in three ways: they can borrow from the banking system, issue equities or issue debt securities such as bonds or notes.

As we established in chapter 2, the basis of banks' existence as financial intermediaries is that of transaction and information costs. This applies as much to international financing as it does to domestic financing. Over the 1980s international banks were beset by problems such as bank failures in the US and the sovereign debt crisis, which have reduced the credit standing of many banks and thus the competitiveness of their lending rates. It has therefore been suggested (see, for example, the Cross Report, BIS [1986]) that banks have been losing their comparative advantage in international financing. In addition, information costs have fallen owing to the emergence of a large number of credit rating agencies over the 1980s providing information on credit risks. As a consequence, many of the larger borrowers with good credit rating have found they can raise funds more cheaply through the international capital markets. That is, there was a greater preference, during some periods of the 1980s, for direct financing rather than indirect financing through a bank inter- mediary. This can be seen in table 12.8, which shows the relative volumes of the various forms of international finance over the 1980s.

Net international bank lending, which is made up of syndicated credits as well as short-term lending, was a declining proportion of total net international financing over the period 1980 to 1985. This is due to a switch from bank financing to indirect financing through the capital markets, a process known as securitisation, for the reasons outlined above. Eurobonds were the main alternative long-term funding security to bank intermediation in the early 1980s. In the mid-1980s, short- to medium-term direct financing through the issue of euronotes also ermerged to compete with syndicated bank lending. However, this pro- cess of securitisation appears to have been halted and possibly reversed since 1986. The reason for this is principally the renewed growth in bank lending, which can be explained by the ambitious expansion of the Japanese banks over the latter half of the 1980s (discussed in chapter 7) and the increase in corporate restructuring in the US and UK financed largely by debt. In addition, issues of international securities are subject to considerable volatility owing to linkages with stock markets. The global stock market crash in 1987 halted the growth in international securities issues, with bond issues only reaching per-crash levels again in 1989. Looking to the future, the factors which led to the expansion of bank lending in the late 1980s look unlikely to be repeated, whilst the spread of securitisation habits to Europe and the pressure on banks to

Table 12.8 *Breakdown of international financing, 1980–89 ($bn)*

	1980	1981	1982	1983	1984	1985	1986	1987	1988	1989
Net international bank lending[a]	160.0	165.0	95.0	85.0	90.0	105.0	200.0	300.0	225.0	330.0
Net international bond issues[b]	28.0	36.5	58.5	59.0	84.0	123.0	159.7	107.8	137.1	171.6
Net euronote issues[c]					5.0	10.0	13.0	23.4	19.5	6.9
International equity issues					0.2	3.5	15.5	20.0	9.0	14.9
Total international financing minus double counting[d]	188.0	201.5	153.5	144.0	179.2	241.5	388.2	451.2	390.6	523.4
	8.0	6.5	8.5	14.0	24.0	58.0	82.7	51.2	66.6	68.5
Total net international financing	180.0	195.0	145.0	130.0	155.2	183.5	305.5	400.0	324.0	454.9
Bank lending as % of total financing	89.0	85.0	66.0	65.0	58.0	57.0	65.0	75.0	69.0	73.0

Notes:
[a] As defined in table 4.5 in chapter 4.
[b] Completed international bond issues (as distinct from announced bond issues recorded in table 12.1 above) minus redemptions and repurchases.
[c] Completed euronote placements (as distinct from announced issues recorded in table 12.4 above).
[d] Purchases of bonds by banks and bonds issued by banks used to underpin international lending activities.
Source: Bank for International Settlements, annual report, various years.

unload assets from their balance sheets to meet the new capital adequacy requirements (discussed in chapter 17) suggest that securitisation may be a long-run trend.

It is a mistake, however, to equate securitisation with dis-intermediation. Banks are actively involved in the securities markets in arranging the issue of securities, underwriting or providing guarantees of liquidity in the euronote markets. Banks are also the important players in the derivative markets, such as swaps, futures and options, which underlie many security market transactions. Banks often act as counterparties in swap transactions or perform a transformation of characteristics as they construct tailor-made option and futures retail contracts from the wholesale standardised contracts traded on the exchanges. It can be argued, then, that securitisation has not led to a greater exclusion of banks from the international financing process but that banks have transferred intermediation business that appeared on the balance sheet to fee-earning business that is conducted off-balance sheet. Banks can be seen to have adapted, and more importantly innovated, in response to the changing preferences of international borrowers. The innovation that has taken place has tended to blur the boundaries between traditional intermediation and securities transacting.

12.7 Conclusion

In this chapter we have looked at the development of euro-securities markets, which are the international equivalents of domestic securities markets discussed in chapters 8, 9 and 10. These grew rapidly over the 1980s and represent one facet of the internationalisation of finance.

Chapter 13

Financial futures and options

13.1 Introduction

Financial futures trading commenced in the US in 1972. This was followed in September 1982 with the establishment of the London International Financial Futures Exchange (LIFFE), which became the first financial futures market in Europe. Other markets for financial futures in Europe include the Marché à Terme d'Instruments Financiers (MATIF) in Paris, European Options Exchange in the Netherlands, Copenhagen Stock Exchange and the Irish Futures and Options Exchange. LIFFE provides facilities for dealing in financial futures and also in traded options on futures. At the time of writing (autumn 1990) LIFFE has agreed a merger with the London Traded Options Market (LTOM), which provides dealing facilities in sixty-six options on individual shares and two options on the FT-SE 100 Share Index. The average number of contracts traded per day on LIFFE and LTOM during the period January to May 1990 was 145,000 and 33,600 respectively. The merger will be completed during 1992 and the new exchange will be called the London International Financial Futures and Options Exchange. This exchange will be the largest futures and options exchange in Europe.

As shown in table 13.1, futures and options in general have seen a very rapid rate of growth over recent years. One of the reasons for this spectacular rate of growth is the the high degree of volatility experienced in interest rates, inflation and exchange rates since the collapse in 1971 of the fixed exchange rate regime established by the Bretton Woods agreement; see chapter 14, figures 14.1 and 14.2 for more details. In particular, the growth in the quantity of primary securities issued has led automatically to a higher volume of secondary market transactions and therefore a greater demand for hedging instruments and hence financial futures and

Table 13.1 *Futures and options exchanges: % share of total lots traded, 1985–89*

Region	Exchange	1985	1987	1988	1989
London	Baltic	0.1	0.1	0.1	0.1
	IPE	0.1	0.2	0.3	0.5
	LIFFE	0.8	2.0	2.5	3.1
	LFOX	0.6	0.4	0.7	0.6
	LME	0.7	0.7	1.4	1.4
	LTOM	0.7	1.9	1.5	1.8
	Total	3.1	5.2	6.6	7.5
United States	CBOE	35.8	28.7	20.5	19.8
	CBOT	17.0	16.0	21.4	18.1
	CME	12.5	11.2	12.0	13.9
	Total (US)	94.1	84.0	80.7	78.1
Canada	Total	0.3	0.4	0.6	1.1
Europe	EOE (Amsterdam)	1.7	1.7	1.6	2.1
	MATIF (Paris)		1.9	3.0	4.0
	Total (Europe)	1.8	5.5	6.1	7.1
Far East	Total	0.7	4.8	6.0	6.2
World total no. of contracts (millions)		416	635	547	657

Note: CBOE = Chicago Board Options Exchange, CBOT = Chicago Board of Trade, CME = Chicago Mercantile Exchange, EOE = European Options Exchange, IPE = the International Petroleum Exchange, LFOX = London Futures and Options Exchange, LIFFE = London International Financial Futures Exchange, LME = London Metals Exchange, LTOM = London Traded Options Market, MATIF = Marché à Terme d'Instruments Financiers.
The Baltic, IPE, LFOX and LME are derivative markets for commodities.
Source: *Bank of England Quarterly Bulletin*, November 1989, p. 521.

options. The rapid growth of information technology and consequent reduction in transaction costs have also played a role by stimulating the development of new trading strategies which enabled agents to use financial futures as a means of reducing risk. This aspect of the role of financial futures and options is considered in greater detail in chapter 14.

In addition to the fast rate of growth, table 13.1 shows the relative importance of the various centres. The Chicago markets still account for over 50 per cent of total world trade in financial futures, although the other markets have experienced a faster rate of growth over recent years and have, therefore, reduced the dominance of the Chicago markets.

In section 13.2 we will examine in outline the general organisation of LIFFE. It is unlikely that the forthcoming merger will change the operating system to any great extent, so the following discussion will continue to provide an indication of how futures markets operate. The role of financial futures and options will be discussed in sections 13.3 and 13.4 respectively. Section 13.5 presents a survey of the empirical evidence concerning the efficiency of this type of market.

13.2 The organisation of LIFFE

A financial futures contract can be defined as an agreement to sell or buy a quantity of a financial instrument on an organised market or exchange at a future date and at a price specified at the time of making the contract. In contrast, an option confers the right, but not the obligation, to the purchaser to buy (a 'call' option) or the right to sell (a 'put' option) financial instruments at a standard price and times in the future. The distinction between traded and 'over-the-counter' (OTC) options is that the former can be bought from and sold to parties other than the original writer (i.e. seller) of the option. The market in the underlying or actual financial instrument is called the cash market and the options or futures market the derivative market.

Although a range of financial instruments are the subject of futures transactions, the number is, as shown in table 13.2 below, limited. A further restriction applies since the transactions are available only in specific quantities, e.g. on LIFFE the standard unit of trading is £500,000 for three-month sterling deposits, US$1,000,000 for three-month eurodollar deposits, £50,000 for the long gilt futures. The minimum unit of trading decreases as the maturity of the underlying cash market security increases owing to the increase in its price volatility. In all futures and options exchanges, delivery of the security is also made on specific

Table 13.2 *Futures and options contracts available at LIFFE*

Interest rate	Unit of trading
Three-month sterling deposits (short sterling)	£500,000
Three-month eurodollar deposits	US$1,000,000
Three-month euromark deposits*	DM1,000,000
Three-month ecu deposits*	ECU1,000,000
Long gilt	£50,000
German government bond (Bund)	DM250,000
US Treasury bond (US T-Bond)	US$100,000
Japanese government bond* (JGB)	¥100,000,000
Stock index	
FT-SE 100 Index*	Valued at £25 per full index point, i.e. £52,500 at 2,100.0

Source: LIFFE.

dates according to a fixed sequence of months with the cycle of March, June, September and December being the most common. The cycle usually extends up to two years in advance, but in some cases the cycle can extend up to four years. These limitations reduce the flexibility of the contracts available as compared with, say, the provision of tailor-made forward foreign exchange contracts provided by the banks as was discussed in chapter 10. On the other hand, the provision of standardised contracts enables trading to be carried out at a low cost since the buyers and sellers know precisely what they are trading.

The second general point to note is that, although the transactions are originally made between two parties on the exchange, the two resulting contracts are then transferred to LIFFE's clearing house, which clears and guarantees all transactions carried out on the exchange. LIFFE has a zero net position since it has acquired both sides of the trade. This system has a number of advantages. First, the risk of default is eliminated for both parties to the transaction since it is borne by the exchange. In order to protect itself against default, the clearing house requires both parties to deposit cash against the transaction (the 'initial margin') and this margin is revalued on a daily basis to take account of movements in the price of the underlying security (the 'variation margin'). A further protection is gained by restriction of dealing facilities to 'members' of LIFFE who, themselves, are representatives of a wide range of financial institutions. Second, it enables transactions to be 'closed out' before the maturity date since the party wishing to terminate the agreement merely takes out an exactly opposite liability. In fact over 90 per cent of agreements are closed out before the maturity date and we shall discuss the reasons for this in section 13.3.

The contracts available on LIFFE in October 1990 are shown in table 13.2. It should, however, be remembered that this list can be only indicative of what contracts will be available as it is likely that new contracts will be developed. For example, at the present time futures markets are considering the possibility of introducing futures contracts for re-insurance, and a new ECU bond futures contract was launched in March 1991.

Except for those contracts marked with an asterisk, LIFFE also provides options on the futures contracts listed in table 13.2. Up to 1990, LIFFE also provided facilities for trading in futures and options in currencies, but these were suspended in 1990. For the pound against the US dollar, traded options are still available (i) against cash on the Philadelphia stock exchange (units of £31,250 per contract) and (ii) against futures at Chicago.

The relative importance of the various contracts over the years since the formation of LIFFE is shown in table 13.3. The table shows the

Table 13.3   *LIFFE: volume of transactions, 1982–89 ('000 transactions)*

	1982	1984	1986	1988	1989
Futures					
Short sterling	40.3	341.2	958.8	3,538.0	7,131.3
British pound	42.4	145.5	41.5	7.3	4.6
Bund				315.2	5,330.0
DM	7.2	28.3	16.3	4.1	2.2
Dollar/mark			0.5	0.1	0.1
Eurodollar	122.3	1,023.5	1,106.5	1,647.5	2,063.6
Euromark					951.6
Ecu					15.9
FT-SE		73.2	122.3	465.1	1,028.0
JGB				121.6	117.1
Long gilt	28.7	774.7	2,168.0	5,586.8	4,062.5
Medium gilt				54.1	2.6
Short gilt			61.3	0	0
Swiss franc	1.2	12.7	5.9	2.7	1.2
US T-Bond		167.3	1,546.0	2,042.3	966.9
Yen	590.0	11.8	7.8	2.6	3.3
Total futures	242.6	2,578.2	6,484.9	13,787.2	21,681.0
Options					
Dollar/mark			8.5	1.7	0.1
FT-SE			2.8	1.4	0
Long gilt			278.8	1,141.2	726.7
British pound			105.2	8.7	1.1
Eurodollar			38.7	76.2	81.5
Short sterling				444.8	824.1
US T-Bond			52.5	84.4	75.9
Bund					469.0
Total options			486.6	1,758.4	2,178.4
Total exchange	242.6	2,578.2	6,971.5	15,545.6	23,859.4

Note: column totals may not agree with row totals owing to rounding errors.
Source: LIFFE.

dramatic growth in total number of transactions from 242,592 in 1982 to 23,859,399 in 1989. The statistics also demonstrate the importance of short-term interest rate contracts and the FT-SE futures. The decline of currency futures and options is also apparent. The probable reason for this is that the over-the-counter (OTC) market offers comparable products which are perceived by traders to be more advantageous. As far as currency futures are concerned, the forward market provides a similar and flexible opportunity to hedge against future exchange rate changes through either fixed or option dated forward contracts. This eliminates the necessity of having to sell the instrument in the market, although similar resale facilities are available if required by entering into a spot sale of the currency in the market which offsets the original forward contract. Similarly OTC options contracts can be arranged with banks which meet the traders' requirements. It is understood that such contracts have shown a considerable degree of growth, with London as an important centre, though no official statistics exist. However, a 1986 BIS study suggested that the two largest markets in New York and in London were approximately equivalent in outstanding amounts and turnover, with outstanding foreign exchange options in each market amounting at that time to roughly $10 billion.

Dealing on LIFFE must be carried out through members. On receipt of an order from a customer, the member transmits this order to their booth on the trading floor. Trading is carried out by the 'open outcry' system during the period 8 am to 4.15 pm and by LIFFE's Automated Pit Trading System (APT) between 4.30 pm and 6.00 pm. Whilst scenes from the trading floor or pit initially convey the impression of utter chaos, it is claimed that this system ensures that all orders receive equal treatment and that it is therefore fair. However, all this could change. Apart from the APT system discussed above, Reuters have developed a screen trading system which is to be used as an after-hours market for some of the products traded in Chicago, and there is a feeling within the industry that this system will eventually be extended to all dealing. As noted earlier, the order is then transferred to the clearing house. Immediate day-to-day supervision of the market is vested in the board of the exchange which has established a market supervision department to carry out self-regulation. Ultimate supervisory authority lies with the Bank of England, which exercises general surveillance over all London exchanges.

13.3 The nature of financial futures

In order to demonstrate the nature of financial futures it is necessary to describe their function. As is the case for all traded financial instruments (see chapter 7), three uses of financial futures are traditionally identified. These are 'hedging', 'trading' (or, perhaps more appropriately, speculation) and 'arbitrage'. In practice, however, it may be difficult to make this a clearcut and unambiguous distinction since financial institutions are making greater use of derivative markets for the purpose of asset/liability management.

Hedging can be considered a defensive operation by risk-averse operators to insure themselves against adverse movements in, for example, interest or exchange rates. As an outline of this function prior to consideration of particular hedging operations in detail, consider the position of an operator who buys a three-month sterling deposit financial future. If current actual interest rates fall then the value of the future will increase, since it is offering higher rates than can be obtained in the market place. Conversely, if current actual interest rates rise then the value of the financial future will fall, since actual deposits will earn higher rates of interest. Consequently the price of the financial future will move in the opposite direction to the movement of interest rates. Thus it is possible for an agent to offset – at least partially – the effects of movements in interest rates by profits or losses on the value of the financial future by selling the futures contract back to the market. The basic trading rule is that if the trader's cash position will be adversely affected by higher-than-anticipated interest rates, then a futures contract should be sold. Conversely, if it is lower rates that worry the trader, then a futures contract should be bought.

We now illustrate the procedure more precisely, using as an example the three-month sterling interest rate futures contract. A company has obtained a loan of £1,000,000 at a rate of 12 per cent from the money markets which is due to be rolled over on 1 June. The company is concerned that interest rates will change, with a probability that the loan will be rolled over at a higher rate. In order to protect itself the company sells two three-month sterling interest rate financial futures (each valued £500,000) which are due for delivery after 1 June – it is of critical importance that the delivery date of the futures contract is later than the date when the risk to be hedged disappears, otherwise there will be a period of time when potential changes in prices of the cash instrument are not hedged. Assuming the current interest rate is 12 per cent, the price of each contract is 100 minus the annual rate of interest, i.e. 88 in this example. The price of the contract will move up or down in minimum amounts of 0.01 per cent, which are known as a 'ticks' or basis points. The value of a tick varies for each type of financial future but may, in this case, be derived by applying the 0.01 per cent rate of interest to the face value of a £500,000 contract for one-quarter of a year and is therefore £12.50. On 1 June the company will buy the two contracts back from the exchange.

We can now examine the effect of this transaction if interest rates had risen to 14 per cent per annum on 1 June. The first point to note is that the company will bear extra borrowing costs of £5,000 for the next quarter owing to the rise in interest rates of 2 per cent per annum. We next look at the futures market transaction, and we initially assume that the futures price has also moved in line with the cash market rate.

(a) Sells two contracts at 88 (rate of interest 12 per cent).
(b) Buys back two futures at 86 (rate of interest 14 per cent) on 1 June.
(c) Gains 200 ticks per contract, i.e. 400 at £12.50 = £5,000.

In this case the higher cost of interest is exactly matched by the profit on the two futures transactions.

If, on the other hand, interest rates had fallen, then the company's borrowing cost would have fallen but this would have been offset by the loss on buying back the futures contract. This clarifies what the company has gained from its financial futures operation, namely that the uncertainty surrounding the future interest rate on its borrowing cost has been removed. It is important to realise that the company has not necessarily made a gain on its futures transactions. In fact, in the case of an interest rate fall, it would have incurred a loss but it would have reduced the uncertainty of future costs. This example also illustrates the reason why most contracts are 'closed out', i.e. reversed before the time for delivery of the futures contract since the offsetting gain/loss on the futures contract is realised when the futures contract is closed out.

The precision of the hedge in the above example is due to the fact that we have assumed that the price of the futures contract has moved exactly in line with the cash market rate. This degree of precision is unlikely to occur in practice and, to understand why, we need to consider a concept known as basis. This may be defined as:

$$\text{Basis} = \text{Cash Price} - \text{Futures Price}.$$

In the example quoted above, the basis is zero at the start and the finish of the hedging operation. It is quite common, however, for a non-zero basis to exist since the cash and futures prices are subject to different influences. In particular, the futures price will reflect the market's view of the level of the interest rate in the future. If we return to the above example, and consider the case where the futures price at the time the hedger sells the contracts is not 88 but rather 87.50. The existence of a futures price of 87.50 and an analogous cash price of 88.00 (100 − 12) implies that the market expects interest rates to rise in the period up to the date of the futures contract. The basis at the start of the hedge is therefore (88.0 − 87.5) or 0.5. If the basis is different at the time the hedger 'closes out', then the hedge will not be perfect. To illustrate this point, consider the position if the futures price had been 86.00 on 1 June (i.e. a zero basis given an interest rate of 14 per cent). Then the gain on the hedge would have been 150 (87.50 − 86.00) ticks per contract or £3,750 in total. In this case a partial hedge has been achieved since the gain on the futures contract does not cover the additional interest charges on the rolled-over loan. It is also quite possible that the change in basis could work in favour of the hedger. For example, if the futures price was 85.00 on 1 June (i.e. a basis of 1.0) then the gain would have been 250 ticks per contract or £6,250 in total. A further point worth nothing is that, if the futures contract purchased by the hedger had been for delivery in June, then it is quite likely that the basis on 1 June would have been close to zero. This is because, as the delivery date on the futures contract approaches, the cash price and the futures price tend to equality because the influences on the two contracts are identical on the delivery date. As will be shown below, any difference between the two prices would lead to arbitrage.

A non-zero basis can occur for a number of reasons (see Kolb [1988] for further discussion). If the basis is close to zero when the contract is being taken out, then it is sensible to choose futures contracts that mature soon after the disappearance of the risk to be hedged. In general, however, cash and futures prices do exhibit a fairly high degree of correlation so that basis risk (the risk of movements in basis) is less than outright risk (the risk of an unhedged positions) as long as the characteristics of the instrument being hedged are not very different from those of relevant futures instrument.

We now turn to examine the role of trading or speculation in the operation of financial futures markets. The provider of a hedge can protect himself by negotiating an offsetting contract. In the example of the company treasurer quoted above, the purchaser of the futures may at that time be able to identify a customer who wishes to buy two similar contracts. In this instance the financial institution providing the hedge has incurred no risk since it has two offsetting contracts, with windfall gains on one contract matching windfall losses on the other. In practice it is highly unlikely that the quantity of hedging demanded for a change in one direction will exactly match that required in the opposite direction, so that traders fill the gap by making the market and therefore provide a useful economic function.

Trading is basically a non-defensive activity undertaken by those agents willing to bear the risk of price changes. Their income comes from two sources, which in practice may be difficult to distinguish. First, there is the reward for undertaking risk and, second, the potential profits to be earned from taking a correct view of the future course of the prices of the underlying cash market securities. Financial futures are a particularly useful vehicle for speculation since (i) transaction costs are low and (ii) there is no need to purchase or sell the underlying instrument and the cash outlay is restricted to the initial margin (typically varying between 0.1 per cent and 6 per cent of the face value of the contract) and the variation margin, thus offering potential for high degrees of leverage. Thus if the price of the underlying security is expected to rise they will go long, i.e. buy financial futures, or alternatively if the price is expected to fall they would go short, i.e. sell financial futures. Clearly this is a risky operation and losses will be incurred if the prices move in the opposite direction to those anticipated by the trader. We use the long gilt futures contract as an illustration of the potential for trading contracts. Again we would like to emphasise that this is just one particular example of a wide range of potential trading activities available.

As was pointed out in chapter 8, prices of gilts are sensitive to interest rate changes, and the degree of sensitivity increases directly with the outstanding maturity of the stock in question. Assume that a trader feels that the next round of publications of the various official statistics will be more favourable than has hitherto been the case. He also feels that this is likely to lead to a reduction in interest rates which has not fully been reflected in the current prices of gilt-edged stock. He therefore purchases one unit of gilt futures £50,000 nominal value for the next delivery date after the publication of the last in the round of the official statistics he considers relevant. Assume that the relevant contract is trading at £102–25, that is, £102 and 25/32nds. The minimum price movement is 1/32nd, with a tick valued at £15,625 for this contract. If he is correct and the statistics on balance are sufficiently favourable to permit a fall in interest rates, then gilt prices will rise and so consequently will the gilt futures contract, so that the trader will make the expected profit. It should be emphasised that the profit is entirely dependent on the accuracy of the trader's forecast as against that implicit in market prices.

The third activity in futures markets refers to arbitrage to take advantage of price anomalies between either (i) the underlying cash market instruments and the futures or (ii) different futures contracts. Such price anomalies are likely to be quite small and short lived since other traders will quickly perceive the opportunity of making a profit with minimal risk. As one example we consider the position of the long gilt futures contracts. This contract can be carried out by delivery of a specified gilt-edged stock. The current specification broadly refers to any stock maturing between the years 2003 and 2009 inclusive, but excludes convertible and index-linked stocks. Thus if the prices of the futures and underlying stocks are misaligned it may be possible to borrow funds, purchase the misaligned deliverable stock and sell an appropriate futures contract. This is called cash and carry arbitrage. Little risk is attached to such an operation provided all the contracts are undertaken simultaneously. Anomalies between the prices of future contracts may occur between (i) different types of contracts (such as, for example, between the various three-month interest rate futures noted in section 13.2) or (ii) between different delivery dates of the same futures contract. This latter arbitrage is known as spreading.

In addition to the three traditional uses discussed above, futures markets can be used to vary a portfolio's overall maturity structure by altering the maturity of individual securities. For example, the average maturity of a portfolio can be 'synthetically' reduced by the sale of, say, a long gilt futures in five months' time and using a 'deliverable' gilt from the portfolio to complete the transaction. Thus the maturity on the security has been changed from its previous term to five months and the new redemption value is the price implied by the futures contract. Similarly, the average length of a portfolio of short-term securities can be lengthened by purchasing a series of short-term contracts.

We have completed our discussion of futures contracts and we now turn to discuss the nature of options.

13.4 The nature of options

Options give the purchaser, in return for a premium, the right to buy (a 'call' option) or the right to sell (a 'put' option) a financial instrument at an agreed exchange rate (the 'striking' price) at a specified date or dates. No obligation is imposed on the buyer to carry out the obligation, so he will choose to do so only if it is profitable for him. Two classes or types of option can be distinguished. As was discussed in section 13.2, an option can be either an OTC option or a traded option. OTC options have to be either exercised or allowed to lapse. Traded options offer the additional choice to the holder of reselling them on the market. In fact, as we shall see later, it is more likely that a traded option will be resold rather than exercised. Trading on organised option markets can be for the purposes of both speculation and hedging and it is the presence of speculators which provides liquidity for the market. Options can be further categorised into American and European options. An American type of option can be exercised at any date up to the expiry of the option, whereas the European type can be exercised only on a specified date. The options traded on LIFFE are all of the American type.

Premia for traded options are quoted in market statistics and we show in table 13.4 the relevant details for options on the Philadelphia Stock Exchange for the pound versus the dollar at close of trade on 10 October 1990. The detail contained in table 13.4 can be interpreted in the following way. A trader can purchase a call option (i.e. the right to buy pounds) expiring in November at a strike/exercise price of $1.875 per £1 for a premium of 9.20 cents per £1. For March expiry and the same strike price the premium is 9.79 cents per £1. Similarly, the purchase of a put option (the right to sell) with a strike price of $2.000 per £1 and December expiry would require a premium of 7.11 cents per £1.

We use the quotation for November calls and puts at a strike price of

Table 13.4 *Philadelphia Stock Exchange £/$ options as at 10 October 1990: £31,250 (cents per £1)*

Strike price ($)	Calls				Puts			
	Oct	Nov	Dec	Mar	Oct	Nov	Dec	Mar
1,875	9.10	9.20	9.33	9.79	–	0.70	1.41	3.56
1,900	6.60	7.04	7.31	8.02	0.04	1.22	2.01	4.56
1,925	4.11	5.17	5.57	6.49	0.07	2.02	2.91	5.71
1,950	1.97	3.61	4.11	5.20	0.29	2.88	4.05	7.06
1,975	0.53	2.43	3.00	4.12	1.37	4.24	5.47	8.55
2,000	0.07	1.65	2.08	–	3.29	5.89	7.11	–
2,025	0.01	1.08	1.56	–	5.67	7.77	8.94	–

Source: *Financial Times*, 11 October 1990.

$1.875 per £1 to derive the diagrams used to illustrate the profit and loss situation for the purchaser and the writer of the option. In the first example, the purchaser of a call option will exercise it to purchase sterling only if the market spot rate rises above $1.875 per £1. At market prices lower than this rate it is more profitable for the trader to purchase sterling in the market so that his loss is restricted to the 9.2 cents premium paid on taking out the option. The break-even point occurs when the actual spot rate is $1.967 per £1 so that the premium just matches the gain on the option contract of $0.092 (or 9.2 cents). In effect, therefore, the purchase of the call option has fixed the maximum price to be paid for pounds at $1.967 per £1. As the spot exchange rate rises above $1.967 per £1, the purchaser obtains profits which in theory are unlimited but in practice are limited to the likely range of market fluctuations. The position for the seller (i.e. the 'writer') of the option is the mirror image of that of the purchaser. Figure 13.1 illustrates the above situation.

The position in the case of the purchase of a put option is the reverse of that in the case of a call option and is illustrated in figure 13.2. For an exercise price of $1.875 per £1, the option will be exercised only when the market spot rate for sterling falls below $1.875 per £1. At prices above $1.875 it is more profitable to sell the sterling in the market. Consequently the break-even price for the purchaser is $1.868 per £1 when the profit on the sale of sterling just matches the premium paid, i.e. $0.007 (0.7 cents). As the spot exchange rate falls below $1.868 per £1, the purchaser makes gains which in theory are only limited by an exchange rate of zero but, in practice, are again limited by the likely range of fluctuations. As for the case of a call option, the position of the writer is the mirror image of that of the purchaser.

Remember, the exercise of an option lies entirely in the hands of the

Figure 13.1   Profit and loss on a call option

Figure 13.2   Profit and loss on a put option

purchaser. The writer has no control over whether the option is exercised or not. It is in the nature of a contingent liability which may or may not be incurred. As far as the purchaser is concerned, an option contract is analogous with an insurance policy: the premium for the option represents the premium paid for the policy and the risk insured is the downside risk of an adverse exchange rate movement, with the purchaser taking all the benefits of a favourable movement.

The price of an option contract can be divided into two components:

(i) The *intrinsic value* is the gain which would be realised if an option were exercised immediately. In the case of a call option it is the excess of the spot price over the exercise price. This represents the gain that can be made by exercising the option immediately and selling the currency in the market. For a put option, the intrinsic value is the excess of the exercise price over the spot rate, which represents the profit derived from buying the currency in the market and exercising the option to sell the currency at the strike price. In the above example, the spot rate for the pound was \$1.966–\$1.968 per £1 at the close of trading on 10/10/90 – remember the lower figure represents the price at which the bank will buy sterling and the higher figure the price at which the bank will sell sterling. For a strike price of \$1.875 per £1 the intrinsic value for a call option is \$0.091 (1.966 − 1.875) or 9.1 cents. Similarly for a put option at a strike price of \$2.000 per £1 the intrinsic value is \$0.032 (2.000 − 1.968) or 3.2 cents. The intrinsic value is always positive or zero.

(ii) The *time value* represents that part of the premium not represented by the intrinsic value. For example, given an intrinsic value of 9.10 cents per £1 and a premium of 9.20 cents per £1 for November expiry of a call option with a strike price of \$1.875 per £1, the time value is \$0.001 or 0.1 cents. Time value cannot be negative and will approach zero at an increasing rate as the option nears expiry. This is can be seen from table 13.4 where the time value of a call option at a strike price of \$1.875 per £1 expiring in March is 0.69 cents (9.79 − 9.10) as compared with the value of 0.1 cents for November expiry and zero for expiry in October.

When the intrinsic value of an option exists the option is said to be 'in the money'. For a put option, if the strike price is less than the current spot rate, then the option is said to be 'out of the money'. A call option is said to 'out of the money' if the strike price is more than the current price. If the exercise (strike) price is equal to the spot price then the option is 'at the money'. Time value is at its maximum value for a given expiry date when an option is at the money and tends to zero for deeply out of the money and deeply in the money options. It can be seen in table 13.4 that the intrinsic value for a call option expiring in November with an exercise price of 1.975 is \$0.009 or 0.9 cents per £1. The time value of this option is therefore 1.53 cents (2.43 − 0.9) as compared with 0.01 cents for the deeply in the money call option with a exercise price of 1.875. This can be rationalised intuitively by considering the position of a deeply out of money option. The further the option is away from the strike price, the more unlikely it becomes that it will be exercised. Hence both the value to the holder and the risk to the writer are reduced, thus lowering the premia required for taking on the risk. For an in the money option, intrinsic value exists, so that the holder incurs the risk of this value being eroded by adverse movements in the spot price. As far as the writer of the option is concerned, the adverse movement to the holder would be a gain for the writer. The larger the intrinsic value, the greater the risk of erosion of the intrinsic value. Thus the premium will compensate the buyer of the option with a reduced time value in the premium and the writer will be willing to grant the lower premium owing to the lower risk involved. The presence of the time component in the price of an option means that it is likely that the holder will sell the option in the market rather than exercise it. To illustrate this point, consider the case of a call option expiring in December with a strike price of $1.875 per £1. The premium is 9.33 cents per £1 which, given the then ruling spot exchange rate spread of $1.966–$1.986 per £1, implies an intrinsic value of $0.091 per £1 and a time value of $0.0023 per £1 (0.23 cents). Sale of the option in the market would permit the holder to extract the time value for himself and he could buy the pounds in the market for the lower figure of $1.966 per £1.

The price of an option depends on a number of factors and can be derived by mathematical formulae including various forms of the Black–Scholes formula. More intuitively it is possible to identify the main factors influencing the price of an option. In the case of a call option, the lower the exercise or strike price the more likely it is to be exercised and therefore the higher the price. The second factor is the current spot price. In this case the higher the spot price the more likely the option is to be exercised. Two other factors are the volatility of the price of the underlying cash asset and the maturity of the option. The option is more likely to be exercised (i) if the price of the cash instrument is volatile and/or (ii) the greater the length of time before the option expires. Anything which increases the probability of the option being exercised raises the price of the option, i.e. the premium. In the case of a put option, the premium would be raised if the direction of the first two factors is reversed, i.e. the option will be more valuable (i) the lower the price of the underlying cash instrument and/or (ii) the higher the strike or exercise price.

A wide range of transactions is available in futures and options markets, including both defensive and speculative. It might be expected therefore that price anomalies between and within the various securities and options would be quickly eliminated, so that market prices would reflect all available information; i.e. the market would be efficient. It is to this aspect that we now turn in section 13.5.

13.5 The efficiency of futures markets

Futures and options are derivative markets so that their prices are a function of the anticipated movements in the price of the underlying cash market asset. It is therefore possible to impute equilibrium prices from the prices of options and futures. Efficiency requires that these imputed prices should provide accurate forecasts. The literature on the efficiency of these markets is more limited than that for the cash markets and therefore our survey of the evidence is more restricted. We briefly describe studies of the role of options prices in the stock market and foreign currency markets and of futures in relation to the foreign currency markets and the US treasury bill futures market.

The methodology adopted by Manaster and Rendleman [1982] in respect to the stock market was to use option prices to calculate the market's implied equilibrium stock price using the Black–Scholes formula for close-of-market option prices on all listed options exchanges for the period 26 April 1973 to 30 June 1976 (approximately 37,000 observations). This price was compared with another estimate of the equilibrium price given by the actual observed stock price and the divergence between these two estimates of the unobservable equilibrium price calculated. If this divergence is related to future movements in stock price then there is a suggestion that option prices contain some information not contained in the observed price. Manaster and Rendleman find that a relationship does exist between these two variables but simulation of an *ex ante* trading rule suggested that this information was not sufficient to generate significant economic profits.

The methodology used by Manaster and Rendleman was adopted by Tucker [1987] for a study of the foreign exchange market using the implied exchange rates in comparison with the forward rate to derive a profitable trading strategy. The data base consisted of 608 observations of options for sterling, Deutschmark, Swiss franc, Japanese and yen over the period November 1983 to August 1984. The assumption of interest rate parity and the observed forward rate were incorporated into the calculation of the implied equilibrium exchange rate. This resulted in a trading rule which suggested that, when the implied spot rate is greater than the observed spot rate, then the currency options market assessment is that the forward rate is underpriced so that the currency should be bought forward. In a result similar to that obtained by Manaster and Rendleman, Tucker also found that, whilst the deviation between the observed and implied spot rates was a statistically significant determinant of future returns, this information was insufficient to generate significant economic profits.

Cavanaugh [1987] looked at the potential to use futures contracts prices to generate profits. The data represented daily changes in the logarithm of futures prices for delivery of currency on specific days. Fifteen series for the Canadian dollar and sterling were examined by Cavanaugh and he found evidence of serial correlation. Test of simulated trading strategies suggested that this dependence could have been exploited by members of the exchange to generate profits in excess of those obtained by a policy of buy and hold. Because of the higher costs of trading involved, it was also suggested that these opportunities for profit could not have been exploited by non-members.

Finally in this section we look at a study carried out by Elton, Gruber and Rentzler [1984] based on intra-day quotations for treasury bills (cash and futures) for the period 6 January 1976 through 22 December 1982. Elton *et al.* note that an investor can purchase an *N*-day treasury bill in either of two ways using the futures market:

(i) Purchase an *N*-day treasury bill in the cash market.
(ii) Purchase a (91 + *N*)-day treasury bill in the cash market and sell a treasury bill in the futures market for delivery in *N* days. Deliver the (91 + *N*)-day bill against the futures contract.

An efficient market implies that the returns on the two strategies should be the same after allowance for transaction costs. Three strategies are examined. First, there is the simple strategy of purchasing the lower-priced instrument. Second, an arbitrage strategy could be followed whereby the lower-priced instrument is purchased and this is financed by shorting the higher-priced instrument. The third strategy examined is a swap whereby holders of the higher-priced instrument liquidate their holdings and use the proceeds to purchase the lower-priced instrument. Elton *et al.* find that profits can be made from all three strategies, suggesting that the US treasury bill futures market is not perfectly efficient. Since the study does not depend on any assumptions concerning an equilibrium model, these are direct tests of efficiency rather than joint tests of efficiency and a particular equilibrium model.

13.6 Conclusion

We have surveyed the development of the financial futures markets in London and find that these markets have grown rapidly. The conditions for this rapid growth, i.e. the observed volatility of asset prices in the related cash markets, are likely to continue and use of these markets is therefore likely to grow both in volume and number of securities traded in the future as they offer traders some opportunity to hedge against adverse price movements. The question of the efficiency of these markets is, like the other markets surveyed, an open question. In this connection it is relevant that many of these markets are relatively new and that the operators may still be on a learning curve.

Chapter 14

Managing risk via the financial markets

14.1 Introduction

In this chapter we survey the various methods that are open to traders to manage risk. The risks we are concerned with arise in connection with unforeseen changes in exchange rates and interest rates. Quite obviously a rise in interest rates raises both costs to borrowers and also returns to lenders. Similarly, changes in exchange rates alter the domestic currency equivalent of foreign currency. This is easily demonstrated by reference to the sterling equivalent of $500,000 at exchange rates of $1.95 per £1 and $2.0 per £1. The sterling equivalent is £256,410 at the former rate but only £250,000 at the latter rate. Thus a person making a payment denominated in dollars benefits as sterling appreciates from $1.95 to $2.0 per £1 but the recipient of a payment denominated in dollars loses out. This causes problems for the traders. In a similar way changes in interest rates cause problems for the borrower and lender when these are made at floating rates of interest.

In this chapter we discuss how firms may attempt to manage this risk. This type of risk has increased in severity since the beginning of the 1970s owing to the increasing volatility of prices on security markets. This is demonstrated in figures 14.1 and 14.2, which show changes in volatility in representative exchange and interest rates since 1964. In the case of figure 14.1, exchange rate volatility for the $/£ exchange rate is represented by the annual standard deviation of percentage monthly changes. The picture shown before 1970 is one of relative stability, with the exception of the year 1967 when sterling was devalued. With the change from fixed to floating exchange rates at the beginning of the 1970s a step increase in volatility can be observed and this increase has persisted until 1990. Interest rate volatility is measured by the annual standard deviation of

Standard deviation

Note: Volatility = standard deviation of % monthly changes.
Source: ESRC Data Bank.

Figure 14.1   Exchange rate volatility: dollar/pound exchange rate, 1964–89

monthly changes. It seems inappropriate to use percentage changes when the level of the rate itself was subject to such a range of values and the cost/benefit to the trader depends on the absolute magnitude of the change. The changes themselves depicted in figure 14.2 are more volatile than those for exchange rates shown in figure 14.1, but generally interest rate volatility is more pronounced in the 1970s and 1980s than during the 1960s. This is particularly true of the late 1970s and early 1980s. The

Standard deviation

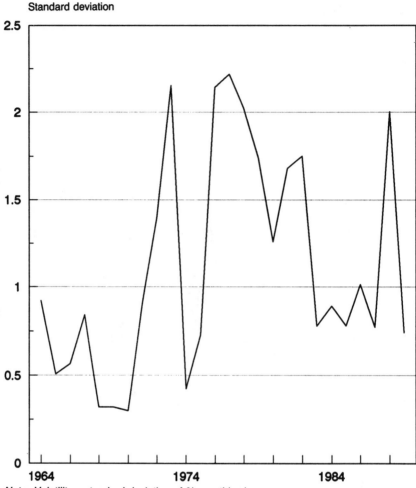

Note: Volatility = standard deviation of % monthly changes.
Source: ESRC Data Bank.

Figure 14.2   Interest rate volatility: treasury bill discount rate, 1964–89

general picture revealed by these two figures is, then, one of increasing volatility of exchange and interest rates, which in turn enhanced the uncertainties faced by firms.

In section 14.2 we discuss in more detail the precise nature of exchange and interest rate risk before proceeding in section 14.3 to discuss how firms can use internal methods of managing exchange rate risk. In section 14.4 we discuss external methods of managing exchange rate risk and in section 14.5 the management of interest rate risk. Our conclusions are presented in section 14.6.

14.2 Nature of risk

Exchange rate risk can arise in a number of different ways. First there is transaction risk, which arises because the exchange rate has changed between the date of the commitment and the date the payment is made or received. For the exporter, uncertainty is increased by the possibility of exchange rate changes if the commodity is invoiced in foreign currency and his costs are primarily defined in terms of domestic currency. A similar problem arises for importers, who find the domestic currency costs of their inputs denominated in foreign currency rising and falling in an unpredictable manner. This raises the possibility of unforeseen windfall losses or profits making foreign trade considerably more risky than domestic trade. It also makes it difficult for firms engaged in foreign trade to quote prices for fear of exchange rate changes altering costs.

It is important to define when this risk is incurred. It arises from the date the commitment is entered into. In the case of exports, this dates from the time the price quotation has been communicated to the purchaser. This may be a special quotation or it may date from the time a price list is circulated to actual or prospective customers. In a similar manner, for an importer the risk dates from the time he has communicated his acceptance of the purchase of the goods from the foreign company. It is also important to realise that, in the case when the trade is priced in one currency and payment is to be made in another, it is the currency in which the good is priced that is subject to exchange rate risk. If, for example, payment is to be made in dollars, then if both the domestic currency and that used as the unit of account move against the dollar in the same proportion, no extra exchange rate risk is involved.

The second type of exposure to exchange rate changes is defined as translation risk. This arises when it is necessary to value overseas assets and liabilities for their incorporation into a consolidated balance sheet. If a company has net surplus or deficit of assets defined in non-domestic currencies, then the balance sheet valuation will change as the relevant exchange rate alters. This particular exposure would not pose serious difficulties if the changes in the exchange rates were purely random around a relatively constant value. In fact, since the abandonment of fixed exchange rates in 1972, long swings in exchange rates have been observed. Again the nature of the commitment of the asset or liability is relevant. The translation exposure on a short-term liability or asset which is likely to be realised in the fairly near future (say one to five years) is similar to transaction exposure since its renewal might occur at the time of an unfavourable exchange rate. Therefore potential serious translation risk exists for the firm unless these risks are hedged. In contrast, permanent investment in subsidiaries can be treated as non-renewable and therefore imposes a much lower incidence of exposure, though this could be serious if the currency in which the asset/liability is priced has shown a long trend movement against the domestic currency.

The third type of exposure is economic exposure. In this case, changes in exchange rates alter the relative prices of exports and imports. Over time this can adversely affect the position of firms where exchange rates have moved against them or alternatively help those firms whose products are made relatively cheaper by the exchange rate change. This type of exposure is of a long-term nature and is brought about by changes in the volume of sales following a change in the exchange rate. One example of this type of exposure is the pricing of oil in dollars. If the domestic currency depreciates against the dollar, the price of oil rises, adversely affecting those companies whose products have a large oil component. It should be emphasised that the exchange rate which matters for international trade is the real exchange rate, which may be defined as the nominal rate corrected for price changes. Thus, if nominal rates always moved to correct differing rates of inflation in the countries concerned, then the dangers arising from economic exposure would be considerably reduced. In fact there is a considerable volume of evidence suggesting that purchasing power parity does not exist in the short run, so that changes in real exchange rates do occur. There is little a company can do to protect itself against this type of risk except to diversify its products and production centres.

The final type of risk can be termed hidden exposure. A firm may not be directly affected by exchange rate changes since its products may be sold entirely to domestic customers and its raw materials bought from domestic producers. Despite this concentration on the domestic market, the firm would be exposed to indirect transaction and economic risk via one of its suppliers. Similarly, exchange rate change may beneficially affect potential competitors from abroad. An alternative form of indirect exposure can arise from the operation of a subsidiary which is itself affected by exchange rate changes in a third market even if the currencies of the principal and its subsidiary are linked together by fixed exchange rates.

So far we have concentrated on exchange rate exposure, but interest rate exposure may be analysed in the same way. Transaction exposure occurs through changing interest payments or receipts following a change in the interest rate structure. Translation exposure can occur through changes in the value of financial assets held originating from changes in interest rates. This is particularly applicable to the position of investment institutions that hold large volumes of long-term financial securities. Economic exposure arises from changes in interest rates which affect the general business environment as well as having an impact on firms according to the degree of leverage, i.e. the proportion of capital raised by way of loans as distinct from equity finance. Thus a rise in interest rates will reduce consumer demand and therefore generally raise the cost of investment and impose costs on particular firms that have undertaken to raise finance by way of loans subject to interest rate adjustment.

In the following section we discuss how firms may reduce exchange rate exposure by methods internal to the firm and in section 14.3 the role of methods external to the firm.

14.3 Managing exchange rate risk: internal methods

A number of methods exist offering a means of managing exchange rate risk and which are internal to the firm. These include (i) doing nothing, (ii) forecasting exchange rate movements, (iii) invoicing or accepting invoices denominated only in domestic currency and (iv) operating a foreign currency bank account. In summary, the individual firm has a choice of doing nothing or hedging. The first option offers the lowest cost but the least protection against exchange rate exposure, whereas hedging offers the highest degree of protection but also the highest cost because of the number of transactions involved.

The first method of managing exchange rate risk is therefore to do nothing and accept the spot rate at the time the payment is made or received. Appeal to the efficient markets hypothesis suggests that the current spot rate may well be the best available forecast of the future spot rate. In this case the most profitable policy for the firm would be to rely on the future spot rate for conversion of the foreign currency. Two problems arise with this approach. First, there is a distinct possibility that the foreign exchange market does not conform to the efficient markets hypothesis and that therefore the current spot rate is not the 'best' forecast of future exchange rates. Second, the firm may value certainty or near certainty of the domestic currency equivalent of the foreign currency receipt or payment; in other words it may be risk-averse in this respect. To illustrate this point, a firm is able to plan its pricing policy if it knows in advance the sterling value of future imports and exports. This may well be preferable to a trading system that lowers the average domestic currency cost of imports and raises the average domestic currency receipts for exports if this policy involves relatively large gains and losses around the average. It is quite possible that the firm, in these circumstances, may place a higher value on certainty than on profitability in areas where it lacks expertise.

The policy of relying on the future spot rate to convert foreign currency into domestic currency is really nested in the second option, i.e. that of forecasting. In reality, doing nothing is equivalent to using the current spot rate as the optimal forecast of future spot exchange rares. It may, however, be the view of the firm that it can improve on the current spot rate as a predictor so that it forecasts the future pattern of spot exchange rates itself. The policy for the firm to manage exchange rate risk would then be to forecast and to choose between internal and external methods of managing the risk in the light of a comparison of its internal forecasts and the constellation of market spot rates, forward rates and option prices. In a similar manner the firm could speed up payments in foreign currency (or purchase of the foreign currency) when the domestic currency was expected to depreciate and retard conversion of foreign currency receipts into domestic currency. The converse behaviour would occur when the domestic currency was expected to appreciate. This overall strategy of forecasting would be consistent with the view that the foreign exchange market does not conform to the efficient markets hypothesis. Apart from the comments made above with respect to risk aversion, the strategy of forecasting the future pattern of exchange rates also suffers from the defect that it requires resources to develop the expertise necessary to provide accurate forecasts. The firm may feel that its available resources are more profitably directed towards its primary functions.

The third internal method is to require invoices to be denominated in domestic currency. In this case there is no exchange rate exposure as far as the transaction component is concerned. However, this exposure has not been eliminated but rather transferred to the foreign purchaser or supplier of the goods. It is also more than likely that the foreign purchaser of goods would not be willing to accept invoices denominated in the domestic currency of the supplier which, given the existence of competition, would be likely to cause loss of orders. In effect, transaction exposure has been changed into economic exposure.

The final internal method of managing exchange rate risk is to operate foreign currency bank accounts. As long as receipts and payments are in balance over a reasonable period of time, the exposure on receipts would match and offset the exposure on payments in a specific foreign currency. This type of account could also be allowed to run into deficit by way of an overdraft for a short period of time, provided this overdraft was eliminated by future receipts of that currency. This type of risk management has only a limited application since it does require receipts and payments of that currency to cancel each other out over a reasonably short period of time. A persistent balance, particularly a persistently growing balance (either in deficit or surplus), leaves the firm open to exchange rate exposure on both a transaction and a translation basis.

It was seen that internal methods offer the firm only limited scope to manage exchange rate risk, so we now turn to discussing the external methods open to the firm.

14.4 Managing exchange rate risk: external methods

In this section we discuss how a firm might manage exchange rate risk by having recourse to the financial institutions and markets. A number of such methods exist and these are the use of (i) the forward exchange market, (ii) temporary foreign currency loans and deposits, (iii) forfaiting, (iv) options and (v) back-to-back loans. We do not consider the use of currency futures because they seem to play a less important role in the management of exchange rate risk than in the case of other financial risks.

We discussed the forward exchange market in chapter 11 where it was seen that it is possible to purchase or sell foreign currency for delivery at a future date at a rate agreed at the time of the transaction. For example, if a trader was due to receive $500,000 in three months' time, he could sell the $500,000 forward for sterling, thus fixing the rate for conversion into sterling in three months' time. Clearly this method of managing risk provides the trader with certainty of the domestic currency equivalent of the foreign currency receipts or payments. For example, if the relevant forward rate was $1.9398 per £1, then the sterling value of the $500,000 is £257,758.53. Again it is worthwhile emphasising that the firm does not make a profit by trading in the forward exchange market. At the time of the conversion out of or into foreign currency the spot rate may be higher or lower than the agreed forward rate of $1.9398 per £1. In fact our survey of the empirical evidence on the efficiency of the forward rate as a predictor of the future spot rate suggests that the forward rate will deviate from the future spot rate because of the existence of a risk premium. In other words, the trader will on balance pay a premium to the provider of the forward exchange as a compensation for the transfer of risk. Thus the trader's gains arise purely from knowing what the rate will be, i.e. he has purchased certainty, which, in the case of the above example, means he is sure that he can convert the $500,000 into £257,758.53. Even here a caveat must be raised. The certainty is only obtained provided the second party (i.e. the person buying or selling the goods) does not default. If he fails to complete his part of the transaction, the original trader is left with a forward contract not matched by a future spot receipt or payment, so that he then has a foreign exchange rate exposure.

A further restriction on a straightforward contract is that it applies to a fixed date, whereas in many commercial transactions the precise date of receipt of or payment in foreign currency is uncertain. One way around this is to choose an option date forward contract. This provides the right to buy or sell foreign currency up to a particular date. The disadvantage with this type of purchase is that the bank will offer the contract at the rate most favourable to itself. Thus, for a contract to sell sterling for an option contract for three months forward, the bank would select the highest rate out of the spot and individual outright forward rates up to three months. Conversely, in the case of an option date forward contract for the bank to purchase sterling, it would apply the lowest of the relevant rates. The trader can mitigate the impact of the adverse (from his point of view) selection of rates by entering into overlapping option date forward contracts so that, for example, receipts of foreign currency expected in instalments over the next three months might be covered by an option forward contract for one month for a proportion of the total receipts and the balance by way of an option forward contract for two to three months. A further restriction may occur because the forward market for the desired currency is very thin or in the extreme non-existent. This may be overcome by exercising two forward contracts. In the case of a future receipt of a thinly traded currency, for example, it may be possible, given the importance of the dollar in international financial transactions, to (i) sell dollars forward for domestic currency and (ii) simultaneously buy dollars forward for the thinly traded currency. By this method the firm has achieved an indirect forward sale of the currency concerned.

A firm can use temporary foreign deposits and loans to achieve the same degree of protection against transaction exposure as is afforded by forward transactions. Reverting to the example of the future receipt of $500,000, the firm can achieve protection in the following manner:

(i)   Borrow $500,000 from a bank for three months at the time of entering into the contract leading to the receipt of dollars.
(ii)   Convert the dollars into sterling at the current spot exchange rate.
(iii) Deposit the sterling received in a three-month interest-bearing sterling deposit.

The dollar loan is then paid of by the $500,000 receipt in three months' time. The sterling equivalent of the $500,000 depends on the two interest rates (the dollar and the sterling deposit) and the spot exchange rate loan. Since all these rates are known, this strategy fixes the sterling equivalent of the future receipt of dollars. In the case of a payment of $500,000 by a firm, steps (i) to (iii) above are reversed, that is:

(i)   Borrow for three months the sterling equivalent of the quantity of dollars which will increase to $500,000 when invested. Alternatively the firm could use any spare cash holdings to finance step (ii).
(ii)   Convert the sterling into dollars at the current spot rate.

(iii) Invest the dollar receipts from (ii) above into a three-month interest-bearing dollar deposit.

On maturity of the deposit, the dollars are then used to make the dollar payment. In principle, the cost of using this type of strategy should be the same as using the forward exchange market since it is in effect equivalent to covered interest arbitrage discussed in chapter 11, and interest rate parity would imply that no profits can be made through moving funds between various centres.

The third method of avoiding transaction exposure is to use a technique known as forfaiting. This involves transferring the risk on to a bank by obtaining domestic currency from the bank in return for the transfer of the foreign currency debt to the bank. The most common types of debt instruments transferred are promissory notes and bills of exchange and the usual currencies are Deutschmarks and US dollars. The base interest rate for the transaction would be the relevant eurocurrency rate and, in addition, the bank would charge a commitment fee representing the delay between the agreement and the delivery of the instrument and the risk of exchange rate changes.

Options also offer a method of managing exchange rate risk. As noted in chapter 13, options give the purchaser, in return for a premium, the right to buy (a 'call' option) or the right to sell (a 'put' option) at an agreed exchange rate (the 'striking' price) at a specified date or dates. No obligation is imposed on the buyer to carry out the obligation, so he will choose to do so only if it is profitable for him. Remember, the exercise of an option lies entirely in the hands of the purchaser. The writer has no control over whether the option is exercised or not. As was demonstrated in chapter 13, an option contract is analogous to an insurance policy, with the premium for the option representing the premium paid for the policy and the risk insured is the downside risk of an adverse exchange rate movement, with the purchaser taking all the benefits of a favourable movement. Options are also particularly useful in the case of contingent exposures, for example in the case of a tender in foreign currency. If the firm does not win the contract, there is no need for the foreign currency and the option will be exercised only if it offers the chance of immediate profit because it is 'in the money'. Similarly, the firm may wish to take out options because the precise quantity of foreign exposure is not known, e.g. in the case of an uncertain volume of sales of goods abroad or alternatively in the case of domestic sales requiring imported raw materials. In such cases the firm can use options to provide a hedge against foreign currency exposure.

OTC options would be arranged as a private contract with a bank and offer the advantage that the conditions attached to the contract exactly match those required by the purchaser. In contrast, traded options are standardised and may not therefore match the precise quantity requirements of the purchaser. For example, the sterling options quoted on the Philadelphia Stock Exchange are denominated in units of £31,250. On the other hand, they offer the additional benefit of being able to be sold on the market rather than just being exercised or allowed to lapse. The suspension of currency options on LIFFE suggests that the disadvantage of standardised contracts outweighs the advantage of tradeability. Various option strategies are possible and we use the quotations for December delivery on the Philadelphia Stock Exchange at close of trade on 10 October 1990 listed in table 13.4 to illustrate these various strategies. This table is reproduced for the convenience of the reader.

In the case of options the trader has a choice of exercise rates. If he purchases, for example, a Dec call option with a strike price of $1.875 per £1, the premium is 9.33 cents implying a maximum price for the purchase of pounds of $1.9683 per £1 (1.875 + 0.0933). Thus the trader is sure that the minimum quantity of sterling obtained for a future receipt of $500,000 is £254,026.32. If the spot rate at the time of receipt of the dollars is less than $1.875, then the option will not be exercised and the trader will purchase the sterling in the market at the lower price but lose the option premium, Similarly at strike prices of $1.975 and $2.025 per £1, the maximum prices rise to $2.005 and $2.0406 respectively. In a similar manner, buying Dec put options with strike prices of $1.875, $1.975 and $2.025 per £1 fix the minimum price obtained by the sale of sterling at $1.8609, $1.9203 and $1.9356 respectively. It can be seen that the analogy to insurance is very close. The higher the premium paid, the greater the degree of protection against the downside risk of adverse changes in the spot exchange rate. This leaves the trader a choice of strategies in which

Table 14.1 *Philadelphia Stock Exchange £/$ options as at 10 October 1990: £31,250 (cents per £1)*

Strike price ($)	Calls				Puts			
	Oct	Nov	Dec	Mar	Oct	Nov	Dec	Mar
1.875	9.10	9.20	9.33	9.79	–	0.70	1.41	3.56
1.900	6.60	7.04	7.31	8.02	0.04	1.22	2.01	4.56
1.925	4.11	5.17	5.57	6.49	0.07	2.02	2.91	5.71
1.950	1.97	3.61	4.11	5.20	0.29	2.88	4.05	7.06
1.975	0.53	2.43	3.00	4.12	1.37	4.24	5.47	8.55
2.000	0.07	1.65	2.08	–	3.29	5.89	7.11	–
2.025	0.01	1.08	1.56	–	5.67	7.77	8.94	–

Source: *Financial Times*, 11 October 1990.

there is a trade-off between protection and cost. More complex strategies are discussed below.

One such strategy goes by the name of a vertical spread and involves the simultaneous purchase and sale of options with different exercise prices. In the case of a vertical bull call spread (so called because of the expectation of rises in the exchange rate), the trader would buy a call option with a strike price of say $1.975 per £1 at a premium of 3.0 cents and write (sell) a call with a higher strike price say $2.025 per £1 at a premium of 1.56 cents. Thus the premium income incurs a loss of 1.44 cents (3.0 − 1.56) or equivalently $0.0144. At a spot rate below $1.975 per £1, neither option is exercised and the trader's loss is 1.44 cents. At spot rates between $1.975 and $2.025, only the purchased call option is exercised so the trader benefits from the increasing profitability of this option. At the rate of $2.025 per £1 the trader's profit (compared with the spot rate) is at a maximum since thereafter any profit on the purchase of the call option is matched on a one-for-one basis by the loss on the option sold. At a spot rate of $2.025 per £1, the trader's profit (as compared with the spot rate) is given by the profit on the option purchased minus the loss on the premium, i.e.

$$(\$2.025 - \$1.975) - \$0.0144 = \$0.0356 \text{ or } 3.56 \text{ cents}$$

In this case the trader has given up the potential unlimited gain above a spot rate of $2.225 per £1 offered by a simple call option purchase with a strike price of $1.975 per £1 in return for a lower premium, i.e. 1.44 cents as against 3.0 cents. In terms of hedging, the trader has ensured a minimum sterling equivalent for, say, $500,000 of £251,332.06 {500,000/ (1.975 + 0.0144)} provided the spot exchange rate remains below $2.025 per £1. As the rate rises above $2.025 per £1, he is fully exposed to potential losses. A trader would use this strategy in the case where he thought that the exchange rate was likely to rise above the current spot rate but not by any great amount.

In an analogous manner a trader who believed that the spot rate was likely to fall from the current level but not to any great extent would buy a put again, say with a strike price of $1.975 per £1 (premium 5.47 cents) and sell a put with a lower strike price, say $1.950 per £1 (premium 4.05 cents). At an exchange rate greater than $1.975 per £1 neither option would be exercised and the trader's loss is limited to the premium deficiency of 1.42 cents per £1. At rates below $1.975 per £1 but above $1.950 per £1, only the put option purchased is exercised, and below $1.950 per £1 both options are exercised. Thus the trader's maximum profit at $1.950 per £1 is $0.0108 or 1.08 cents ($1.975 − $1.950 − $0.0142). Again the trader has given up the opportunity of obtaining an unlimited profit at rates below $1.950 per £1 in return for the lower premium of 1.08 cents per £1. In terms of hedging, the trader, who has to make a payment of $500,000, has ensured a maximum sterling cost of £254,556.56 provided the spot rate remains above $1.950 per £1 {500,000/ (1.975 − 0.0108)}. As the spot rate falls below $1.950 per £1, the trader is fully exposed to potential losses. This type of strategy is called a vertical bear spread.

The vertical spread strategy is also called a 'collar' because of the restricted range of protection compared with a traditional option. Note that this restricted range of protection is obtained through payment of a reduced premium. This type of trade can be gainfully used by either a hedger or a speculator. In the case of a hedger, it is no longer a pure hedge since the firm has taken a view on the likely direction and magnitude of future exchange rate movements. A diagrammatic presentation of profit/loss situations is shown in figure 14.3.

The concluding types of option trading strategies examined are concerned with volatility trading. These are (i) straddles, (ii) strangles and (iii) butterflies. In each case the operator takes a view on the likely course of movements in exchange rate volatility and backs this view by entering into an appropriate option strategy. For this reason these strategies are more likely to be adopted by speculators and writers of options than by firms using the market as a facility to hedge.

A straddle involves writing or purchasing a call and put option at the same strike price. In the case of a sale of straddle (sometimes called a short straddle) the writer could, for example, write (sell) a December call and a December put each with a strike price of $1.975 per £1. The combined premium received from the sale would be 8.47 cents per £1 (5.47 + 3.0). At the strike price (i.e. $1.975 per £1), neither option would

Figure 14.3   Profit and loss for vertical spreads

be exercised. At spot exchange rates below $1.975 per £1, only the put option would be exercised and the break-even point for the writer of the option occurs where the loss on this option is just matched by the combined premium receipts. This occurs at a spot exchange rate of $1.8903 per £1. In a similar way, as the spot exchange rate rises above $1.975 per £1, only the call option is exercised and the break-even rate is $2.0597 per £1 (i.e. $1.975 + $0.0847). Whilst the rate remains within the two bounds ($1.975 and $2.0597) the speculator will profit but otherwise faces unlimited loss. This type of trade is likely to be used by a speculator who believes that volatility is not likely to increase to any great extent, and it is often therefore called a bear straddle.

In contrast, a speculator who believes that volatility is likely to increase will buy a straddle (a 'long' or 'bull' straddle). In this he would purchase a call and put option for the same delivery date and strike price. Using the above example as an illustration, he could purchase a December call and put each with a strike price of $1.975 per £1. In this case he pays out the combined premium of 8.47 cents per £1 and this is his maximum loss. His profit is unlimited if the spot exchange rate rises above $2.0597 per £1 or falls below $1.8903 per £1. In both cases of long and short straddles, the speculator is forming a view not of the direction of the exchange rate movement but rather of its volatility or the likelihood of it moving beyond specified limits. The profit and loss situations for both types of straddle are shown in figure 14.4.

The second type of volatility strategy is a strangle. It is similar to a straddle, with the same underlying rationale, but two different strike prices are involved and this lengthens the area of maximum profitability in the case of a short straddle or maximum loss in the case of a long

Figure 14.4 Profit and loss for a straddle

Figure 14.5   Profit and loss for a strangle

straddle. In the case of a short strangle, the speculator could write a December call with a strike price of $2.000 per £1 (premium 2.08 cents) and a December put with a strike price of $1.950 per £1 (premium 4.05 cents). The combined premium income is 6.13 cents per £1 (2.08 + 4.05). At spot rates below $1.950 per £1 only the put option is exercised so that the break-even point is $1.8887 per £1 ($1.950 − $0.0613). Between rates of £1.950 and $2.000 per £1, neither option is exercised so the speculator earns a profit of 6.13 cents per £1. At rates above $2.000 per £1, only the call option is exercised and the break-even point is $2.0613 per £1 ($2.000 + $0.0613). The case of a long straddle can be illustrated by the same example but in this case the speculator purchases the two options. Consequently his maximum loss is given by the combined premium income, and positions of profit are given when the spot exchange rate either falls below $1.8887 per £1 or rises above $2.0613 per £1. A diagrammatic representation of the profit and loss situations for strangles is shown in figure 14.5.

The final option strategy considered is a butterfly. A butterfly strategy is also similar to a straddle, with the same underlying rationale of trading against movements in the volatility of exchange rates. In this strategy, however, a floor is provided for the maximum loss or a ceiling to the maximum gain. Purchase of a butterfly (a long butterfly) entails buying an out-of-the-money call, writing two at-the-money calls and buying an in-the-money call. As an illustration of this strategy the calls purchased could be:

	Strike price ($ per £1)	Premium (cents per £1)	When exercised spot rate ($/£)
In the money	1.925	5.57	>1.925
At the money	1.975	3.00	>1.975
Out of the money	2.025	1.56	>2.025

The combined premium income represents a net loss of 1.13 cents. At a spot rate below $1.925, no option is exercised so the maximum loss is the negative premium income, i.e. 1.13 cents per £1. Up to a spot rate of $1.975 per £1, only the in-the-money option is exercised, so the point of maximum gain is ($1.975 − $1.925 − £0.0113) per £1, i.e. $0.0387 per £1 or 3.87 cents per £1. At rates above $1.975 per £1 but below $2.025 per £1, the two at-the-money options (written) are exercised, so losses on these offset the profits gained on the in-the-money option purchased. The maximum loss occurs at a spot rate of $2.025 per £1 because after this point the out-of-the-money call is exercised. Consequently the gain on the two call options purchased is matched on a one-for-one basis by the loss on the two call options sold. The maximum loss is therefore the gain on the option with a strike price of $1.925 per £1 less the loss on the two options written with a strike price of $2.025 less the net premium deficiency {i.e. ($2.025 − $1.925) − 2($2.025 − $1.975) − $0.0113} per £1, i.e. $0.0113 per £1 or 1.13 cents per £1. Selling a butterfly (a short butterfly) would entail the reverse procedure, i.e. writing an in-the-money call, buying two at-the-money calls and writing an out-of-the-money call. The profit and loss situation would be precisely opposite to that illustrated for the above example, i.e. a maximum loss of 3.87 cents per £1 and a maximum profit of 1.13 cents per £1. The profits and losses for this situation are illustrated in figure 14.6. As noted above, the two figures illustrate the essential difference between a butterfly and a straddle; that is, the maximum loss or gain is restricted to a fixed amount.

One of the problems for traders suing options as a strategy to manage risk is that the premium has to be paid in advance, or 'up front' in the jargon. Partly in response to the reluctance to make payments up front, a number of variants have been developed in the OTC sector. These variants have been given a number of names according to the marketing strategy of the institution itself, but a generic title would be 'hidden premium' options. These are a sort of hybrid between normal forward contracts and options. The trader due to receive dollars would enter into a forward contract to purchase sterling, but one with a break point at which the trader could break out of the forward position and transact at the spot rate. No up-front premium is involved, as the cost would be

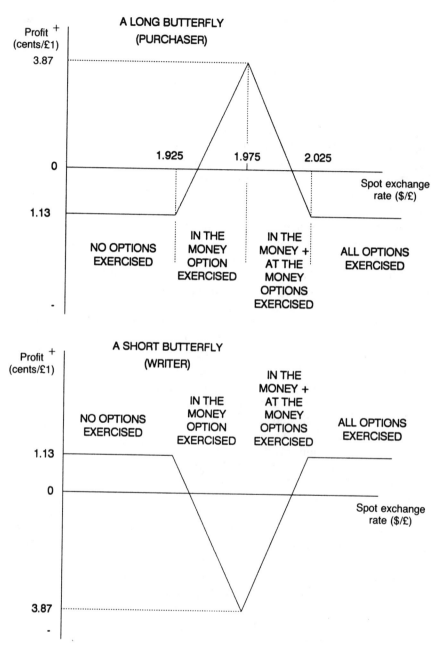

Figure 14.6   Profit and loss for a butterfly

incorporated into the forward rate. Clearly, in view of the added protection, the forward rate would be less advantageous than for a standard forward contract: a higher rate in the case of purchases of, or a lower rate in the case of sales of sterling. As an illustration, consider again the situation of the receipt of $500,000. The normal forward rate discussed earlier was assumed to be $1.9398 per £1. For the illustration of the principle behind hidden premium options, we assume that the rate for a forward contract with a break at $1.90 per £1 is $1.9980 per £1. This gives the trader the right to break the contract if the spot rate at the maturity of the contract is less than $1.90 per £1. If on maturity the spot rate was $1.80 per £1, the following transactions are implied, leaving the trader with net receipts of £264,870.14:

	£
Sale of $500,000 at the forward rate ($1.9980)	250,250.25
Purchase of $500,000 at the break rate ($1.90)	−263,157.89
Purchase of $500,000 at the spot rate ($1.80)	277,777.70
Net receipts	264,870.06

Note that by this strategy the trader has protected himself against the loss of falls in the spot rate against the forward rate *below* the break rate. At the same time the trader has protected himself against rises in the spot rate above the agreed forward rate. The protection strategy in the case of sale of sterling would be the mirror image of that discussed above for the purchase of sterling. The trader would enter into a contract with an enhanced forward rate but one which provided a break if the spot rate rose above a specified break rate.

The final method of using the market to hedge exchange rate risk is to arrange a back-to-back loan. Back-to-back loans can take two forms parallel loans or swaps. Multinational corporations use these types of loans for subsidiaries wishing to raise finance in foreign currencies. Assume there are two parent companies, one in the UK and one in the USA, each with a subsidiary in the country of the other parent company. The UK parent company lends in sterling to the subsidiary of the US company located in the UK and the US parent company lends in dollars to the subsidiary of the UK company located in the US. Thus each subsidiary company has a loan and cash denominated in the currency where it operates and has, therefore, avoided exchange rate exposure. If each parent company had borrowed in its domestic currency, it would then have to transform the loan into foreign currency for the use of its subsidiary and it would therefore be exposed to exchange rate risk.

Swap loans involve the exchange of debts denominated in different currencies. Thus a firm with easy access to the UK capital market may wish to finance an investment in the US. If it is possible for that firm to find a corresponding US firm which has easy access to the US capital market but wishes to finance a sterling investment, then both firms could gain by swapping their respective liabilities for repayment of the debt principal and interest payments. Such parallel and swap loans may be arranged through banks.

Finally we look at currency exchange agreements, which are in essence similar to swap loans. Returning to the example used to illustrate the parallel loan, the two parent companies would agree to lend to each other, the US company to the UK company in dollars and the UK company to the US company in sterling. These loans would then be passed on to their subsidiaries so that each subsidiary has a loan denominated in the desired currency. The repayment terms including any interest differentials would be agreed at the time of the original load, thus removing any exposure to subsequent exchange rate movements.

We now turn to examine strategies to manage interest rate risk.

14.5 Managing interest rate risk

We shall spend rather less time discussing interest rate risk, not because we regard this type of risk as being of less importance than exchange rate risk but rather because many of the strategies have already been discussed in the previous sections.

Internal methods of managing interest rate exposure take the form of doing nothing or forecasting, with all the inherent problems examined at the beginning of section 14.3.

External methods of managing risk include use of the futures market, of options and of interest swaps. In section 13.3 we illustrated the position of a company treasurer who wished to hedge against a rise in rates of interest by selling a financial futures short-term deposit. We also noted that the hedge may be less than perfect owing to a change in basis. We also emphasised that the hedger should sell futures if he was harmed by rising interest rates but buy futures if his position was adversely affected by falls in interest rates. As a second similar example, although not strictly an interest rate hedge, we consider the position of an investor due to receive a cash payment of £1 million on 1 July. On 1 May the investor is concerned that stock market prices will have risen, so he decides to protect himself by purchasing FT-SE 100 Index futures. These are priced at one-tenth of the value of the actual index during the day. Let us assume that the futures contract for September delivery is priced at 200. The tick (i.e. minimum price movement) is 0.05 and each tick has a value of £12.50, so the total number of contracts required is:

$$£1m \div [(200/0.05) \times 12.50] = 20 \text{ contracts}$$

On 1 July equity prices have risen so that the FT-SE Index stands at 2100. The investor will then be able to close out his futures transaction by selling the futures at 210 per contract at a total value of £1,050,000 (20 × [(210/0.05) × 12.5]) i.e. a profit of £50,000 compared with the purchase price of £1 million. This will offset – at least partially – the increased cost of the purchase of equities.

As was noted in table 13.2, a range of interest rate futures are provided, including domestic and foreign rates of interest, short and long-term rates. This offers a number of possible strategies to manage interest rate exposure. However, a single interest rate contract is likely to involve more than one instance of exposure. Thus a loan which is to be rolled over every three months for one year involves four instances of, rather than a single, risk. This can be covered by utilising a strip hedge, i.e. taking out sales of four futures contracts, one for each time the loan is to be rolled over. This may prove to be difficult if the market for distant futures is illiquid. An alternative strategy is to employ a rolling hedge. Successive hedges are obtained on the earliest interest rate revisions only. Another strategy is to take out a 'piled-up' hedge, in which futures amounting to a multiple of the loan would be taken out. Thus if the interest rate on the loan is to be reassessed four times, futures contracts equal to four times the loan would be sold. These contracts would be closed out and renewed at each of the reassessment dates. The advantage of piled-up hedges is that they avoid distant futures, but on the other hand they incur a large number of contracts and therefore commission charges.

OTC options are provided by some banks and LIFFE also offers options on interest rate futures on some of the most important contracts (see table 13.2 for details). This provides hedging opportunities in the same way as was discussed for exchange rate exposure in the previous section for fixing maximum and minimum rates of interest. However in this case it is important to note that options on futures guarantee maximum or minimum prices of the futures contract, but, unless exercised on the maturity date of the options contract, this does not guarantee a maximum or minimum rate of interest. This is because the futures price may diverge from that of the cash instrument owing to a change in basis, as was examined in chapter 13.

Finally in this section we discuss the nature of interest rate swaps. An interest rate swap entails the exchange by two parties of interest rate payments of a different character based on a notional principal amount. Three types of swap are probably the most important. These are coupon swaps, basis swaps and cross-currency interest rate swaps. We have already examined the third category in section 14.4 above and so we will now concentrate on the two remaining categories, which involve swaps denominated in the same currency. An example of the first type of swap is to exchange a floating interest rate loan for a fixed-rate one. This may be carried out to eliminate the risk of changes in interest rates. Note again that the benefit of this strategy is the subsitution of certainty for uncertainty. This swap may be carried out directly by the two liability holders or alternatively through a bank acting as an intermediary. In the latter case anonymity is preserved. A second type of interest rate swap is a basis swap, where a loan with interest rates based on one key rate is swapped for another loan based on an alternative key rate (e.g. a LIBOR rate for, say, a local authority rate). In both cases it may be possible for a borrower with a low credit rating to obtain a lower charge than would otherwise be the case.

14.6 Conclusion

We have examined a wide range of strategies for firms to manage exposure to risk. Since these risks have increased since the early 1960s it is not surprising that the number of instruments available to hedge risk has also increased. This is just one further example of financial innovation.

Chapter 15

The single European market in financial services and economic and monetary union

15.1 Introduction

The general principle of a single market for Europe was embodied in the Treaty of Rome in 1957. However, little was done over the 1960s and 1970s as the individual member states of the EC concentrated attention on their own domestic economic problems. The impetus for achieving the objective of a single market came in 1985 with the publication of an EC Commission White Paper *Completing the Internal Market*, promoted by the then Vice President of the Commission, Lord Cockfield. Momentum was achieved by setting a target date of 1992 for completion of the single market. To this end the White Paper detailed 300 measures designed to remove physical, technical and fiscal barriers to trade within the Community. The introduction of the principle of qualified majority voting in the EC Council on most issues, whereby no individual member state can veto a proposal, also helped to speed up the decision making process. This is illustrated by the passing of the Single European Act in 1987, soon after the White Paper.

The underlying objective for a single European market is to benefit consumers and producers by a variety of methods, but most importantly by reducing costs through the removal of non-tariff barriers to trade, increased competition and the ability to operate on a larger scale thereby obtaining the benefits of economies of scale. These developments should in turn promote greater efficiency of firms operating within the EC and thus strengthen their ability to compete in world markets, with the prospect of increased growth in EC economies.

In this chapter we will examine in section 15.2 the progress so far in achieving a single market in financial services. In section 15.3 we will discuss some of the likely effects of a single market in financial services for UK-based financial intermediaries. Finally in section 15.4 we will briefly consider the complementary developments towards achieving economic and monetary union within the EC.

15.2 A single European market in financial services

Progress has been slower in tackling barriers to trade in financial services compared to physical goods. This is despite the economic importance of financial services, which is estimated at 8 per cent of EC GDP (higher in the UK – see table 2.7). Also, given the important role of the financial system in encouraging and facilitating investment and hence economic growth, the removal of barriers to trade in financial services will have effects wider than those directly impinging on the financial services industry.

The main barriers to trade in financial services are:

(i)   market entrance requirements
(ii)   differences in prudential standards
(iii) differences in rules of market conduct.

In terms of (i) a basic right of establishment already exists in the EC for providers of financial services. That is, a firm from one EC member state can set up an operation in another EC member state and compete on an equal basis with other firms in that member state, provided they establish local offices in conformity with the rules and regulations of that member state. This falls short of a true single market and recent negotiations have been aimed at giving the right to firms to trade financial services throughout the EC on the basis of a single authorisation 'passport' from their home member state. To ease doubts about the completeness or rigour of home country regulatory regimes, attention is being directed at harmonising key prudential standards. This harmonisation aims to remove (a) host country concerns about the possible failure of foreign firms and (b) concerns about 'unlevel playing fields' whereby a firm operating in one member state but subject to lighter and therefore lower-cost regulation under its home member state regulations may obtain an unfair advantage in the market in which it operates.

The main headings under which financial services are being liberalised by EC legislation are collective investments, banking, investment services and insurance. We now consider the principal developments to date in each of these areas.

Collective investments
The EC directive harmonising the laws relating to the authorisation of Undertakings for Collective Investment in Transferable Securities

(UCITS), which for the UK refers to unit trusts, was implemented in 1989. Once authorised at home, UCITS will be free to market its units anywhere in the EC subject only to compliance with local marketing regulations.

Banking
The first attempt at harmonisation of banking across the EC was the First Banking Directive of 1977. This laid down minimum legal requirements for credit institutions to be authorised in member states and created a basic right of establishment. The Second Banking Directive, which obtained EC Parliamentary approval in November 1989, takes the harmonisation process considerably further. Rather than large-scale harmonisation, the aim of the Second Directive was to establish the minimum harmonisation of prudential standards to entitle a credit institution authorised in one member state to provide core banking services throughout the EC under the passport scheme, outlined above. The harmonisation standards roughly correspond to those set out in the Basle proposal discussed in chapter 17. The core banking services referred to are listed in table 15.1.

Investment services
The Second Banking Directive also covers securities trading by credit institutions. A complementary directive covering investment services by non-banks is also under discussion. This together with an associated directive for the minimum harmonisation of capital adequary standards would give investment firms a similar home country authorisation passport to the one implemented for banks.

Insurance
Progress has been slower in developing freedom to provide insurance on an EC-wide basis. Freedom of establishment was provided in 1973 for non-life insurance and 1979 for life insurance. Further progress has been difficult to achieve, with the main breakthrough being the Second Non-Life Insurance Directive, which was implemented in 1990. This provided freedom to provide cross-border insurance services for large commercial risks. Harmonisation of long-term business on the basis of the passport principle is taking longer to achieve because of considerable differences between member states in terms of taxation of savings, prudential supervision, group pension arrangements and social security systems.

A complementary Directive on the Liberalisation of Capital Movements, requiring the removal of all capital controls in the EC, was adopted in June 1988 and largely put into effect during 1990. The UK has of course been free of capital controls since 1979.

Table 15.1   *Second Banking Directive: Business Which is Integral to Banking and Shall be Included within the Scope of Mutual Recognition*

---

1.   Deposit taking and other forms of borrowing
2.   Lending – including: consumer credit
                                    mortgage lending
                                    factoring
                                    trade finance
3.   Financial leasing
4.   Money transmission services
5.   Issuing and administering means of payment (credit cards, travellers cheque and bankers draft)
6.   Guarantees and commitments
7.   Trading for own account or for account of customers in:
     (a)   Money market instruments (bills, CDs, etc.)
     (b)   Foreign exchange
     (c)   Financial futures and options
     (d)   Exchange and interest rate instruments
     (e)   Securities
8.   Participation in share issues and the provision of services related to such issues
9.   Money broking
10. Portfolio management and advice
11. Safekeeping of securities
12. Credit reference services
13. Safe custody services

Source: Annex to Second Banking Directive, European Commission, 1989.

15.3   Likely effects of the liberalisation of EC financial services

To examine the potential effects of a single market in financial services we draw upon the Cecchini Report [1988], published by the European Commission. The Cecchini Report's section on financial services is based on an analysis by Price Waterhouse. The methodology of the report was to make a comparison between the price charged for a particular service in one member state with the average of the four lowest member state prices. The member states considered were Belgium, France, Germany, Spain, Italy, Luxembourg, Netherlands and the UK. A selection of the results of the study are presented in table 15.2.

The Cecchini Report attempts to predict the effects of competition in financial services with the arrival of a single market by assuming that where prices are higher than the average of the four lowest then the price will fall by half the difference. Such assumptions are questionable for a number of reasons. First, the figures may not be based on a comparison

Table 15.2 *Percentage differences in the prices of standard financial products compared with the average of the four lowest national prices*

Service	Description of service	Belgium	Germany	Spain	France	Italy	Luxembourg	Netherlands	UK
Banking services									
Consumer credit	Annual cost to consumer of 500 ECU. Excess interest rate over money market rates	−41	136	39	n.a.	121	−26	31	121
Credit cards	Annual cost assuming 500 ECU debit. Excess interest rate over money market rates	79	60	26	−30	89	−12	43	16
Mortgages	Annual cost of home loan of 25,000 ECU. Excess interest rate over money market rates	31	57	118	78	−4	n.a.	−6	−20
Commercial loans	Annual cost (including commissions and charges) to a medium-size firm of a loan of 250,000 ECU	−5	6	19	−7	9	6	43	46
Insurance services									
Life insurance	Average annual cost of life insurance	78	5	37	33	83	66	−9	−30
Home insurance	Annual cost of fire and theft cover for house valued at 70,000 ECU with 20,000 ECU contents	−16	3	−4	39	81	57	17	90

Source: Cecchini Report [1988], Table 6.1.

of like with like; for example, a consumer loan in the UK may have a different default rate, and hence a different interest rate, when compared to a consumer loan in Spain. Similarly, when comparing insurance premiums, the variation in premium rates may reflect variations in expected claims. In other words, some variation in prices may be justifiable given the idiosyncratic nature of individual markets. Also, whilst it is likely that some business will flow to low-cost producers, assuming a competitive market emerges, this process may take some time to occur owing to, for example, price-insensitive consumers, cultural factors which favour the home producer and the costs involved in setting up a distribution network.

With these drawbacks in mind, the figures in table 15.2 provide some indication of where UK producers face competition or where they have scope for expansion into other EC countries. One area where UK consumers face high cost is consumer credit, where interest rates are approximately 9 per cent above money market rates. It should be noted though that building societies have entered into competition with banks in this market since the Price Waterhouse study was conducted, following liberalisation of building societies (discussed in chapter 5). In addition, with the four main countries of the EC at the high end of the credit price range it is doubtful that there will be much competition from other EC banks in the UK market. One area where the UK has a cost advantage is in mortgage lending. The Spanish mortgage market in particular offers the most scope to UK banks and building societies in their expansion into EC countries. However, the wide variation in legal and institutional arrangements for mortgage lending in EC countries may slow down any expansion.

The benefits of a single market in financial services are undermined by exchange rate fluctuations between EC member states' currencies which create uncertainty and therefore would inhibit cross-border trade. Moves towards economic and monetary union between member states and in particular to closer linkage of exchange rates through the Exchange Rate Mechanism can therefore be seen as complementary to the creation of a single market. It is to these developments we now turn.

15.4 European economic and monetary union

The Delors Report, prepared in 1989 by the Committee for the Study of Economic and Monetary Union, provides a broad framework for the transition towards monetary union in Europe. The report recommends three stages in a 'progressive realisation of economic and monetary union'. The first stage began in July 1990 and is aimed at accomplishing liberalisation of financial markets (in particular the removal of exchange controls), enlargement of the membership of the Exchange Rate Mechanism (ERM) of the European Monetary System (EMS) and a change in the mandate of the Committee of Central Bank Governors. The second stage envisages the establishment of a European System of Central Banks (ESCB) which would initially operate alongside the national monetary authorities. The third stage proposes the irrevocable fixing of exchange rates, with a possible replacement by a single currency and the transfer of monetary authority to the ESCB.

Stage one of the report has been largely implemented whilst the details of stage two and three are, at the time of writing, being discussed at an intergovernmental conference. In the next section we examine the nature of the ERM, which is at the heart of stage one of EMU. We then consider the nature of the European currency unit (ECU), in particular its relationship to the ERM. Finally we discuss the Delors proposals regarding stages two and three of EMU and consider some alternative proposals to these, in particular the proposal for an evolutionary stage two advocated by the UK government.

The Exchange Rate Mechanism (ERM)
The history of the ERM can be traced back to the breakdown of the Bretton Woods system of fixed exchange rates in 1971. Attempts were made to create a European successor to Bretton Woods with the establishment of the European currency 'Snake' in 1972. This arrangement was designed to narrow fluctuating margins between EC currencies. Sterling participated in the early months of the Snake but withdrew to follow a floating-rate regime. The Snake had mixed success, with other currencies withdrawing in its first years of operation leaving just five currencies participating in 1978. The Snake was replaced by the more durable ERM in March 1979. A number of realignments were undertaken in the early years of the ERM but there have been no general realignments since January 1987. The most recent entrants to the ERM are the Spanish peseta (June 1989) and sterling (October 1990). These two currencies are permitted fluctuations of up to 6 per cent around agreed central rates with other currencies, whilst the other currencies are allowed fluctuations of 2.25 per cent. The wider bands for the peseta and sterling are recognised as transitional. The only EC currencies which presently do not participate in the ERM are those of Greece and Portugal. The various relationships between participating currencies are set out in a parity grid which indicates the intervention obligations of the participating central banks. The parity grid following the entry of sterling (which remains in force until a realignment) is reproduced in table 15.3.

When a currency approaches its upper or lower limit in the parity grid then the appropriate central banks must buy or sell currency, with-

Table 15.3 *Bilateral central rates and selling and buying rates in the EMS Exchange Rate Mechanism from 8 October 1990*

		B.Fc/L.Fc. 100 =	D. Kr. 100 =	Fr. Fc. 100 =	DM 100 =	I£1 =	Lit 1,000 =	Fl 100 =	Pis 100 =	£1 =
Belgium/ Luxembourg: B.Fc/L.Fc.	S	–	553.000	628.970	2,109.50	56.5115	28.1930	1,872.15	33.6930	64.6050
	C	–	540.723	614.977	2,062.55	55.2545	27.5661	1,830.54	31.7316	60.8451
	B	–	528.700	601.295	2,016.55	54.0250	26.9530	1,789.85	29.8850	57.3035
Denmark: D.Kr.	S	18.9143	–	116.320	390.160	10.4511	5.21400	346.240	6.23100	11.9479
	C	18.4938	–	113.732	381.443	10.2186	5.09803	338.537	5.86837	11.2526
	B	18.0831	–	111.200	373.000	9.9913	4.98500	331.020	5.52600	10.5976
France: Fr.Fc.	S	16.6310	89.9250	–	343.050	9.18900	4.58450	304.440	5.47850	10.50550
	C	16.2608	87.9257	–	335.386	8.98480	4.48247	297.661	5.15981	9.89389
	B	15.8990	85.9700	–	327.920	8.78500	4.38300	291.040	4.85950	9.31800
Germany: DM	S	4.95900	26.8100	30.4950	–	2.74000	1.36700	90.7700	1.63300	3.13200
	C	4.84837	26.2162	29.8164	–	2.67894	1.33651	88.7526	1.53847	2.95000
	B	4.74000	25.6300	29.1500	–	2.61900	1.30650	86.7800	1.44900	2.77800
Ireland:	S	1.85100	10.00870	11.3830	38.1825	–	0.510246	33.8868	0.609772	1.16920
	C	1.80981	9.78604	11.1299	37.3281	–	0.498895	33.1293	0.574281	1.10118

Table 15.3 Continued

I£	B	1.76950	9.56830	10.8825	36.4964	—	0.487799	32.3939	0.540858	1.03710
Italy:	S	3,710.20	20,062.0	22,817.0	76,540.0	2,050.03	—	67,912.0	1,222.30	2,343.62
	C	3,627.64	19,615.4	22,309.1	74,821.7	2,004.43	—	66,405.3	1,151.11	2,207.25
Lit	B	3,546.90	19,179.0	21,813.0	73,157.0	1,959.84	—	64,928.0	1,084.10	2,078.79
Netherlands:	S	5.58700	30.2100	34.3600	115.2350	3.08700	1.54000	—	1.84050	3.52950
	C	5.46286	29.5389	33.5953	112.6730	3.01848	1.50590	—	1.73345	3.32389
Fl	B	5.34150	28.8825	32.8475	110.1675	2.95100	1.47250	—	1.63250	3.13050
Spain:	S	334.619	1,809.40	2,057.80	6,901.70	184.892	92.2400	6,125.30	—	203.600
	C	315.143	1,704.05	1,938.06	6,500.00	174.131	86.8726	5,768.83	—	191.750
Pis	B	296.802	1,604.90	1,825.30	6,121.70	163.997	81.8200	5,433.10	—	180.590
United Kingdom:	S	1.74510	9.43610	10.7320	35.9970	0.964240	0.481050	31.9450	0.553740	—
	C	1.64352	8.88687	10.1073	33.8984	0.908116	0.453053	30.0853	0.521514	—
£	B	1.54790	8.36970	9.5190	31.9280	0.855260	0.426690	28.3340	0.491160	—

Notes: S = Exchange rate at which the central bank of the country in the left-hand column will sell the currency identified in the row at the top of the table.

C = Bilateral central rate.

B = Exchange rate at which the central bank of the country in the left-hand column will buy the courrency identified in the now at the top of the table.

Source: Bank of England Quarterly Bulletin, November 1990.

out limit, to keep the exchange rate within the fluctuation limits. For example, the £/DM central rate was set at 2.95, implying upper and lower limits of 3.132 and 2.778 based on a permitted 6 per cent fluctuation either side. If the £ came close to reaching its lower limit then this would trigger the Bank of England to intervene to buy £s for DMs at the rate of 35.997 (i.e. its selling rate for the DM) and the Bundesbank to sell DMs for £s at the rate of 2.778. Of course, these upper and lower limits for the £/DM rate may only be reached as long as the £ does not reach its limits against any of the other currencies beforehand.

The aim of the ERM is to reduce exchange rate volatility between participating member currencies and to bring about convergence of inflation. The experience of the ERM countries since 1983 suggests that it has been largely successful in achieving these aims. The exact role of the ERM in achieving these aims has been the subject of much debate in the academic literature and the interested reader is referred to Haldane [1991] for a review of this literature.

European currency unit (ECU)
The ECU, first introduced in 1978, is a composite currency made up of all the national currencies of the EC. The amount of each currency in the composite is determined by reference to items such as share of that

Table 15.4   *The composition of the ECU*

Currency	Amount[a]	Weight[b] (%)
Deutschmark	0.6242	30.30
French franc	1.332	19.29
Sterling	0.08784	12.60
Lira	151.8	9.83
Dutch florin	0.2198	9.47
Belgian franc	3.431	7.78
Peseta	6.885	5.33
Danish krone	0.1967	2.51
Drachma	1.44	1.12
Irish punt	0.008552	1.11
Escudo	1.393	0.77
		100.00

Notes:
[a] These amounts have applied since September 1989.
[b] Weights based on exchange rates on 18 October 1990.
Source: Bank of England Quarterly Bulletin, November 1990.

country's currency in intra-EC trade and EC GDP. The amounts are normally revised every five years, with the last revision taking place in September 1989. At 18 October 1990 the Deutschmark had a weight of around 30 per cent and sterling around 12 per cent; however, even with unchanged amounts, the weights of the currencies will constantly change as the currencies strengthen or weaken against each other (see table 15.4).

The ECU is the basis of a divergence indicator for the ERM. Each currency in the European Monetary System (EMS), that is, the ERM currencies plus the Greek drachma and the Portugese escudo, have a central rate against the ECU (shown in table 15.5). The divergence indicator compares an ERM currency's market rate against the ECU with its ECU central rate, expressing the difference as a proportion of its maximum divergence spread (MDS). The MDS is the maximum percentage divergence of a currency from its ECU central rate before it reaches its bilateral limit against other currencies in the ERM. An MDS of 75 per cent is used as a threshold for action to correct the divergence, although in practice it is possible for a currency to reach its bilateral limit without crossing the 75 per cent MDS threshold.

EMU after stage one
It was mentioned above that stage one of EMU came into effect in July 1990. Progress after stage one is, at the time of writing, more uncertain, with the detail and timing of arrangements being discussed at an inter-governmental conference. The target date for stage two has, however, been set for 1 January 1994. The Delors proposals regarding stage two

Table 15.5 *ECU central rates of EMS currencies*

Currency	
Deutschmark	2.05586
French franc	6.89509
Sterling	0.696904
Lira	1,538.24
Dutch florin	2.31643
Belgian franc	42.4032
Peseta	133.631
Danish krone	7.84195
Irish punt	0.767417

Source: *Bank of England Quarterly Bulletin*, November 1990.

were for closer cooperation of economic and monetary policy between member stages. However, the details of stage two were not formulated clearly in the Delors Report and the handing over of responsibility for monetary policy in EC member states to the new European Central Bank was not scheduled to occur until stage three.

The lack of detail in the Delors Report about stages two and three has led to a number of proposals aimed at either providing the details or putting forward alternative schemes to the Delors plan. For example, Giovannini [1990] argues that the Delors plan does not rule out exchange rate realignments during stage two, and goes on to state that instability in foreign exchange markets may lead governments to realign, which would lead to a 'de facto dismemberment of the zone of monetary stability provided by the EMS'. He therefore suggests that, to achieve credibility during the transition to full monetary union, pressures in the foreign exchange markets should be met by an acceleration to full monetary union rather than realignment. This, it is argued, would give credibility to the fixed bilateral parities during the transition. At the same time, the European Central Bank should begin operating in stage two through the agencies of the Exchange Rate Stabilisation Authority – with responsibility for bilateral exchange rate intervention – and the Board of Central Bank Governors – acting as a consultative body to national central banks to coordinate monetary policy.

Detailed proposals on the structure and operation of the European Central Bank (ECB) have come from the Board of Central Bank Governors (see Lomax [1991] for further discussion), the proposed ECB will be an independent institution, 'owned' by the national central banks, with the national central bank governors sitting on its governing council. The national central banks will act as the administrative arms of the ECB. It is clear from this that the national central banks will have to be independent of their national governments. We discussed in chapter 3 the issue of greater independence for the Bank of England. The decision of the UK government to join the ERM, and therefore to maintain the exchange rate within the fluctuation limits against other ERM currencies, means that the government's freedom of manoeuvre on setting interest rates has been reduced. That is, financial policy determination is already partly independent of government. If the ECB is finally established, then the government will have to pass legislation to make the Bank of England independent of government. There is therefore greater pressure than ever before to make the Bank of England independent. Even under the UK government's own proposals for an evolutionary stage two, discussed below, an independent institution having influence over UK monetary policy is envisaged.

The UK government rejects the Delors proposals for stages two and three (see HM Treasury [1989] and [1990]). It argues that full monetary union implies the same interest rates in each member state and therefore a precondition to full monetary union is economic convergence. However, there are clearly structural differences between the economies of the EC countries and it will take some time to achieve economic convergence. The UK government therefore argues that a more practical way forward after stage one is to adopt an evolutionary approach to monetary union. The two principal elements of the UK proposals are for a new currency, the Hard Ecu, and a new European institution, the European Monetary Fund (EMF). The Hard Ecu differs from the ECU described in the previous section in that it would be not an average currency but a new thirteenth currency in the ERM. The Hard Ecu though would be the strongest currency in the ERM by virtue of the feature that its central ERM parity could never be devalued against any other ERM currency. It is argued that this strength would make it an attractive currency to hold. The value of the Hard Ecu would be guaranteed by the EMF, which in turn would be controlled by the various national central banks. Now, the Delors report rejected the idea of a parallel currency on the grounds that this would lead to new monetary creation. A particular feature of the Hard Ecu proposal, however, is that each national bank is obliged to maintain the Hard Ecu value of any holdings of its own currency. So that as (i) the Hard Ecu became an increasingly attractive currency to hold and (ii) the EMF accumulated holdings of weaker national currencies as it exchanged them for Hard Ecus, then the EMF would have the right to require the repurchase of national currencies by the issuing central bank. This, it is argued, would meet the above criticism of a conventional parallel currency. The EMF would be required to (i) manage Hard Ecu interest rates and (ii) bring downward pressure on inflation. As holdings of Hard Ecus built up in the EC, then the actions of the EMF would have an increasing impact on national monetary authorities, who would have to respond to the actions of the EMF. For example, if Hard Ecu interest rates were raised, causing a flow of funds into Hard Ecus and out of national currencies, the obligation to repurchase national currencies would put pressure on national authorities to raise their national interest rates. Thus the key idea behind the UK proposals is that the market would dictate the move towards the replacement of national currencies with Hard Ecus and hence the extent of the influence of the EMF on national monetary authorities. It should also be noted that the supranational EMF would begin operating in stage two (compared with the European Central Bank which in the Delors plan does not take over responsibility for monetary control until stage three). An interesting feature of the UK proposals is that the EMF institution is an independent body which would have an increasing amount of influence over UK monetary policy. This appears to be in conflict with the UK government's previous position on the independence of the Bank of England.

15.5 Conclusion

In this chapter we have briefly summarised the main developments in the move towards greater integration amongst EC countries in terms of trade in financial services and economic and monetary union. The final outcome of these developments is uncertain, as at the time of writing the timing and extent of the moves towards integration are uncertain. What is clear, though, is that, given the momentum for change and the changes already agreed, a greater degree of European integration is inevitable.

Chapter 16

The efficiency of the UK financial system

16.1 Introduction

The criticisms against the UK financial system are generally based on the following rationale. Growth of UK GNP has been less than that of many other countries during the post-1945 period. Over this period gross domestic capital formation has been lower in the UK than in other countries and this has caused the lower rate of growth of GNP. In turn this lower level of investment has been caused by deficiencies in the UK financial system. Complaints have focussed on the excessive amount of resources devoted to speculation on secondary markets, inadequate provision of funds for investment, excessive cost of capital, and short termism, i.e. excessive concentration on the short term as opposed to the long term. Such criticisms have come from a wide range of sources, not just the left in political terms. For example, a Conservative chancellor referred to market operators as 'teenaged scribblers'. Nevertheless these arguments appear to be rather tenuous in the absence of other confirmatory evidence. It is factual to note that both the rate of growth and also the level of investment have been lower than those observed in many other continental countries. This, as any student of statistics knows, does not of necessity indicate a causal relationship flowing from the lower level of investment to the lower rate of growth. It could be plausible to argue that the lower rate of growth in the UK has led to ('caused'?) the lower level of investment or that they were both caused by a third variable. Similarly it is a large step to assume that, in the absence of other confirmatory evidence, the lower level of investment has been caused by deficiencies in the financial system. Equally it is true to add that additional evidence may well support these criticisms.

It is as well at this stage to remind the reader of the functions of the financial system discussed in chapter 1. These are the provision of (i) a payments mechanism, (ii) a mechanism for financial intermediation between surplus and deficit units, (iii) primary and secondary markets so that portfolio holders can adjust their portfolios and (iv) various financial services such as foreign exchange, pension provision, insurance, etc. As can be seen from the opening remarks, most of the complaints have centred on functions (ii) to (iv) rather than on the provision of the payments mechanism. Consequently we concentrate on these aspects of the financial system in the following assessment though, in view of the large volume of literature on this topic, we are able only to indicate the main themes of the various arguments. In section 16.2 we will examine the efficiency of the the various markets and in section 16.3 discuss the nature of short termism, which is perhaps the most consistent criticism raised. In section 16.4 we return to other potential deficiencies within the UK economy which may have resulted in the slower rate of growth, and we present our conclusions in section 16.5.

16.2   Efficiency of the financial system

In chapter 7 we reviewed the various meanings of the word 'efficiency' as applied to financial markets. These were (i) allocative efficiency, (ii) operational efficiency and (iii) informational efficiency.

Allocative efficiency
Allocative efficiency is a broad concept and is likely to be achieved provided the market is giving out correct signals (i.e. that informational efficiency is achieved) and that incentives exist to follow the direction of these signals. There is just one proviso to this statement and this concerns the possibility that certain types of undertakings may not be able to obtain finance owing to gaps in the market.

   The proposition that it is difficult for entrepreneurs to obtain small amounts of capital to finance the start-up of a company or to expand it in its early years is of long standing. In 1931 the Macmillan Committee on Finance and Industry brought attention to such a gap in the provision of finance (the 'Macmillan Gap') and as a consequence the forerunner of the 3i Group (previously Investors In Industry – owned by the clearing banks and the Bank of England) was established in 1945. In 1971, the Bolton Committee in its report highlighted both an 'equity gap' in terms of raising long-term finance below £250,000 (£1 million in current price terms) and an information gap where small firms were unaware of sources of finance or could not present a reasoned request for finance. The Wilson Committee also reported on the financial problems of small companies in 1979 and also highlighted the information gap and commented on the difficulties for small firms in obtaining venture capital (i.e. for high-risk ventures with little track record). Over the 1980s there were a number of developments which have gone some way to closing the finance and information gaps identified. What follows is a brief summary of these developments – more detailed surveys can be found in *Bank of England Quarterly Bulletin*, (February 1990) and Boocock [1990].

With regard to the information gap, the Department of Trade and Industry has set up a number of Small Firm Information Centres, providing free information and advice. In addition, a number of Regional Development Agencies and other specialised agencies have been established which also provide advice. There has also been a growth in venture capital providers which provide equity and other forms of long-term capital to small/medium firms at both the early stages of development (e.g. seed capital) and later stages (e.g. expansion, management buy-outs/ins. Institutions offering this type of financing can be divided into two broad groups: first, captive funds, which are subsidiaries of the major UK pension funds, insurance companies and banks and obtain their finance from the parent company; second, independent funds, which raise capital for investment from a wide variety of sources, including private investors and some financial institutions. In 1988 the independents accounted for approximately 66 per cent of the amount invested by venture capital funds, with captive funds accounting for most of the rest. The distinction between captive and independent is not so clearcut though, with most independent funds having some links with financial institutions and captive funds having some degree of independence.

The finance provided by the venture capital industry substantially increased over the 1980s so that in 1988 over £1 billion was invested. However, there was a change in the nature of the finance provided over this period, illustrated in table 16.1. There was an increasing emphasis on financing buy-outs, buy-ins and acquisitions at the expense of start-up and other early-stage financing. UK corporate restructuring over the latter half of the 1980s led to the sale of non-core businesses by many diversified companies as they reverted to core activities. These sales were often to incumbent management (management buy-out) and financed by venture capital funds. This type of financing was attractive to venture capital funds as it was less risky than the traditional investment and usually offered a quicker exit route (i.e. realisation of the fund's investment) through a trade sale or flotation.

Two government initiatives in the early 1980s also addressed the funding gap for small companies. The first was the Loan Guarantee Scheme (LGS), which was introduced in 1981 following a recommendation of the Wilson Committee. The aim of this initiative is to encourage banks and some other credit institutions to supply medium-term (two

Table 16.1   *UK venture capital financing by financing stage, 1984–88 (% of total invested)*

Financing stage	1984	1985	1986	1987	1988
Start-up	17	13	16	8	5
Other early-stage	10	6	7	4	2
Expansion	39	36	27	22	27
Buy-out/in & acquisition[a]	28	38	44	63	62
Secondary purchase[b]	5	6	5	3	4
Other	1	1	1		
Total (£m)	228	279	396	795	1,006

Notes:
[a] Buy-out/in – the purchase of an existing company as a going concern.
[b] Secondary purchase – the acquisition of existing shares in a company from another venture capital firm or other shareholders.
Source: *Bank of England Quarterly Bulletin*, February, 1990.

to seven years) loan finance, up to a maximum of £100,000, where the risks involved would normally mean the loan request is rejected. The government guarantees 70 per cent of any loan approved and the borrower pays a premium on top of the normal interest rate. The scheme was extended indefinitely following a review by the government in 1989. This suggests that the government perceives there is a funding gap requiring a scheme of this sort. The scheme has been criticised, though, as it provides loan finance, whereas equity risk capital is considered more appropriate for small growing companies.

The second government initiative was the Business Expansion Scheme (BES) introduced in the 1983 Finance Act. This is designed to attract investors to provide equity finance to non-quoted companies, by giving tax relief to investors at the marginal rate paid for amounts up to £40,000 per annum. This tax relief is to compensate investors for the extra risks involved. Most finance of this sort is obtained by companies making a direct issue of shares to the public. The advantage to the company is that investors cannot sell shares purchased under the scheme before five years have elapsed without losing the tax relief. BES funding can be used for a variety of activities and it is believed that investors' preferences have increasingly moved away from venture capital type funding, so that in 1988 only 2 per cent of venture capital funding came from this source compared to 20 per cent in 1984.

Despite the developments in funding for small business over the 1980s and in particular the growth in venture capital providers, it is still widely believed that there exists an equity gap for amounts below £100,000.

There is also some evidence to suggest that a gap exists in second-stage equity funding for amounts between £100,000 to £250,000.

Operational efficiency
It is difficult to obtain hard evidence concerning operational efficiency, but what we can obtain is indirect evidence from the structure of the financial system and also the cost of capital. In a competitive system we would expect to see inefficiencies competed away and, in the long run, profits to be 'normal', reflecting the degree of risk involved in the industry. As we have seen in earlier chapters, the UK financial system has certainly been subject to a large degree of liberalisation in areas of pricing and range of business conducted. To take just a few examples, in recent years we have seen the relaxation of controls over the banking industry, and the death of some cartels, such as Big Bang on the stock exchange removing fixed commissions and opening up the exchange to a greater degree of competition. The building societies' interest rate cartel has also ended and, as a consequence, the mortgage market is now a 'competitive price-driven' market. The incidence of competition has increased not only in the domestic context but also on an international scale. The abolition of exchange controls allows residents to invest overseas without restraint. As we have seen in chapter 4, a large number of foreign banks now operate in London. Consequently it would be reasonable to expect that the increased competitive environment would have led to a greater degree of efficiency.

We certainly have seen a fairly high degree of financial innovation, i.e. the development of new markets and financial instruments. In chapter 13 we discussed the development in London of a major new financial market, namely the London International Financial Futures and Options Exchange (formerly called LIFFE). The increased volume of trading on this market noted in chapter 13 indicates a successful development. New instruments have been developed and extended, such as in the commercial paper market, together with all those available to manage risk as indicated in chapter 13. Nevertheless, critics have pointed to the volume of trading carried out on the major markets and in particular the stock exchange and the foreign exchange market. With reference to the stock exchange, we noted in table 8.1 the low proportion of funds raised by firms through new issues of equity and debentures and the consequent importance of internally generated funds as a source of business finance.

One other aspect of the operational efficiency of markets concerns the cost of capital. A number of commentators have argued that the cost of capital is higher in countries such as the UK and US compared with other countries such as Germany but in particular Japan. Perhaps one of the most recent and widely quoted studies was that carried out by McCauley and Zimmer [1989], which claimed that the real cost of funds after tax was some 3 per cent higher in the UK than in Germany and Japan. The main reasons given for this difference are (i) higher saving ratios, and (ii) lower risk premia. These reasons are not unambiguous with respect to their theoretical underpinning. If real returns on savings are lower in some countries, then, given the current level of globalisation of the nature of finance, it would be expected that international arbitrage would lead to funds moving out of countries with a lower rate of return in favour of centres with higher real rates of return. This would tend to lead to real rates of return being equalised across international centres. The second reason put forward suggests that high levels of inflation lead to volatility of nominal returns and a higher risk premium. Marsh [1990] suggests that examination of the gap between the risk-free return and the return on equities shows that risk premia were higher in Japan than in the UK. This is supported also by the fact that the standard deviation of stock market returns was higher in Japan than in other countries. Marsh also argues that McCauley and Zimmer have used an inappropriate measure of the cost of equity capital in their study, i.e. the inverse of the price/earnings ratio, which is inappropriate because it makes no allowance for future growth potential. The correct measure is the risk-free real rate of interest plus a premium for investing in equities. However, a contrary argument must also be raised at this juncture. High nominal rates of interest can cause cash flow problems, particularly for firms with high gearing. It could be claimed that nominal interest rate stability permits firms to utilise a more highly geared capital structure, with its cost advantage, without the danger of a financial crisis owing to restrictive monetary policy. Clearly this has not been the case for UK firms during periods of high nominal interest rates (to take just one example, Brent Walker in 1990). All in all it seems that cost of capital may well be higher in the UK than in other countries but that the extent of the margin has been exaggerated. Furthermore, any higher cost due to higher nominal rates of interest must be the responsibility of the government for permitting higher and more volatile rates of inflation rather than of the financial system.

One final criticism concerns the response of the financial system to firms in difficulty. It is often claimed that the financial institutions are too keen to foreclose on debt rather than allow sufficient time for a firm to recover its former position of financial strength. This is, of course, the classic dilemma for banks. Do they force the firm into bankruptcy and accept the loss without a chance to recoup their losses or do they lend additional funds, thus incurring additional risk, in the hope of obtaining repayment of all lending eventually? The criticism suggests that the banks and other lenders often follow the first course of action. There appears to be some force in this argument since the Bank of England has been negotiating with the commercial banks to produce an agreed procedure in the event of a company with a liquidity crisis. Basically the approach is to provide funds for the company to keep it afloat until such time as a considered judgement can be made about its long-term future. The funds are to be provided by the lending banks in proportion to their existing exposure. A lead bank is to be identified to keep the other creditors informed. This is necessary because of the large number of banks often lending to a single firm. For example, in the case of the troubled Goodman International empire in Ireland, it was reported that thirty-three different banks were involved in lending the equivalent of £500 million. The lead bank is likely to be the bank with the largest exposure. Finally, in this interval all other lending to the company should be suspended.

Informational efficiency

It has been argued that excessive amounts of resources have been devoted to speculation as distinct from the raising of capital. A similar objection could be raised against the operation of the foreign exchange market, where the daily volume of trading dwarfs any requirement to finance UK overseas trade. The counter-argument is that the speculators are necessary to ensure that prices of the various securities reflect all available information. The aim of the speculator is to make a profit. He does this by identifying securities which are incorrectly priced in the market and purchasing those which are identified as under-priced and selling those identified as over-priced. In this manner the speculator contributes to market efficiency in the informational sense. Correct decision making will reward the speculator and, in the same way, the inefficient speculator who makes wrong decisions will be penalised. A 'Darwinian' process will ensure the survival of efficient speculators at the expense of the inefficient ones. Speculation will, therefore, be stabilising. However, it is of course perfectly possible to argue that the process is not as efficient as that described above. Whilst persistently inefficient speculators must leave the market through shortages of finance, it is quite possible (though improbable over a long period) that successive waves of inefficient speculators will appear on the market leading to the existence of destabilising speculation.

A second criticism arising from the relative volume of speculative activity on financial markets points to the likelihood of increased volatility of market prices. It is quite probable that this increased volatility may have detracted from the efficiency of the market mechanism by obscuring the price signals given out by the market. Some casual empirical support for an adverse effect of market volatility on business operation is given by the rapid growth of hedging instruments such as financial futures since

1980. However, the real test of these criticisms must be whether the market conforms to the efficient markets hypothesis or not. Clearly no market can be absolutely efficient in the sense that market prices always fully reflect all available information. The acid test is more sensibly one of examining whether market prices usually reflect all available information so that the market approximates to the efficient markets hypothesis. In this connection we examined the efficiency of the stock market (chapter 8), the bond market (chapter 9), the foreign exchange market (chapter 11) and the financial futures market (chapter 13). Our conclusions were not decisive in either direction, but it is certainly true to say that no conclusive evidence was presented against market efficiency in the informational sense.

A second aspect of informational efficiency concerns the advice given by City analysts about the advisability of purchasing equity in a company. In this connection the *Observer* (28 October 1990) provided an interesting commentary on analysts' reports on Polly Peck, which foundered in the autumn of 1990. Throughout 1990 a considerable number of analysts were recommending the purchase of Polly Peck shares on the ground that the shares were undervalued. At least ten analysts were quoted as re-commending the purchase and some with a repetition of a buy and hold strategy even as late as September. It is patently obvious that the advice was ill founded and this may raise doubts on this aspect of the City's work. This, incidentally, adds additional support to the efficient markets hypothesis, since, at least in this case, market experts failed to beat the market.

We now turn to discuss short termism, which is perhaps the main thrust of common criticism of the UK financial system.

16.3 Short termism

In general terms, short termism can be defined as a climate in which companies concentrate on short-term profits rather than long-term investment. Associated with the concept of short termism is the view that the financial system suffers from myopia. One aspect of this view on short termism is the belief that the takeover mechanism contributes to companies concentrating on short-term issues because of the necessity of having to look continually over their shoulders, as it were, to identify possible predators. This is particularly true in times of falling share prices. This is largely a consequence of the type of financial system that exists in the UK. As we saw in chapter 2, the financial systems in the UK and US can be broadly categorised as market based. Thus financial markets play an important role both in terms of raising long-term capital and in changing corporate control. In bank-based financial systems such as those of Germany and Japan, in contrast, the banks play a greater role in providing external finance. The finance provided by banks consists of loans and equity, so that the banks often take a more active role in the running of the companies they finance. In particular they will often initiate changes in management and sometimes ownership. However, such changes are carried out without hostile confrontation.

Certainly it is true that expenditure on takeovers has increased over the last ten years, but the question remains whether or not this will have encouraged the growth of short termism. The role of the financial system in mergers and acquisitions is highlighted by the advisory fees earned both from the predators and the victims. The fact that such fees add to a bank's profitability without incurring any of the balance sheet restraints imposed through prudential control provides an additional stimulus for banks to engage in this type of business. A counter-argument would suggest that takeovers are part of the discipline of the market and are necessary to provide a spur for the stimulation of efficiency and the removal of inefficient managements. However, the discipline is rather a blunt instrument which may threaten efficient as well as inefficient companies.

Protagonists of the view that the financial system is responsible for short termism suggest that the equity of a company is subject to a dual valuation situation. First, there is what may be called the normal valuation, when the price of equity reflects the marginal trading in company shares between portfolio investors. There is, however, a second valuation which occurs when a potential bidder is attempting to acquire control of a business so is bidding for the whole of the company's equity. In this case the share price will rise above the normal price and the difference between the two prices is the bid premium. This provides an incentive for shareholders, particularly the institutions, to accept the bid because it is unlikely that the share price will continue to remain at that level in the absence of the predator. The source of the bid premium can be construed to be the increased efficiency with which the firm taken over is managed or alternatively increased economies of scale attributable to the integration of the firm into the predator's operations. An alternative view of the source of the premia is, however, that they represent the anticipated profit through asset stripping, including sale of assets, and perhaps the acquisition of pension fund surpluses. In this case the bid premia represent a transfer from the other stakeholders in the firm such as employees to the predator company without conferring any benefit to the economy as a whole.

In the UK the investment institutions dominate holdings of equities in companies, so it is their decisions which matter as far as the success of takeovers are concerned. In this connection it is important to note that the institutions have incentives to accept takeover offers for reasons other than that described above. Fund managers prepare statistics every quarter and therefore have an additional incentive to accept bids for companies whose shares are held in their portfolios to boost the quarterly performance of the fund that they manage. This also raises the question of their commitment to the company whose securities are held in their portfolios. In general they seem quite reluctant to become involved in the management of these firms, possibly owing to a lack of expertise. A second possible reason is that the possession of detailed knowledge of any firms would make it more difficult for them to deal in their securities for fear of falling foul of insider trading legislation. A further reason for a 'hands off' approach to the management of the companies is the number of different funds which are likely to hold the equity of any one individual company. This general situation is contrasted with the position of other countries where the banks provide a major source of funds for industrial and commercial companies. It appears that these banks are more firmly committed to their clients and are represented in top management and have, therefore, a voice in the firms' policy making process. However, changes may be taking place in the UK financial system. A number of insurance companies and issuing houses are trying to devise a new form of intermediary operating between the institutional shareholders and the company itself. This new intermediary would represent the large shareholders without holding or trading shares itself. It would be expected that such an intermediary would be able to demand management information without falling foul of the law. Logically it would also be able to change directors and call in consultants. It could obtain the power to enforce its demands through being granted proxy votes by the institutional shareholders.

The general tenor of the argument put forward in the previous paragraph depends on the hypothesis that share prices do not reflect the long-run profit potential of the company concerned, in other words that the efficient markets hypothesis is breached since some facets of information are not fully reflected in the price of equity. Marsh [1990] disputes this with the aid of an illustration derived from the valuation of ICI shares according to a standard valuation model. The then current share price and price of capital for ICI imply

that the market is expecting ICI's dividends to grow at the rate of 13 per cent per annum. In turn this implies that of ICI's current market capitalisation, only 8 per cent is attributable to the current year's dividend, only 29 per cent can be explained by the present value of dividends expected over the next five years and only 50 per cent by the value of the dividends expected over the next 10 years. (Marsh [1990])

Marsh admits that analysts' judgements on the cost of capital are tentative, but nevertheless the figures are not suggestive of short termism in share valuation. This point seems to us to be critical since if the price of equity is representing, albeit as an approximation, the long-term profit potential of firms then the search for short-term profits by fund managers will not provoke short-term profit decisions by firms. A fund manager will seek to identify shares which are incorrectly valued and then buy in the case of undervalued shares or sell from his portfolio any shares which he considers to be overvalued. Consequently, even though his actions are motivated by short-term gains, he is in fact moving share prices towards their correct price. Clearly, if the market is not efficient in an informational sense then the foregoing argument is not correct and his actions will be stimulating short-term behaviour.

A further consideration concerns the influence of investment on the price of a company's shares. There is a not inconsiderable volume of evidence derived from the USA to suggest that the announcement of long-term investment often enhances the value of a company's shares – see, for example, McConnell and Muscerella [1985]. This implies that investment is not of necessity an activity to be avoided for fear of inducing takeover bids through lower share prices. In this connection it may also be argued that the perception that investment and dividend payments are necessarily an alternative source of demand for a company's resources is incorrect. Successful investment projects will enhance a company's profit making potential and therefore dividends in the long run.

16.4 An alternative explanation of short termism

An alternative explanation of short termism is provided by Marsh [1990]. This is based on the view that it is the management itself which is subject to myopia or 'managerial short termism'. A number of arguments are presented to support this hypothesis. The first point concerns the system of remunerating top managers. It appears that only a small proportion of managers' remuneration is directly linked to the performance of the corporation. Furthermore, the majority of executive schemes that are in existence are based on short-term indicators such as accounting profit. The underlying argument is that such schemes may provide an incentive for executives to pursue short-term objectives at the expense of a long-term strategy. One example would be an investment proposal which provides benefits in the long run but which is perceived to have an adverse effect on profits in the next few years.

Second there is the role of investment appraisal. It is often argued that current profitability influences the divisional allocation of capital budgets. The problem arises because profitability is assessed via accounting profits and this may provide incorrect signals for investment appraisal, which should be based on discounting methods. It also appears that, in practice, the payback method of investment appraisal is still used by UK managers to assess investment projects – see Marsh [1990] for survey evidence. The problem with this method of investment appraisal is that it concentrates on the short term only and ignores any long-term profits which occur after the break-even time has been reached. If true, this would also provide an important explanation of short termism.

The third broad strand of the argument that managers suffer from myopia can be considered under the heading of a perceived lack of investment opportunities. One reason for this could be poor labour relations, with a heavy incidence of restrictive practices leading to a dilution of the benefits from innovation and investment. A second reason could be the uncertain economic climate due to the higher inflation rates experienced in the UK, which have led to the imposition of restrictive monetary policies from time to time. The resulting uncertain economic climate would not be expected to provide a spur to the development of long-term strategies by firms. A further argument offered is the lower investment in education and training in the UK as compared with other developed nations.

In the following section, we discuss possible remedies for short termism.

16.5 Remedies for short termism

Assuming that short termism is a problem for the UK economy, the proposal of adequate remedies requires identification of its causes. One reform which would draw fairly wide support is a change in the method of remuneration of managers by providing incentive schemes which link their salaries to the medium-term (say in the region of five years) market value of their companies. Sykes [1990] suggests that the rate would typically be in the range of 5–10 per cent and also that penalties should accrue for non-performance. This would require both an extension of incentive schemes and and also the replacement of the role of short-term accounting profits within existing schemes. Presumably extension of such schemes would require fiscal incentives to be provided by government. Benefits would accrue in the form of an incentive directed towards the adoption of long-term strategies by firms. Furthermore, the risk element coupled with the incentives should assist in the correct allocation of managerial resources within the UK economy.

A similar proposal advocates the extension of the appointment of non-executive directors and the separation of the duties of managing director and chairman of a company. Advocates of this strategy claim that this would provide a more independent element in the board of directors and remove an element of passivity and self-selection. It would also facilitate a more objective assessment of past policies and remedies where appropriate. A basic requirement for this strategy to be successful is that the non-executive directors must be genuinely independent and not just 'old cronies' of the existing directors.

The above two proposals could presumably be facilitated by persuading shareholders to take a more active and discerning role in the management of firms. This in reality entails the investment institutions taking a more active role in the management because, in general, individual's shareholdings are dwarfed by those held by the institutions, with the result that proposals by individuals have little chance of acceptance. The problem with institutions taking a more active role in the management of individual firms in their portfolio is, as we have seen earlier, twofold. First, they probably lack the expertise and would therefore be involved in additional expenditure to recruit the requisite qualified staff. Second, the possession of inside knowledge would inhibit share dealings and could therefore detract from market efficiency. For similar reasons it is advocated that banks should become more like banks in Germany and Japan by being closely identified with their borrowers. This would include lending by way of equity and becoming involved in management decisions.

Further remedies suggested depend on the view that short termism is attributable to the deficiencies of the financial system – for such a view see, for example, Cosh *et al.* [1990]. They argue that such remedies as those indicated above will require a fairly long time to implement. It is therefore suggested that some 'grit' should be introduced into the takeover mechanism. First, terms of reference to the Monopolies Commission should be broadened so as to enable a better distinction between takeovers which result in economies of scale and greater efficiency of operation and those which are designed to gain profits by asset stripping. Currently, criteria are restricted to the effect on competition, which provides a reasonably clear framework for decisions. Extension of the criteria to incorporate public interest would permit the authorities to filter out, albeit judgementally, takeovers which were not designed to increase efficiency of operation. Further restraints could be introduced by requiring all contested bids to be submitted to the Monopolies Commission. Another suggestion on similar lines takes the form of restricting the voting rights of newly acquired shares for a specific period of time after the acquisition such as twelve months. Similarly it is also suggested that the threshold at which a predator is obliged to make an offer to all shareholders is reduced from the current 29.9 per cent to a lower figure such as 14.9 per cent (Plender [1990]). Both these measures would increase the cost and difficulty of making predatory bids, especially where they are contested.

A further proposal along these lines advocates the imposition of tax penalties on share transactions to encourage the institutions to take a longer view in their portfolio decisions. This seems to us to be a step in the wrong direction for three reasons. First, the existence of a secondary market provides liquidity, so that existing individuals as well as institutions can change the composition of their portfolios. Restriction on this important function may well reduce the willingness of individuals to hold equity in their overall portfolio of wealth. Second, as we have noted earlier, dealing by institutions is a mechanism which pushes equity prices towards their true value. Third, imposition of taxes on share dealings on the London Stock Exchange would force business away to other international stock exchanges. It is quite likely that attempts to tax dealings on other exchanges would create massive scope for evasion. It would therefore in all probability be ineffective and costly to operate.

16.6 Conclusion

Certain facets of the debate appear to be clear. Short termism is generally perceived to be a problem for the UK economy. Investment has been lower in the UK economy and this is presumably due, at least in part, to short termism. Certain of the proposed remedies command fairly widespread support. These include the proposals for the introduction of long-term incentives for managers and increased representation of genuinely independent non-executive directors. Beyond this, little agreement on either the causes or the remedies exists. Those who believe that the volume of takeovers is excessive advocate legal or quasi-legal restraints on the takeover process. Believers in the efficient markets hypothesis argue that such restraints would do more harm than good.

Chapter 17

Regulation of the financial system

17.1 Introduction

The type of regulation which we are discussing in this chapter is termed prudential regulation since it is designed to ensure prudent behaviour by financial institutions. In contrast to the rest of the financial sector, prudential regulation of banks has been the subject of analysis over quite a long period of time. Consequently the major part of the following discussion in both this section and section 17.2 will be directed to prudential control of banks. We will review the system of prudential control of the investment industry in section 17.3 and present our conclusions in section 17.4. The remainder of this section provides a brief survey of recent bank failures and an examination of the type of risks faced by the banking industry.

Regulation of banks must be examined against the background of bank failures experienced in previous years. Any major problem results in changes in the regulatory environment as the regulators try to block any loophole in the rules. Concentrating on events this century, the greatest incidence of bank failure occurred in the US between the years 1929 when then were 25,000 banking firms and 1934 when the number had been reduced to 14,000. These failures led to the introduction of fairly restrictive bank legislation such as single-state operations, which have remained characteristic of the US banking scene until today, although these restrictions are currently under review.

Broadly speaking there were no further major problems until 1973, which saw the start of the fringe bank crisis in the UK. Over the early 1970s, following rapid credit expansion which was a consequence of the introduction of the policy of 'competition and credit control', many secondary (or 'fringe') banks increased their deposits rapidly and lent a large proportion of these funds to property, related companies. Following a slump in property values in 1973, the secondary banks began to experience difficulties. As a consequence the inter-bank market, upon which the secondary banks were heavily dependent for deposits, dried up for all but banks of good standing and in addition deposits were withdrawn from the secondary banks. At the end of 1973 the Bank of England, seeing the problem as one of illiquidity, stepped in and organised a rescue of the secondary banks which has come to be known as 'the lifeboat'. Under this operation the Bank of England sought the help of the clearing banks in recycling the deposits they had gained following the withdrawal of deposits from the secondary banks. However, the problems in the property market which had caused the loss of confidence in the secondary banks deteriorated further over 1974 and several of the banks receiving support under the 'lifeboat' moved into a position of insolvency. Whilst a few banks were allowed to fail, the majority were kept going. The Bank of England's intervention was justified in the following way (*Bank of England Quarterly Bulletin*, June 1978):

The Bank thus found themselves confronted with the imminent collapse of several deposit-taking institutions and with the clear danger of a rapidly escalating crisis of confidence. This threatened other deposit-taking institutions and if left unchecked, would have quickly passed into parts of the banking system proper. While the UK clearing banks still appeared secure from the domestic effects of any run . . . their international exposure was such that the risk to external confidence was a matter of concern for themselves as well as for the Bank. The problem was to avoid a widening circle of collapse through the contagion of fear.

At the height of the rescue operations, total lending amounted to over £1 billion. This crisis led to a rethink of banking supervision and subsequently to the introduction of the Banking Act of 1979, which provided the first legal codification of the Bank of England's regulatory powers. This Act required the licensing of banks and deposit-taking institutions, and also transferred the duty of supervision entirely to the Bank of England.

Further major failures occurred in 1974, namely Bankhaus Herstatt (Germany) and the Franklin National Bank (US). The latter was the twelfth largest bank in the US. Also in the US, 1984 saw the failure of Continental Illinois Bank, which was the eighth largest bank in the US. In this year the Johnson Mathey Bank failed in the UK – this failure is discussed in detail below. Other bank failures occurred over a range of countries including Denmark, Canada and Ireland.

The Johnson Mathey Bank (JMB) faced financial difficulties which resulted in the Bank of England purchasing the JMB bank for £1 on 1 October 1984 from its parent company Johnson Mathey PLC with a view to rescue and subsequently resale, which has now been carried out. This was the first rescue of an ailing bank by the Bank of England since the lifeboat operation of 1974. The Bank of England sought to justify the rescue of JMB with arguments similar to those used to justify the lifeboat operation, in particular the fear of contagion if JMB were to collapse. There were also reasons put forward which were specific to the JMB case. JMB was one of a group of five gold bullion dealers which jointly fixed the price of gold on a twice-daily basis in London. It was feared that the other gold bullion price fixers might have encountered liquidity problems if JMB were allowed to collapse, which would have put in jeopardy London's position in the international bullion market.

The rescue of JMB, like the lifeboat operation of 1974, involved the participation of other banks and the clearing banks in particular. These banks were persuaded by the Bank of England to provide indemnities against potential loan losses by JMB in order to keep JMB's credit lines open. This time, however, the clearing banks publicly objected to being forced into the rescue of JMB. As Goodhart [1988] argues:

In today's more competitive conditions, the banks at the centre of the system frequently see the failing bank as being a relatively imprudent competitor. Why then, they feel, should they penalise their own shareholders for the sake of such a competitor?

Goodhart goes on to argue that the clearing banks' reaction in the JMB affair 'is a clear warning now that the Bank of England, and other central banks, may find it increasingly hard, if not impossible, to persuade other commercial banks to assist them in future rescue packages'. Goodhart suggests that this should lead to a consideration of alternative strategies to deal with a future illiquidity/insolvency problem, and we consider one such alternative (namely deposit insurance) in the next section.

There are other issues highlighted by the JMB affair (see Hall [1987a] for further discussion) which merit comment. It can be argued that the act of rescuing JMB introduced moral hazard into the banking system, that is, other banks may act less prudently in the belief that the Bank of England will not allow them to fail. The Bank of England, however, has stated that the rescue of JMB was a special case and does not imply that all banks in difficulties will be rescued, but, as Hall [1987a] argues, 'no amount of exhortation is likely to persuade market operators to ignore the Bank's actual deeds in the market place'.

The JMB affair also opens to question the adequacy of the supervisory arrangements and authorisation procedures at that time. The supervisors of JMB did not chase up late quarterly returns and allowed JMB to postpone meetings with Bank staff. Also the escalating problems of JMB were not seen by the supervisors despite the breaches of the Bank's guideline on loan exposure. The Bank expects to be notified of any single non-bank exposure of over 10 per cent of the bank's capital. In its 1985 report, the Bank of England stated that two large exposures at end-June 1983 were reported to be 15 per cent and 12 per cent of capital (in fact these were understated and the 'true' figures were 26 per cent and 17 per cent respectively) and at end-June 1984 were reported to be 38 per cent and 34 per cent ('true' figures being 76 per cent and 39 per cent respectively). Leaving aside the understatement, the Bank's guideline on loan exposure was known to be breached, with the problem getting worse, well before JMB had to be rescued. The Bank, however, has stated that breaches of this guideline are commonplace and that complete observance of this rule would be too restrictive. The catalogue of incompetence by JMB management, reported in the Bank of England's report for 1985, also calls into question the adequacy of the vetting arrangements undertaken by the Bank.

One final issue raised by the JMB affair is the role of auditors in the supervision process. The auditors of JMB, Arthur Young, were sued and an out-of-court settlement reached involving the payment of compensation to the Bank of England without admission of negligence by the auditors.

As indicated above, occurrence of bank failure provides the trigger for further regulation but, before looking at the detail of the system of control, we examine why financial institutions are subject to a degree of prudential regulation and supervision. This contrasts with the position of industry and commerce in general where imprudent behaviour (other than illegal activities such as fraud) likely to lead to bankruptcy is the concern of the owners and shareholders rather than any supervisory authority. In discussion of the reasons for prudential control of the financial system, we follow the direction of most of the early literature on this topic, which was focussed on prudential control of the banks rather than the financial system as a whole.

First of all we need to examine the nature of the risks faced by banks. These can be categorised as (i) systemic failure arising from deposit withdrawals, (ii) price risk, (iii) default risk, (iv) fraud and mismanagement risk and (v) regulatory risk.

Systemic risk arises from the fact that banks' assets and liabilities have a particular feature which may render them liable to financial difficulties even when they are basically sound. Their liabilities are very liquid, often withdrawable on demand, whereas a large proportion of their assets are in the form of loans and advances which are illiquid owing to both (i) the difficulty of securing repayment at short notice and (ii) the absence of a wide secondary market in bank debt. Consequently, exercise of the right to withdraw by a large number of depositors (i.e. a run on the bank) may cause failure of a bank which is perfectly viable in the sense that the discounted value of its assets exceeds that of its liabilities. This problem is enhanced by the procedure followed by banks in the event of a run occurring. Until insolvency is declared, the bank is obliged to pay out the full amount of any deposit withdrawn. Once insolvency is declared, the depositors must await realisation of the bank's assets in the company of other creditors and have their claims assessed by the courts. Thus, in the event of a rumour of difficulties being faced by a bank, there is likely to be a run on that institution since it is in the interest of each depositor to be at the head of the queue. In fact the risk is wider than that so far discussed since, for similar reasons, the 'run mentality' can spread to other banks, even though these banks may not be in difficulties. This is because depositors have only imperfect information about a bank's safety. If they see one bank in difficulty, they do not have the information to assess whether the problems are specific to that bank or affect all banks. In such circumstances it is rational for depositors to withdraw funds from sound banks in order to fully guarantee safety for their deposits. Thus the run can spread through the banking system. An unregulated banking system is therefore susceptible to swings in public confidence and this provides one of the main reasons why the banking system is regulated. This danger is termed 'systemic risk' or contagion.

Price risk refers to the possibility of asset prices changing in a manner which will have adverse effects on the bank's financial position. A good illustrative example of price risk is given by the current position of the savings and loans associations in the US. If assets are held with a longer maturity duration than liabilities, then unanticipated rises in interest rates will cause losses unless the lending is at floating rates of interest. It is estimated (see, for example, Benston and Kaufman [1988]) that at least 500 savings and loans associations were merged or failed since 1981 because of this type of risk. Open currency positions also incur a price risk since unanticipated changes in the relevant exchange rate risk will result in windfall gains or losses to the bank concerned. Involvement of a bank in futures or options also leaves it exposed to the risk of price changes. The final type of price risk occurs when an institution is forced to sell an asset to obtain funds quickly. The necessity of a speedy sale may prevent the bank from seeking out the most advantageous deal thus incurring some form of loss. This is in effect a liquidity risk. Price risk in general has increased owing to the rising volatility of asset prices illustrated in figures 14.1 and 14.2.

The risk of default is endemic in bank lending and arises for example from changes in economic climate which will induce failure of some firms.

The impact of monetary restraint, with its accompanying high interest rates, on firms with a large percentage of capital in the form of debt provides a good illustration of increased risk of default due to a changing economic climate. Another potential source of debt failure arises from country risk, which refers to the failure by foreign governments and other borrowers to repay loans. The problem of sovereign lending was examined in chapter 4. As was discussed in chapters 3 and 4, a bank can reduce the incidence of default risk by spreading its lending activities over a wide number of customers so that failure of any one customer imposes only a light burden on the bank. Banks can also further reduce the incidence of this type of risk by applying an adequate system of scrutiny of loan applications. Nevertheless default risk is always present for banks.

Fraud and mismanagement offer further risks to banks. In the UK there does not appear to have been any instance of fraud on a scale sufficient to cause the failure of a bank until the case of the Bank of Credit and Commerce International (BCCI), which was closed down in July 1991. In the US it seems that fraud has been the reason for the failure of some savings and loan associations. Yang [1987] reports that fraud and other misconduct were the principal reason for the failure of some thirty associations in California between 1983 and 1986. Mismanagement is a fairly general cause of difficulties for all concerns, financial or otherwise, and was probably one of the main reasons for the 1984 failure of the Johnson Mathey Bank in the UK.

The final type of risk faced by a bank is the potential impact of the regulatory environment, which may impair the safe and efficient operation of a bank. One example of this type of risk in the UK was that, in the past, banks were subject to imposed lending restraints as part of the government's monetary policy. Similar restraints were not imposed on lending by the building societies.

For the sake of ease of exposition, we have examined these risks as though they were independent of each other. In fact they are interdependent in a number of ways. Thus, for example, inefficient management is likely to lead to inadequate scrutiny of loan applications and hence greater default risk. Price risk can be reduced by appropriate interest rate pricing and taking a balanced currency position. Liquidity risks can be avoided by holding a sufficient level of highly liquid assets. Fraud can be prevented by good internal supervision as well as the supervision provided by auditors.

We now turn to examining the justification for external regulation of banks in the light of the risks examined above. The first reason offered concerns systemic risk. It is argued that the financial system is subject to waves of confidence and so external regulation is necessary to prevent financial panics. A second reason offered for the control of banks is that the social costs of a major bank failure are far more wide reaching than the failure of a single firm. Failure of any firm affects shareholders. The difference is that the customers (i.e. the depositors) of a bank are likely to be much larger in number and wider in geographical distribution than those of a comparable commercial undertaking. In addition there is the adverse impact on the function of channelling savings to prospective investors, which is likely to lower the aggregate level of investment within an economy.

A third reason offered for prudential control is the possible lack of sophistication of the general public. It is argued that they lack the expertise to differentiate between safe and risky investments. One consequence of this is that the public would be likely to accept a higher return without analysing any extra risk which may be involved. This problem is reinforced by the difficulty of obtaining adequate statistics to assess the risk or safety of an individual institution. Balance sheets tend to conceal the type of lending and the risks involved. In addition, as we saw in chapter 2, banks' existence is partly based on asymmetric information since banks have access to information not available to depositors. Adequate risk assessment requires information supplementary to that contained in the financial reports. The justification of regulation under this heading may be conveniently summed up as depositor protection.

As we have seen in chapters 3 and 4, banks are currently under a considerable degree of pressure resulting from a variety of reasons such as the sovereign debt overhang, bad debts arising from company failure due to high interest rates and falling property values and keen competition. These facets provide a fourth reason for supervising banks, which is the prevention of banks undertaking excessively risky operations in an effort to restore their financial position. There is also the feeling that excessive competition may lead to underpricing of services which, in turn, has an adverse effect on long-run profitability and, therefore, the viability of banks. This fear is compounded by the fact that the 'correct' price for a new service may be difficult to determine without experience extending over an adequate period of time.

The final reason offered for prudential control of banks is the prevention of 'undesirable' firms or individuals entering into an industry in which the preservation of confidence is so vital. A supporting argument is that the industry offers considerable scope for fraud and that, therefore, this restraint is essential.

It should also be noted that the arguments so far presented favour regulation of banks. Nevertheless certain caveats can be entered against the exercise of excessive prudential control over banks. The first consideration is the incontrovertible fact that regulation imposes costs in the form of real resources on both the regulators and the regulated. The central bank has to employ the expertise necessary to carry out the prudential control and the banks have to employ resources to complete the returns required by the controller. These costs can be relatively high and it is therefore a question of cost – benefit analysis to determine whether the benefits gained by prudential regulation outweigh the costs incurred. Second, there is the danger of the regulation becoming so excessive as to reduce competition, raising costs and lowering the pace of financial innovation. A similar argument is often presented in terms of the institutions capturing the regulator by the introduction of practices favourable to themselves, as for example the introduction of a cartel restraining competition and raising profits. A further argument against regulation is that the form of the regulations will distort the market mechanism by diverting resources to fields of activity favoured by the regulators. Finally by way of arguments opposed to regulation is the danger that onerous regulations imposed in one centre will merely lead to the movement of the activity to centres where regulation is more relaxed. This is, of course, one of the main reasons for the development of off-shore banking and is perhaps the main incentive for a common regulation system across banks operating in different countries, often termed a 'level playing field'. This aspect of prudential control is discussed in the following section.

Most of the protagonists of free banking (i.e. the absence of prudential legislation) originate from the US rather than the UK. One interesting suggestion put forward by Benston (see e.g. Benston and Kaufman [1988]) is for a bank's assets and liabilities to be revalued at market prices and that, when economic capital becomes negative (or perhaps positive but only by a small margin), the bank should be reorganised or taken over. One of the main advantages claimed for this system is that the cost of any bank rescue would be quite small. Second, it is argued that depositors would have increased confidence in the banking system, so that runs on banks would become less frequent. Third, the requirement for much of the system of prudential control would be removed. Implementation of such a system would require periodic revaluation of assets, and this would cause major difficulty given the high proportion of UK bank assets in the form of loans which, as we have already seen, are difficult to recall or sell on a secondary market.

In summing up the arguments for and against prudential regulation of banks, perhaps the most telling argument is the lack of expertise and knowledge possessed by the individual depositor to assess the quality of the bank. The argument in favour of prudential regulation of the financial industry has been framed in terms of banks, but most of the arguments can easily be extended to incorporate prudential regulation of financial institutions in general. The remainder of this chapter will concentrate on the regulation of banks (section 17.2) followed by the investment institutions (section 17.3).

17.2 The UK system of prudential control of banks

The Banking Acts of 1979 and 1987 require banks to be licensed by the Bank of England prior to operating as a bank. The 1979 Act divided the industry into banks and deposit-taking institutions, which was seen by many as first and second division banking. This distinction was removed by the 1987 Act. The licensing procedure requires the Bank of England to be satisfied that the quality of management, range of services and reputation are consistent with the banking status. There is also provision for removal of the licence but this has not yet been carried out for a bank, though licences were terminated for a number of licensed deposit-taking institutions under the 1979 Act. The connection between this requirement and the danger of undesirable firms/individuals entering the banking industry is obvious. Other components of the UK system of prudential control are (i) deposit insurance, (ii) the role of auditors, (iii) liquidity controls and (iv) capital adequacy. These are dealt with in the following sections, together with the problem of international coordination of supervision of banks.

Deposit insurance
The second component of the UK system of prudential control is the existence of insurance of deposits. In the event of failure, depositors would obtain 75 per cent of their deposits refunded up to a maximum of £20,000. The scheme is financed by a flat-rate contribution by banks in proportion to their deposits and is administered by the Bank of England. The advantages claimed for deposit insurance are threefold. First, such schemes are designed to provide for speedy compensation for depositors who then have no need to wait for the completion of the winding up of the institution. Second, systemic risk should be reduced since the incentive to be first in the queue to withdraw deposits is reduced. This point is critically dependent on the public being aware that deposits are insured in this manner. This is far from evident. As an interesting exercise the reader should try asking his friends or a class of students if they know that their deposits are insured! Third, perhaps the hidden rationale for the scheme is that it provides the finance for compensation of depositors without recourse to the government.

Deposit insurance is not without its critics since it is open to a number of objections. It can be argued that the existence of deposit insurance increases the problem of 'moral hazard'. As far as the banks are concerned, the wrath of the depositors may be averted because of the knowledge that they will obtain compensation for any deposit loss. This could act as an incentive to the bank managers to take excessive risks since any profits gained will be theirs but any loss will be borne by the insurer. For similar reasons the depositors may be less careful in their assessment of risk and may select institutions which offer the highest rate of interest on deposits regardless of the risks involved because they know any loss will be reimbursed by the insurer. Presumably the restriction of reimbursement to 75 per cent and a maximum of £20,000 is both an attempt to overcome the moral hazard problem and a recognition that large deposits are likely to be made by persons or institutions with an awareness of the financial risks involved. There is some doubt, however, whether a 25 per cent 'haircut' will prevent a 'run' developing.

Apart from the question of moral hazard, there is doubt over the precise form of insurance charge levied in the UK and most other countries. The charge is levied on the quantity of deposits at a flat rate. Many argue that the charge should be linked to the risk involved, in the manner of car insurance. The problem with this suggestion is who is going to make the risk assessment? It is likely that a central bank would baulk at that type of decision for fear of complaints of discrimination. It also remains a moot point whether ratings provided by private agencies would be satisfactory for the purpose of fixing deposit insurance rates.

The last point to be made about deposit insurance is that it is not likely to be an adequate substitute for prudential control unless central banks are prepared to permit banks to become bankrupt, so that insurance would be seen as protection rather than compensation. This certainly does not seem to be the case as far as the Bank of England is concerned, as the evidence provided by the rescue of the JMB bank suggests that banks will be rescued. Schemes for the overhaul of the UK system of deposit insurance are suggested by Hall [1987b] and Goodhart [1988].

Liaison with auditors

Auditors provide a potentially fruitful source of information concerning the financial position of banks. However, a conflict of duty may arise since the auditors have a prime responsibility to the shareholders of the banks, whereas the role of the supervisors is the protection of the depositors. Following the Banking Act 1987, a relationship between the auditors and the Bank was provided for. The relationship is to be based on trilateral meetings between the auditors, the institution and the supervisors at the Bank. Matters to be discussed include the statutory accounts and the auditors' reports. The reporting accountants are also required to report on the institution's accounting and other internal control systems and the returns provided for prudential control purposes. Meetings are normally to be called by the Bank or by the auditors via the institution concerned. In exceptional cases however, the auditors or reporting accountants could report direct to the Bank. Such exceptional circumstances would have to be of a serious nature, such as, for example, situations where the integrity of the directors or senior management is being questioned.

The connection between the role of auditors and the failure of management in connection with JMB failure accompanied by inadequate internal systems of control and provision of inaccurate returns is self-evident.

Liquidity control
As we have discussed above, one feature of the asset and liability structure of banks which suggests prudential control is the liquid nature of liabilities and illiquid nature of their assets. A bank can fail through inability to meet deposit withdrawals because of lack of liquidity even though it is viable in the long run. Liquidity can be provided in a number of ways including:

(i)   holding sufficient cash or assets which are easily liquidated;
(ii)   holding an appropriately matching portfolio of cash flows from maturing assets;
(iii) maintaining an adequately diversified deposit base in terms of maturities and mix of depositors.

The bank supervisors have the duty to ensure that banks maintain an appropriate mix of all three items discussed above. With specific reference to the liquidity position, no minimum overall liquidity ratio is applied to all banks because it is felt that the allocation of specific assets to a liquidity category is bound to be arbitrary. Banks engage in maturity transformation so that the term structure of their assets is longer than that of their liabilities. Hence control of the liquidity position of banks can be achieved by preparing a maturity ladder showing the accumulated mismatch of short-term assets and liabilities over a variety of time periods up to one year. In this ladder, marketable assets are shown as maturing immediately but are subject to a discount for valuation in the liquidity ladder so as to reflect potential variations in market price, e.g. CDs with less than six months remaining to maturity are subject to 5 per cent discount and those up to five years to 10 per cent discount. The time periods of this maturity ladder are (i) sight – 8 days; (ii) 8 days–1 month; (iii) 1–3 months; (iv) 3–6 months and (v) 6–12 months. It would be expected that the maximum point of excess of liabilities over assets will occur in the first six months. No standards are imposed for any of the periods involved and the position of each bank will be considered in the environment in which it operates.

A further control exists since the Bank is concerned with individual banks' holdings of 'high class' liquidity. High-class liquidity is defined as instruments with which the Bank of England is prepared to deal in its daily operations in the London discount market (see chapter 10), such as eligible bills, local authority bills, etc. No general requirement is imposed on all banks, but the Bank will discuss with each bank their holdings of high-class liquidity. Assessment of its adequacy will be considered against the individual circumstances of each bank.

Capital adequacy

As we have noted in the last section, liquidity is essentially a short-term concept referring to the ability of an institution to meet day-to-day cash outflows, whereas solvency is a longer-term concept referring to the prospective ability of a bank to meet all its liabilities as they fall due. The distinction between liquidity and solvency is not as clearcut as these definitions imply. There is a view that if a financial institution is confidently believed to be solvent then it should be able to borrow through the markets to meet any short-term liquidity difficulties. It follows therefore that the existence of liquidity problems that cannot be resolved through the markets implies that other market participants believe the risk of insolvency for that institution to be high. The reverse is generally not the case, as it is possible to face insolvency problems without any illiquidity problems first showing up, as was the case with the Johnson Mathey Bank.

The view that 'banks with liquidity problems that cannot be solved through the markets implies the bank is likely to be insolvent' is seen by Quinn, the executive director of the Bank of England with responsibility for banking supervision, to be one which is 'absolutist and neglects the vital role that time plays in assessing the quality of a bank's assets, quite apart from being a high risk strategy' (*BEQB*, May 1988). Quinn argues that there are great difficulties in establishing the value of a bank's assets and it is possible for assets to gain or lose value very quickly thus creating liquidity problems. A bank's management may be able to turn round the problem over time or the problem may disappear through an improvement in external circumstances. However, if a bank is denied short-term funding, its capacity to recover claims is put in doubt and other debtors may then stop paying, believing that the institution is likely to become insolvent thus compounding the problem. Thus the Bank of England has placed increasing emphasis on banks' managing their liquidity as part of the overall policy of minimising the risk of insolvency. However, the most important aspect of the Bank's policy in this regard relates to its monitoring of each bank's capital adequacy.

The capital of a bank is seen as financing the infrastructure of the business and providing a cushion to absorb any losses on its assets. As we saw in chapter 2, a bank can minimise any default losses with regard to its loans by (i) limiting the risk of default on individual loans through appropriate selection of borrowers, (ii) reducing the overall risk of its loan portfolio by diversifying and (iii) pooling its risk so as to make the overall risk of default more predictable. This last point enables the bank to cover its expected losses by incorporating a premium in its loan rate of interest. Unexpected loan losses are then covered by the bank's profits in the first instance and ultimately by its capital. Thus the level of a bank's capital is important in assessing the solvency of a bank in adverse circumstances. The underlying principle is that it is the shareholders rather than the depositors who should bear the risks of the business undertaking.

The question of capital adequacy was first addressed by a working party set up by the Bank of England in 1974 which reported in 1975 (see *BEQB*, September 1975). This working party recommended the use of two ratios: the free resources (gearing) ratio and the risk assets ratio. These ratios were further revised in 1979 and the system of assessing capital adequacy that operated throughout most of the 1980s is set out in the *BEQB* of September 1980. The gearing ratio is a very simple measure essentially relating the value of a bank's free resources, that is, broadly the bank's capital minus the value of its infrastructure, to the value of its deposits. Thus it takes no account of the riskiness of the bank's assets and as a consequence is rarely referred to nowadays for supervisory purposes. The risk assets ratio has become the key ratio in monitoring capital adequacy and this relates the value of a bank's capital to the value of its assets weighted according to their inherent riskiness. Whilst this approach related an individual bank's capital to the riskiness of its activities, it did so only to the extent that these activities appeared on the balance sheet. As we have discussed in chapter 4, over the 1980s banks increasingly undertook activities which did not result in a balance sheet entry under normal accounting procedures ('off-balance sheet' business). Thus, in order to measure the adequacy of a bank's capital to all, or at least most, of the default risks it is exposed to, the risk assets ratio has recently been modified to incorporate off-balance sheet business.

The new system of risk weightings and capital definitions is being introduced on a phased basis following an agreement reached under the auspices of the Bank for International Settlements. It is intended that the system, which provides for a common system of prudential control for banks operating in the major industrial countries, will be fully operative by 1993, but in the meantime transitional arrangements are permitted. Under this approach, banks' assets are divided into various categories and each category is given a weighting according to its perceived relative riskiness. Each asset is multiplied by this risk factor and the total of the risk-adjusted assets then related to the bank's capital. A two-step process is involved for off-balance sheet items. First, they are transformed into an on-balance sheet item using standard conversion ratios. Second, the risk weightings are then applied to the converted values. The capital base itself consists of two components: (i) core capital or tier 1 and (ii) supplementary capital or tier 2. The first component broadly represents equity, reserves and retained profits and the second consists of other types of capital liabilities such as subordinated debt instruments (i.e. debt ranking after all other debt for winding up purposes), general provisions and revaluation reserves. Three restrictions are imposed. First, the total of tier 2 components should not exceed a maximum of 100 per cent of tier 1 items. Second, subordinated debt should not exceed a maximum of 50 per cent of the total of tier 1 items. Third, general provisions should not exceed 1.25 per cent of weighted risk assets. A minimum level of 8 per cent is prescribed, but it is not expected that all banks will work to this figure and capital adequacy will be considered for each bank against the background of its operations. Details of capital definitions and asset weightings are included as an appendix to this chapter. Sometimes an informal distinction is made between upper tier 2 capital and lower tier 2 capital. Lower tier 2 capital refers to subordinated term debt, which, as noted above, is restricted to a maximum of 50 per cent of tier 1 capital. All other types of tier 2 capital fall into the upper category.

The theoretical basis of the risk-adjusted asset ratio is perhaps suspect since it is based on the assumption that the risks are independent, otherwise it would not be possible to add the risk-adjusted assets together. Portfolio theory suggests that risks may be interdependent in some instances; for example, a general recession will induce failures of a number of companies. It is difficult, however, to design a scheme which would take this factor into consideration. A second problem arises if the risk factors do not accurately measure the relative degree of risk in each asset. This problem is made worse because the effect of the risk weightings is likely to induce lending favourable to the arbitrarily imposed risk factors and may therefore distort the market mechanism.

Heavy exposure to individual companies imposes a risk over and above that captured by comparing asset risks and capital, as evidenced in the failure of the JMB bank. A bank is therefore required to notify exposure to any individual customer in excess of 10 per cent of its capital (calculated in the same manner as for the risk-adjusted asset ratio). Any exposure in excess of 25 per cent of the capital base requires prior permission of the Bank of England.

Foreign currency exposure provides an additional source of danger to banks since exchange rates can change quickly, imposing potential losses of a major nature. Consequently banks, open dealing positions are restricted to a maximum of:

(i)   10 per cent of capital base for net open position in any one currency,
(ii) 15 per cent of capital base for net open short position of all currencies taken together.

The precise position for each bank would depend on its experience in dealing in foreign currency assets/liabilities and management skills, so it would not be likely that each bank could deal up to the positions discussed above. Again it is notable that the control is based on ensuring that the capital position of a bank is adequate to cover potential losses incurred through open foreign currency dealing positions so as to protect depositors as compared with shareholders from losses.

International cooperation

Banking is an international function, with many banks operating outside the country where their head office is located. Types of foreign banking establishments comprise branches, subsidiaries and joint ventures or consortia. Thus some difficulties could occur for effective prudential control because of ambiguities as to the precise division of the responsibility for supervision. In 1975 the Basle concordat set out guidelines defining the responsibilities of the parent and the host country for supervision. This was reformulated again in 1983. The main principle of these guidelines is that no foreign banking establishment should escape adequate supervision. It was agreed that supervision of consortia should be exercised by the authorities in the country of incorporation. With respect to the other two categories, host authorities are primarily responsible for supervision of their liquidity and foreign currency positions. Capital adequacy is the responsibility of the parent country. It is expected that full consultation and cooperation will take place between the various supervisory bodies.

We now turn to an examination of the supervision of investment institutions.

17.3   Control of investment business

Prior to 1986 the control of investment business was carried out under the provisions of the Prevention of Fraud (Investments) Act 1958. However, at the beginning of the 1980s doubts were being expressed concerning the effectiveness of this Act and these led to the appointment of Professor Gower to review the protection of investors. The Financial Services Act 1986 was based on the Gower Report. In view of the relatively short time this Act has been in force, we are unable to make detailed comments on its effectiveness but will rather review the general nature of the machinery of control.

In general the Act provided for the legislation of investment business. An investment was widely defined to include securities issued by companies, public corporations, central and local government. Units in collective investment schemes were also included, as were futures, options and long-term insurance. Investment business was also widely defined and included dealing, arranging deals, managing collective investment schemes and investment advice. Basically the legislation requires that any person or company carrying out such investment business must obtain authorisation. Provision was included for removal of authorisation in the case of wrongdoing. A compensation fund was set up and provisions made for dealing with complaints by the general public.

The overall regulatory function was delegated to the Securities and Investment Board (SIB). Second-tier regulatory bodies were also set up for the various subdivisions of the investment business and these were called Self-Regulatory Organisations (SROs). The SROs require approval from the SIB before they can operate. Five SROs were established as follows:

The Securities Association (formed by a merger of the Stock Exchange and the International Securities Regulatory Association) (TSA)
The Association of Futures Brokers and Dealers (AFBD)
The Financial Intermediaries, Managers and Brokers Regulatory Association (FIMBRA)
The Investment Management Regulatory Organisation (IMRO)
The Life Assurance and Unit Trust Regulatory Organisation (LAUTRO)

Supervision of the conduct of business is entrusted to these SROs and one of the early tasks for them is to produce rule books for operations within their trade. In this connection it has proved difficult to reach a compromise between broad coverage and a lack of complexity.

The overall objective of the legislation is to achieve protection for investors with involvement of government being the minimum necessary to achieve an operation of a financial system which provides fair rewards without fraud. The strategy adopted was one of self-regulation within a statutory framework. Some felt that a more legal approach would have been desirable on the lines of the US Securities and Exchange Commission. The opposing argument is based on the idea that practitioners are better placed to spot abuses and breaches of rules than an external body carrying out legal obligations. It is probable that the system adopted will be more flexible and faster in the provision of remedies than a court.

17.4 Conclusion

We have surveyed the UK system of prudential control of financial institutions. The main thrust of our argument has been concerned with the banks. Because of the central position of financial institutions as intermediaries between lenders and borrowers, it is generally (but not always) agreed that some form of external control should be exercised over their behaviour to ensure that they act in a 'prudential' or careful manner. However, all financial behaviour involves risk, and prudential control should not be too excessive otherwise competition may be restrained in a manner which leads to excessive operating costs and a lack of financial innovation.

Appendix

A *Definition of capital*

Tier 1: Core capital

(a) Permanent shareholders' equity:
    (i) Allotted called up and fully paid capital/common stock
    (ii) Perpetual, irredeemable non-cumulative preference shares and perpetual non-cumulative preference shares convertible at the issuer's option into common shares with the Bank of England's prior consent
(b) Disclosed reserves in the form of general or other reserves created or increased by appropriations of retained earnings, share premiums or other surpluses
(c) Published retained profit or loss (ie net of anticipated tax, dividends and any other appropriations) arising during the course of current year
(d) Minority interests arising on consolidation from interests in permanent shareholders' equity

less

(e) Goodwill and other intangible assets

and

(f) Current year's unpublished losses

Tier 2: Supplementary capital

(a) Undisclosed reserves and unpublished current year's retained profits
(b) Reserves arising from the revaluation of tangible fixed assets
(c) General provisions: provision against possible losses which have not occurred will be treated as capital subject to the restrictions noted in the main body of the text. Specific provision will not be included in capital

(d) Hybrid capital instruments
   (i)   Perpetual irredeemable cumulative preference shares, and perpetual cumulative preference shares redeemable at the option of the issuer and with the prior consent of the Bank of England
   (ii) Convertible subordinated bonds which are convertible into equity at the issuer's option
   (iii) Approved perpetual subordinated debt
(e) Subordinated term debt
   (i)   Dated preference shares
   (ii) Convertible subordinated bonds not included in d(ii) above
   (iii) Subordinated term loan capital with a minimum original term to maturity of over five years, subject to straight line amortisation in the last five years, leaving no more than 20 per cent of the original amount issued outstanding in the final year before redemption.

Deductions from total capital
(a) Investments in unconsolidated subsidiaries and associates
(b) Connected lending of a capital nature
(c) All holdings of other banks' and building societies' capital instruments.

B   *Risk weight categories: on balance sheet*

0%   Cash, gold bullion held in own vaults or on an allocated basis
      Claims collateralised by cash or guaranteed by OECD central governments or central banks, loans to OECD central governments and central banks, loans guaranteed by non-OECD central governments and central banks where denominated in local currency and funded in that currency
      Certificates of tax deposit
10%   Loans to discount houses, gilt-edged market makers, institutions with a money market dealing arrangement with the Bank of England and those Stock Exchange money brokers which operate in the gilt-edged market, where the loans are secured on gilts, UK Treasury bills, eligible local authority and eligible bank bills or London CDs
      Holdings of fixed-interest securities issued by OECD central governments with a residual maturity up to one year and floating-rate OECD central government securities of any maturity
      Claims collateralised by OECD central government fixed-interest

securities of up to one year, or similar floating-rate securities of any maturity

Holdings of non-OECD central government securities with a residual maturity of up to one year denominated in local currency and funded by liabilities in that currency

20%   Holdings of OECD central government fixed-interest securities of a residual maturity of one year and over or claims collateralised by such securities

Holdings of non-OECD central government securities of a maturity of one year and over denominated in local currency and funded by liabilities in the same currency

Claims on multilateral development banks and claims guaranteed by or collateralised by securities issued by these institutions

Claims on banks incorporated in the OECD and exposures guaranteed (or accepted) by OECD-incorporated banks (UK building societies are treated as banks for capital adequacy purposes)

Claims in gold and other bullion on those market making members of the London Bullion Market Association which are not included in the item immediately above

Claims on banks incorporated outside the OECD with a residual maturity of up to one year and loans of the same period guaranteed by non-OECD banks

Claims on OECD public sector entities and loans guaranteed by such entities

Loans to discount houses which are unsecured or secured on assets other than those listed in the 10 per cent category

Cash items in the process of collection

50%   Loans to individuals and to housing associations registered with the Housing Corporation for the sole purpose of residential occupation, fully secured by a first equitable or legal charge

Holdings of securities issued by special purpose mortgage finance vehicles where the risk to the security holders is fully and specifically secured against residential mortgage loans which would themselves qualify for the 50 per cent weight or by assets which qualify for a weight less than 50 per cent

Mortgage sub-participations, where the risk to the sub-participating bank is fully and specifically secured against residential mortgage loans which would themselves qualify for the 50 per cent weight

100%   Claims on the non-bank private sector

Claims on banks incorporated outside the OECD with a residual maturity of one year or over

Claims on central governments outside the OECD (unless denominated in the local currency and funded in that currency)

Loans guaranteed by claims on non-OECD central governments
or central banks which are not denominated in local currency
and funded locally

Claims on commercial companies owned by the public sector

Claims on public sector entities outside the OECD

Premises, plant, equipment and other fixed assets

Real estate, trade investments and other assets not otherwise
specified

Aggregate net short open foreign exchange position

C   *Credit conversion factors for off-balance sheet items*

100%   Direct credit substitutes including general guarantees of indebtedness, standby letters of credit serving as financial guarantees
and acceptances

Sale and repurchase agreements and asset sales with recourse
where the credit risk remains with the bank

Forward asset purchases, forward forward deposits and the
unpaid part of partly paid shares and securities which represent
commitments with a certain drawdown

20%   Short-term self-liquidating trade-related contingent items (such as
documentary credits collateralised by the underlying shipments)

50%   Note issuance facilities and revolving underwriting facilities

Other commitments (e.g. formal standby facilities and credit
lines) with an original maturity of one year and over

0%   Similar commitments with an original maturity of up to one year
or which can be unconditionally cancelled at any time Endorse-
ments of bills

Source: Bank of England publication BSD/1988/3.

Chapter 18

Conclusions

18.1 Nature of the UK financial system

In this section we provide a brief summary of the nature of the UK financial system and in section 18.2 we discuss the extent to which the financial system impinges on the operation of monetary policy.

In chapter 2 of the book, we defined the financial system as a set of markets and institutions which provide the means of raising finance and which supply various financial services. The institutions we have considered in this book can be usefully subdivided as follows:

1. The Monetary Sector
    Wholesale and retail banks (chapters 3 and 4 respectively), discount houses (section 10.2)
2. Other Deposit-Taking Institutions
    Building societies and finance houses (chapter 5)
3. Long-term Investment Institutions
    Pension funds, life assurance companies, investment and unit trusts (chapter 6)

In a similar manner, discussion of markets proceeded as follows:

1. Introduction to markets (chapter 7)
2. Equity markets (chapter 8)
3. The bond market, including the term structure of interest rates (chapter 9)
4. The sterling money markets (chapter 10)
5. The foreign exchange markets (chapter 11)
6. The euro-securities markets (chapter 12)
7. The newer derivative markets, i.e. financial futures and options markets (chapter 13). This was followed by a discussion of the role of these markets in the management of risk (chapter 14).

The operation of the financial system raises a number of issues. The first concerns how far prudential control should be exercised over the institutions/markets. This was considered in chapter 17. The impact of a single European market and economic and monetary union between EC member states was discussed in chapter 15. Efficiency of the system was examined in two ways. First, consideration of the application of the efficient markets hypothesis (EMH) took place against the background of each of the markets. An agnostic conclusion was reached for all markets, implying that the EMH was still an open question. Second, the broader aspect of the efficiency of the UK financial system was discussed in chapter 16 and here again our conclusions were not firm but tended to point towards efficiency.

By any standard the UK financial system described above is a sophisticated system. It is also an open financial system, without restriction of flows of funds into or out of the country for either residents or non-residents. It is also a financial system which has seen a considerable degree of change in recent years in the development of both (i) new markets (e.g. financial futures) and new instruments (e.g. commercial paper) and (ii) liberalisation in the sense of the removal of controls restricting competition between institutions. At the same times the incidence of prudential control has increased. It is an interesting question whether such a sophisticated financial system impedes or reinforces monetary policy and we now turn to consider this.

18.2   The financial system and monetary policy

Clearly, monetary policy operates through the financial system. For example, if it is desired to raise rates of interest, the initial change is introduced by the Bank of England through its daily operations in the discount market as described in section 10.2. In a similar way, intervention in the foreign exchange markets to influence exchange rates also affects the market makers in the forex. Policy changes may have an adverse effect on the financial institutions involved. The first way in which a problem may arise for the operation of the monetary policy is attributable to the dual function of the central bank, i.e. the Bank of England. As we saw in chapter 3, the Bank has the responsibility of (i) supporting the financial system in its function as a lender of last resort and (ii) operating monetary policy. A fear is sometimes expressed that, if the Bank pressed too hard in its operation of monetary policy, this would cause difficulties for financial institutions such as the banks and discount houses, causing them problems which could lead to a possibility of failure. In a similar way, recent world-wide increases in rates of interest caused problems for debtor nations and led to the sovereign lending problem discussed in section 4.5. Fear of default by debtor nations raises the spectre of bank failure on a large scale. For this type of reason it is sometimes argued that the well-being of the financial system imposes restraints on the operation of monetary policy.

The nature of the financial system may also impose restraints on the effectiveness of different monetary instruments. This is particularly true of the UK system which, as we have seen, is very open, so that restraint in the UK may be avoided by borrowing overseas or by the movement of institutions to off-shore locations.

In the last decade, UK monetary policy has been operated via interest rate changes. A restrictive policy has raised nominal interest rates (and often real rates) quite sharply with a view to dampening down expenditure. An interest rate policy will also alter the cost of borrowing overseas through adjustments to the expected exchange rate as compared with the current rate so as to maintain interest rate parity (if only approximately) as discussed in section 11.4 (see, in particular, equation (11.3)). A problem of course arises with respect to the UK's membership of the ERM (section 15.4) since only limited exchange rate movements are feasible. If domestic policy actions are deemed by market operators to be inconsistent with maintenance of the current exchange rate, then speculative flows will occur on a massive scale. This will happen because market operators have been presented with what has been termed a 'one-way option'. In the case of a probable devaluation, speculators know that an appreciation of the exchange rate is not possible, so that their losses from speculation in favour of a devaluation will be minimal whereas their gains will be substantial if the devaluation occurs. Consequently the operation of a sophisticated financial system may force devaluation of a fixed exchange rate on an unwilling government and frustrate any attempts by monetary policy to protect the exchange rate at its agreed level.

This concentration of monetary policy has been criticised in the past and, in particular, credit controls have been suggested as an alternative/ supplement to interest rate policy. For example, a restrictive monetary policy would entail increasing the severity of credit controls so that the resulting restriction of the supply of funds would reduce the level of aggregate demand. The efficacy of such controls depends critically on the extent to which they can be circumvented. This can occur in two ways. First, new types of domestic financial institutions and/or lending can develop which are outside the area of the controls. This is likely to be quite a slow process, so that it may well be that the authorities have little to fear from this process in the short run. The potentially more serious frustration of credit controls occurs as a consequence of the very openness of the UK financial system. Capital controls no longer exist for domestic residents of the UK and their reimposition is incompatible with EC regulations (stage one of EMU). Consequently imposition of credit controls within the UK could be easily frustrated by overseas institutions or UK institutions operating off-shore branches. For example, restraint on mortgage lending can be avoided by borrowing from a non-resident institution or an overseas branch of a UK institution. Similarly, restrictions on hire purchase on, say, cars within the UK could be avoided by the purchase of the car from an alternative centre within Europe with finance organised at the point of purchase. In the former case it only needs the opening of a UK office to channel lending to the head office overseas. It may be argued that such developments would take some time to come into being but, on the other hand, sophisticated financial systems are likely to take advantage quickly of perceived profitable opportunities. It would seem therefore that credit controls could provide only an extremely short-term alternative to rising interest rates. They also suffer from the disadvantage that their impact is arbitrary and likely to discriminate unfairly between different classes of people. For example, the economically literate will perceive the opportunities offered by borrowing abroad in the face of domestic credit restraints, whereas those who are not so well-informed will be slow to take up that opportunity. Furthermore, such controls interfere with the operation of the price mechanism, the efficiency of which has been one of the main objectives of the policy of liberalisation of the financial system.

Our conclusion is, therefore, that a developed and open financial system does make it difficult to operate non-market types of monetary policy, as the imposition of direct controls is likely to be quite quickly frustrated by the development of new financial instruments and/or sources of funds.

Glossary

ADRs	American Depository Receipts – confer ownership rights to British shares and traded in their own right. Avoids need to register change in share ownership and transactions do not involve stamp duty.
Arbitrage	Buying and selling securities in order to profit from price differences without incurring risk.
Ask price	The price at which a market maker is prepared to sell a security.
Banker's acceptance	A bill of exchange endorsed by a bank, i.e. the bank is guaranteeing the bill. It commands a low rate of discount – see under *bill of exchange*.
Basis	The spread or difference between two rates, such as the difference between the futures price and that of the underlying cash instrument.
Basis-point	One one-hundredth of 1 per cent.
Bearer bond	A bond which is owned by whoever holds it. No registration of ownership is involved – see under *bond*.
BES	Business Expansion Scheme – a scheme set up by the government in 1983 whereby investors can claim tax relief for investment in unquoted companies.
Bill of exchange	An order in writing telling a person to pay a certain sum of money to another at a specific time in the future. Bills are mainly used in foreign trade. The person who promises to pay is said to accept the bill. A prime bank bill is a bill accepted by a high-class bank. A fine trade bill is a bill accepted by a trader with a first-class reputation.

A bill bears no interest rate and is said to be discounted when it is sold for a price less than its maturity value.

BIS   Bank for International Settlements – a bank for European central banks.

Bond   A title issued by the public sector or a company acknowledging the existence of debt. Normally a bond commands a fixed rate of interest based on its nominal value.

Broker   A person who arranges deals between buyers and sellers on behalf of a third party. A broker is not trading on his own account but earns a commission on the deal called a brokerage fee.

CD   A Certificate of Deposit – a negotiable instrument issued by a bank or building society acknowledging an interest-bearing time deposit.

Collateral   Security given for the repayment of a loan.

Commercial paper   An unsecured promissory note issued by commercial firms promising to pay a fixed sum of money normally with a maturity of less than 270 days. This security is usually sold at a discount, i.e. for less than its nominal or face value.

Consortium banks   A subsidiary set up by a number of banks for the purpose of making a large loan(s).

Contingent liability   Debt which comes into existence on the occurrence of some contingency.

Coupon   Fixed rate of interest payable on bonds.

Covered interest arbitrage   Investing in a security denominated in a foreign currency and covering against the exchange rate risk by taking out an offsetting forward transaction.

Cross default clause   A condition of a loan which permits the lender to demand immediate repayment if the borrower defaults on another loan.

Debt rescheduling   Formal rearrangement of both debt service payments and repayment of the principal with new maturities.

Default   Failure of a borrower to make a payment of either interest or principal on the due date.

Discount   The payment of an immediate sum in settlement of a sum due at a later date.

Dividend   Income return on ordinary shares.

ECU   The European currency unit. It is made up of a weighted total of the currencies of the members of the EC.

EMH   The efficient markets hypothesis, which puts forward the view that market prices reflect all available information.

ERM	Exchange Rate Mechanism. The system of semi-fixed exchange rates of participating countries of the EC.
Equity	The part of total capital of a company belonging to the shareholders. In terms of a company's balance sheet it is the residual after deducting liabilities except those due to shareholders from total assets.
Eurobank	Financial institutions that accept deposits and make loans in currencies other than that of the country where they are located (i.e. the 'host country').
Eurodollar	Dollar deposits held at banks located outside the US. More broadly the term can be used for a deposit denominated in any a currency other than that of the host country.
Euronote	Short-term notes or debts issued in the syndicated loan market. Short term usually refers to one-, three- or six-month maturities.
Exercise price	The specified price at which *options* can be taken up or exercised.
Factoring	The act of a financial institution taking over the debts owed to a firm. The price paid for the debts would be less than the nominal amount outstanding, i.e. the debts are discounted and the rate of discount will reflect the relevant interest charge and an allowance for the riskiness of the debt.
Financial futures	A standardised contract providing for the purchase or sale of a fixed quantity of a financial commodity such as foreign exchange, bank deposit, etc. The underlying financial instrument is known as the cash instrument.
Floating rate	An interest rate which is reset at regular intervals – the adjustment usually being made with reference to a key rate such as LIBOR (see below).
Foreign bond	A *bond* issued by a borrower in the capital market of another country.
Forfaiting	Buying a client's debts without the right to reclaim in the event of *default*.
Forward contract	A contract specifying a price for the delivery of a commodity or financial instrument at an agreed date in the future. This contract differs from a futures contract since the contract is not standardised and can be adjusted according to the needs of the purchaser.
Forward premium	The gap between the forward exchange rate and the ruling *spot rate*. If the forward rate is less than

the current spot rate then the currency is at a discount. The premium/discount can be expressed as a annual percentage or in the form of cents, etc. per £1.

FRN

A floating-rate *note*, i.e. a note issued with provision for revision of the rate of interest at periodic intervals (normally three or six months) in line with a key market rate such as *LIBOR*.

Gilt-edged security

A *bond* issued by the UK government.

Hedge

The reduction of risk on exposure to changes in market prices/rates through taking an offsetting position.

IMF

International Monetary Fund. A multilateral agency that assists countries with payments difficulties by arranging rescheduling of debts or new credits.

Index fund

An investment fund which is constructed to track an appropriate stock market index, e.g. FT-SE All Share Index.

Interest rate parity

The requirement that the differences in interest rates between two countries should be matched by the forward exchange rate premium/discount.

Investment bank

A bank that is involved in the commencement, underwriting and distribution of new issues of securities.

Junk bonds

High-risk, high-return *bonds*. Substantial volume of issues to finance buy-outs (leveraged buy-outs) in the US during a wave of corporate restructuring in the late 1980s.

Lender of last resort

An institution, normally the central bank, which underpins the financial system by lending to banks, or more occasionally domestic firms, which are facing a liquidity crisis but are basically sound in the long run.

LIBID

The London Interbank Bid Rate, i.e. the rate of interest paid on deposits in the London inter-bank market.

LIBOR

The London Interbank Offer Rate, i.e. the rate at which banks are willing to lend funds in the London inter-bank market.

LIFFE

London International Financial Futures Exchange. Merged with LTOM to form the London International Financial Futures and Options Exchange in 1992.

LTOM

London Traded Options Market – see *LIFFE*.

Market maker

An institution which undertakes to sell and buy a commodity(ies) or financial instruments(s) on a

	continuous basis. This ensures that others can always buy or sell, thus providing liquidity.
Matching	The practice of securing a distribution of assets which is equal to that of the liabilities in respect of characteristics such as maturity or currency denomination.
Maturity	The time to the expiry of a loan/debt. Original maturity is the time to expiry when the loan was issued.
MBO	Management buy-out. The purchase of an existing company by its incumbent management, usually financed by a venture capital fund.
Merchant bank	Banks which make profits from carrying out services for corporate customers in addition to lending. The types of services are portfolio advice, new issues advice and underwriting, accepting bills of exchange, advising on takeovers and mergers, foreign currency services, etc.
NASDAQ	National Association of Securities Dealers Automated Quotations – the computerised price information system used by dealers in the over-the-counter market (*OTC*) in the US.
NAV	Net asset value per share. The value of assets less liabilities divided by the number of issued shares.
NIF	A note-issuing facility whereby a bank (or more commonly a syndicate of banks) arranges and guarantees the availability of funds from the issue of a succession of short-term notes (commonly three or six months). In the case of these notes not being taken up by the market, the banks will provide the funds.
Note	A short-term financial instrument similar to a *bond*. Unlike a bond, a note is essentially a short-term instrument.
OECD	The Organisation for Economic Co-operation and Development. Membership includes Australia, Austria, Belgium, Canada, Denmark, Finland, France, Germany, Greece, Iceland, Ireland, Italy, Japan, Luxembourg, Netherlands, New Zealand, Norway, Portugal, Spain, Sweden, Switzerland, Turkey, UK and US. Yugoslavia is involved in some instances.
Off-balance sheet business	A type of business which does not create liabilities or assets for banks (or other businesses). Fees are usually generated along with contingent liabilities. Examples are *NIF*, forward exchange contracts, option writing, etc.

Offer price

The price at which a *market maker* is prepared to sell securities.

Off-shore bank

A subsidiary bank, such as a *eurobank*, which operates in a currency other than that of the host country. An alternative definition emphasises business carried out with non-residents in addition to the currency definition.

Options

The right BUT NOT the obligation to buy (a 'call' option) or sell (a 'put' option) a commodity or financial instrument in return for the payment of a premium. The seller of an option is called the 'writer'. An over-the-counter option (*OTC*) is an option which is tailor-made for the purchaser and which cannot be sold. A traded option is an option in the form of a standardised agreement which the purchaser can sell on an organised market. A European-type option can be exercised only on a specific date and an American type of option can be exercised on any date prior to the expiry date.

OTC

Over-the-counter market. An informal dealer-based market.

Perpetual FRN

A *note* issued without provision for redemption.

Primary market

A market for new issues of securities.

PSBR

Public Sector Borrowing Requirement. The amount of money required by the public sector not otherwise raised by taxation.

PSDR

Public Sector Debt Repayment. Repayment of debt by the public sector when it has a surplus.

Repurchase agreement

An agreement to sell securities and repurchase them at a later date; both prices being agreed at the time of the initial sale. This is in effect an agreement to lend money with *collateral* and the two prices would reflect this.

Rollover credit

A loan that is renewed (rolled over) at fixed intervals, with the interest rate being altered in line with a key rate such as *LIBOR*.

Savings and loans association

In the US, an institution which accepts deposits and makes loans, the bulk of which are in the form of mortgages. The equivalent of building societies in the UK.

SEAQ

Stock Exchange Automatic Quotation system.

SEC

Securities and Exchange Commission. US investment regulatory body.

Secondary market

A market for the sale and purchase of existing securities, as opposed to a market for the sale (or issue) of new securities, which is termed the *primary market*.

Securitisation	The process by which existing non-negotiable debt (such as bank loans) is changed into a security which is marketable. The term can also be used in a broader sense to indicate the change of procedure through which debt which was formerly obtained by bank lending (i.e. non-negotiable) is issued in marketable form such as *NIF*, etc.
SIB	Securities and Investment Board. Regulatory body set up by the Financial Services Act to oversee regulation of investment industry. Delegates to *SROs*.
Spot rate	The rate (most commonly exchange) which refers to transactions completed now rather than at some future time. In the case of foreign exchange rate transactions, settlement must be completed within two days.
Spread	The gap between the institution's buying and selling rates for financial securities and foreign exchange. It can also refer to the margin above the base rate such as *LIBOR* at which a specific loan is priced.
SRO	Self Regulatory Organisation. Body authorised by *SIB* to undertake regulation of a designated part of investment industry.
Subordinated debt	Debt which ranks after all other debt for repayment in the event of liquidation.
Swap	An exchange of currencies or of debt with different characteristics such as interest rate type.
Syndicated loan	A loan which is made by a group of banks. Normally one bank or banks act as the lead bank(s) and then arrange to sell all or some of the debt to other banks, who are termed participating banks.
Underwriting	A process whereby financial institutions guarantee that a debt or *equity* issue will be taken up at a specified price. In the event of the market not purchasing all the issue, the institutions will purchase the balance.
USM	Unlisted Stock Market. Second-tier stock market set up in 1980.
Withholding tax	A tax which is deducted at source prior to payment of the interest or *dividends*.

References

Akerlof, G. [1970] 'The market for "lemons": Qualitative uncertainty and market mechanism', *Quarterly Journal of Economics*, 89, 488–500.

Alexander, S.S. [1954] 'Price movements in speculative markets: trends or random walks', *Industrial Management Review*, V, 25–46.

Allen, T.J. [1990] 'Developments in the international syndicated loan market in the 1980s', *Bank of England Quarterly Bulletin*, February, 30, 71–83.

Arrow, K.J. and Hahn, F.H. [1971] *General Equilibrium Analysis*, Holden Day Inc.

Baillie, R.T., Lippens, R.E. and McMahon, P.C. [1983] 'Testing rational expectations and efficiency in the foreign exchange market', *Econometrica*, 51, 553–64.

Bain, A.D. [1981] *The Economics of the Financial System*, Martin Robertson.

Bank for International Settlements (BIS) [1986] *Recent Innovations in International Banking* (the Cross Report), BIS, Basle.

Benston, G.J. and Kaufman, G.G. [1988] *Risk and Solvency Regulation of Depository Institutions: Past Policies and Current Options*, Monograph 1 in Finance and Economics, Saloman Brothers Centre for the Study of Financial Institutions.

Bilson, J.F.O. [1983] 'The evaluation and use of foreign exchange rate forecasting services', in R.J. Herring (ed.) *Managing Foreign Exchange Risk*, Cambridge University Press.

Bjerring, J.H., Lakonishok, J. and Vermaelen, T. [1983] 'Stock prices and financial analysts' recommendations', *Journal of Finance*, 38, 187–204.

Blake, D., Beenstock, M. and Brasse, V. [1986] 'The performance of UK exchange rate forecasters', *Economic Journal*, 96, 986–99.

Blume, M.E. and Friend, I. [1974] 'Risk, investment strategies and the long-run rates of return', *Review of Economics and Statistics*, 56, 259–69.

Boocock, J.G. [1990] 'An examination of non-bank funding for small and medium sized enterprises in the UK', *Service Industries Journal*, 124–45.

Bryant, C. [1987] 'National and sector balance sheets 1957–1985', *Economic Trends*, No. 403, May, 92–119.

Calder, J.R. [1978] 'The stock of consumer durables in the UK', *Economic Trends*, No. 239, 111–24.

Cavanaugh, K.L. [1987] 'Price dynamics in the foreign currency futures market', *Journal of International Money and Finance*, 6, 295–314.

Cecchini, P. [1988] *The European Challenge, 1992: The Benefits of a Single Market*, Gower Publishing Group.

Copeland, L. [1989] *Exchange Rates and International Finance*, Addison-Wesley.

Cosh, A., Carty, J., Hughes, A., Plender, J. and Singh, A. [1990] *Take-Overs and Short-Termism in the UK*, Institute of Public Policy Research, Industrial Policy Paper No. 3.

Davis, E.P. [1990] *International Financial Centres – an industrial analysis*, Bank of England Discussion Paper No. 51.

Davis, E.P. and Latter, A.R. [1989] 'London as an international financial centre', *Bank of England Quarterly Bulletin*, 29(4), 516–28.

Demery, D. and Duck, N.W. [1978] 'The behaviour of nominal interest rates in the United Kingdom 1961–1973', *Economica*, 45, 23–37.

Diamond, D. [1984] 'Financial intermediation and delegated monitoring', *Review of Economic Studies*, 51, 393–414.

Dimson, E. and Marsh, P. [1984] 'Unpublished forecasts of UK stock returns', *Journal of Finance*, 39, 1257–92.

Dooley, M.P. and Shafer, J.R. [1976] *Analysis of Short-Run Exchange Rate Behavior: March 1973 to September 1975*, International Finance Discussion Papers No. 76, Federal Reserve System, Washington DC.

Elton, E.J., Gruber, M.J. and Rentzler, J. [1984] 'Intra-day tests of the efficiency of the treasury bills futures market', *Review of Economics and Statistics*, 129–37.

Fama, E.F. [1970] 'Efficient capital markets: a review of theory and empirical evidence', *Journal of Finance*, 84, 499–522.

Fama, E.F. [1975] 'Short term interest rates as predictors of inflation', *American Economic Review*, 65, 269–82.

Fama, E.F. [1980] 'Banking in the theory of finance', *Journal of Monetary Economics*, 6, 7–28.

Fama, E.F. and Blume, M.E. [1966] 'Filter rules and stock market trading', *Journal of Business*, 39, 226–41.

Frenkel, J.A. and Levich, R.M. [1975] 'Covered interest arbitrage: unexploited profits?' *Journal of Political Economy*, 83, 325–38.

Frenkel, J.A. and Levich, R.M. [1977] 'Transactions costs and interest arbitrage: tranquil versus turbulent periods', *Journal of Political Economy*, 85, 1209–24.

Gibbons, M. and Hess, P. [1980] 'Day of the week effects and asset returns', *Journal of Business*, 54, 579–96.

Giovannini, A. [1990] *The Transition to Economic and Monetary Union*, Essays in International Finance No. 178, Department of Economics, Princeton University.

Goodhart, C. [1988] 'Bank insolvency and deposit insurance: a proposal', in P. Arestis (ed.) *Contemporary Issues in Money and Banking*, Macmillan.

Goodhart, C.A.E. [1989] *Money, Information and Uncertainty* (2nd edition), Macmillan.

Goodhart, C.A.E. and Gowland, D. [1977] 'The relationship between yields on short and long-dated gilt-edged stock', *Bulletin of Economic Research*, 29.

Goodman, S.J. [1979] 'Foreign exchange forecasting techniques: implications for business and policy', *Journal of Finance*, 34, 415–27.

Haldane, A.G. [1991] 'The exchange rate mechanism of the European monetary system: a review of the literature', *Bank of England Quarterly Bulletin*, February, 73–82.

Hall, M. [1987a] 'UK banking supervision and the Johnson Mathey affair', in C. Goodhart, D. Currie and D. Llewellyn (eds) *The Operation and Regulation of Financial Markets*, Macmillan.

Hall, M. [1987b] 'The deposit protection scheme: a case for reform', *National Westminster Bank Quarterly Review*, 45–53.

HM Treasury [1989] *An Evolutionary Approach to Economic and Monetary Union*, London, November.

HM Treasury [1990] 'Economic and monetary union: beyond stage one', Chancellor's speech to the German Industry Forum, London, June 20.

Jeanneau, J.G.S. [1989] *Structural Changes in World Capital Markets and Eurocommercial Paper*, Bank of England Discussion Paper No. 37.

Keim, D.B. [1986] 'The CAPM and equity return regularities', *Financial Analyst Journal*, 42, 19–34.

Kindleberger, C.P. [1978] *Manias, Panics and Crashes: A History of Financial Crises*, Basic Books.

Kleidon, A.W. [1986] 'Variance bounds tests and stock price valuation models', *Journal of Political Economy*, 43, 639–55.

Kolb, R. [1988] *Understanding Futures Markets*, Scott, Foresman and Co.

Lancaster, K. [1966] 'A new approach to consumer theory', *Journal of Political Economy*, 74, 132–57.

Leland, H.E. and Pyle, D.H. [1977] 'Information assymetries, financial structure and financial intermediation', *Journal of Finance*, 32, 371–87.

Lever, H. and Huhne, C. [1985] *Debt and Danger: The World Financial Crisis*, Penguin Books.

Levich, R.M. [1979] 'On the efficiency of markets for foreign exchange', in R. Dornbusch and J.A. Frenkel (eds) *International Economic Policy*, Johns Hoptins University Press.

Lewis, M.K. [1987] 'Off-balance sheet activities and financial innovation in banking', *Banca Nationale del Lavoro*, 387–410.

Lewis, M.K. and Davis, K.T. [1987] *Domestic and International Banking*, Philip Allan, Oxford.

Llewellyn, D. [1985] 'The evolution of the British financial system', Gilbart Lectures on Banking, Institute of Bankers.

Logue, D.E. and Sweeney, R.J. [1977] 'White noise in imperfect markets: the case of the franc/dollar exchange rate', *Journal of Finance*, 32, 761–8.

Lomax, D. [1991] 'A European central bank and economic and monetary union', *National Westminster Bank Quarterly Review*, 55–72.

McCauley, R.N. and Hargraves, L.A. [1987] 'Eurocommercial paper and US commercial paper: converging money markets', *Quarterly Review Federal Reserve Bank New York*, 24–35.

McCauley, R.N. and Zimmer, S.A. [1989] 'Explaining international differences in the cost of capital', *Quarterly Review Federal Reserve Bank of New York*, Summer, 7–21.

McConnell, J.J. and Muscerella, C.S. [1985] 'Corporate capital expenditure decisions and the market value of the firm', *Journal of Financial Economics*, 14, 399–422.

McCulloch, J.H. [1981] 'Misintermediation and macroeconomic fluctuations', *Journal of Monetary Economics*, 8, 103–15.

Malkiel, B.G. [1966] *The Term Structure of Interest Rates*, Princeton University Press, Princeton.

Manaster, S. and Rendleman, R.J. [1982] 'Options prices as predictors of equilibrium stock prices', *Journal of Finance*, 37, 1043–57.

Mankiw, G. and Summers, L.H. [1984] 'Do long-term Interest rates overreact to short-term interest rates?', *Brookings Papers on Economic Activity*, 1.

Marsh, P. [1990] *Short Termism on Trial*, IFMA, London.

Meiselman, D. [1962] *The Term Structure of Interest Rates*, Prentice-Hall.

Miles, D. [1989] 'Financial liberalisation, the housing market and the current account', Birkbeck College mimeo.

Modigliani, F. and Shiller, R.J. [1973] 'Inflation, rational expectations and the term structure of interest rates', *Economica*, 40, 12–43.

Modigliani, F. and Sutch, R.C. [1966] 'Innovations in interest rate policy', *American Economic Review*, 56, 178–97.

Newbery, D.M. [1989] 'Futures markets, hedging and speculation', in J. Eatwell, M. Milgate and P. Newman (eds), *The New Palgrave Dictionary of Finance*, Macmillan.

Plender, J. [1990] 'Throw sand in the take over machine', *Financial Times*, 24.

Rybczynski, T. [1988] 'Financial systems and industrial restructuring', *National Westminster Bank Quarterly Review*, 3–13.

Sachs, J. [1986] 'Managing the LDC debt crisis', *Brookings Papers on Economic Activity*, 397–440.

Sachs, J. and Huizinga, H. [1987] 'US commercial banks and the developing-country debt crisis', *Brookings Papers on Economic Activity*, 555–606.

Santoni, G.J. [1987] 'The great bull markets 1924–1929 and 1982–1987: speculative bubbles or economic fundamentals', *Federal Reserve Bank of St Louis Review*, November, 16–30.

Sargent, T. [1972] 'Rational expectations and the term structure of interest rates', *Journal of Money Credit and Banking*, 4.

Shiller, R.J. [1979] 'The volatility of long-term interest rates and expectations models of the term structure, *Journal of Political Economy*, 87, 1190–2119.

Shiller, R.J. [1981] 'Do stock prices move too much to be justified by subsequent changes in dividends', *American Economic Review*, 71, 421–36.

Stickel, S.E. [1985] 'The effect of value line investment survey rank changes on common stock prices', *Journal of Financial Economics*, 14, 121–43.

Sykes, A. [1990] 'Bigger carrots and sticks', *Financial Times*, 31 October.

Taylor, M.P. [1987] 'Covered interest parity: a high-frequency, high-quality data study', *Economica*, 54, 429–38.

Taylor, S. [1986] *Modelling Financial Time Series*, John Wiley.

Tobin, J. [1984] 'On the efficiency of the financial system', *Lloyds Bank Review*, 153, 1–15.

Tucker, A.L. [1987] 'Foreign exchange option prices as predictors of equilibrium forward exchange rates', *Journal of International Money and Finance*, 6, 283–94.

Walmsley, J. [1988] *The New Financial Instruments: an Investors Guide*, Wiley.

Yang, J.E. [1987] 'Fraud is the main cause of failure at S & Ls in California, Congress says', *Wall Street Journal*, 15 June, 6.

Index